EMPATHIC CONCERN

EMPATHIC CONCERN

What It Is and Why It's Important

C. Daniel Batson

OXFORD
UNIVERSITY PRESS

Oxford University Press is a department of the University of Oxford. It furthers
the University's objective of excellence in research, scholarship, and education
by publishing worldwide. Oxford is a registered trade mark of Oxford University
Press in the UK and certain other countries.

Published in the United States of America by Oxford University Press
198 Madison Avenue, New York, NY 10016, United States of America.

© Oxford University Press 2023

All rights reserved. No part of this publication may be reproduced, stored in
a retrieval system, or transmitted, in any form or by any means, without the
prior permission in writing of Oxford University Press, or as expressly permitted
by law, by license, or under terms agreed with the appropriate reproduction
rights organization. Inquiries concerning reproduction outside the scope of the
above should be sent to the Rights Department, Oxford University Press, at the
address above.

You must not circulate this work in any other form
and you must impose this same condition on any acquirer.

Library of Congress Cataloging-in-Publication Data
Names: Batson, C. Daniel (Charles Daniel), 1943– author.
Title: Empathic concern : what it is and why it's important / C. Daniel Batson.
Description: New York, NY : Oxford University Press, [2023] |
Includes bibliographical references and index. |
Identifiers: LCCN 2023006166 (print) | LCCN 2023006167 (ebook) |
ISBN 9780197610923 (hardback) | ISBN 9780197610947 (epub) |
ISBN 9780197610954
Subjects: LCSH: Empathy. | Attitude (Psychology)
Classification: LCC BF575 .E55 .B387 2023 (print) | LCC BF575 .E55 (ebook) |
DDC 152.4/1—dc23/eng/20230314
LC record available at https://lccn.loc.gov/2023006166
LC ebook record available at https://lccn.loc.gov/2023006167

DOI: 10.1093/oso/9780197610923.001.0001

Printed by Sheridan Books, Inc., United States of America

CONTENTS

Introduction: The Empathy Controversy   1

PART I: *What Empathic Concern Is*

1. A Definition—and a Measure   9
2. Distinguishing Empathic Concern from Personal Distress   25
3. Distinguishing It from Other Things Called Empathy   43
4. Necessary Conditions for Feeling Empathic Concern   61
5. Empathic Concern's Evolutionary Roots   77
6. Varieties of Empathic Concern   93

PART II: *Why Empathic Concern Is Important*

7. Motivational Consequences: The Empathy-Altruism Hypothesis   109
8. Behavioral Consequences: Interpersonal Benefits   127
9. Behavioral Consequences: Interpersonal Liabilities   143
10. Behavioral Consequences: Intergroup Benefits   161
11. Behavioral Consequences: Intergroup Liabilities   175
12. Realizing the Potential of Empathic Concern   193

Epilogue   211

Acknowledgments   219

References   221

Index   255

INTRODUCTION

THE EMPATHY CONTROVERSY

Empathy has received a lot of attention since the turn of the millennium. Barack Obama championed it as a vital but underutilized national resource—famously saying in a commencement address at Northwestern University in 2006, "There's a lot of talk in this country about the federal deficit. But I think we should talk more about our empathy deficit." As Obama explained two weeks earlier at the University of Massachusetts–Boston, empathy for him meant "to put yourself in other people's shoes—to see the world from their eyes." (These quotes can be found at https://cultureof empathy.com/obama/.)

In 2009, esteemed primatologist and psychologist Frans de Waal began his Preface to *The Age of Empathy* by announcing, "Greed is out, empathy is in." Citing Obama's speeches about the need to overcome our empathy deficit, de Waal asserted that "empathy is the grand theme of our time" (2009, p. ix).

Not all attention to empathy has been so flattering. Both philosopher Jesse Prinz and psychologist Paul Bloom pointed to problems. Prinz worried that "empathy has been enshrined as the panacea for the world's woes; cultivate it and crime will plummet, poverty will vanish, wars will end" (Prinz, 2014). He had doubts:

> Empathy is not all it is cracked up to be. The assumption that empathy is important for morality can be challenged. Indeed, empathy may even be a liability. (Prinz, 2011a, pp. 214–215; also see Prinz, 2011b)

Bloom offered a parallel but more extensive critique in his 2016 book, tellingly titled *Against Empathy*. Reflecting on empathy's role in responses to the 2012 mass shooting at Sandy Hook Elementary School in Newtown, Connecticut, Bloom previewed his argument:

> Our response to that event, at the time and later on, was powerfully influenced by our empathy, by our capacity—many would see it as a gift—to see the world through others' eyes, to feel what they feel. It is easy to see why so many people view empathy as a powerful force for goodness and moral change. It is easy to see why so many believe that the only problem with empathy is that too often we don't have enough of it.
>
> I used to believe that as well. But now I don't. Empathy has its merits. It can be a great source of pleasure, involved in art and fiction and sports, and it can be a valuable aspect of intimate relationships. And it can sometimes spark us to do good. But on the whole, it's a poor moral guide. It grounds foolish judgments and often motivates indifference and cruelty. It can lead to irrational and unfair political decisions, it can corrode certain important relationships, such as between a doctor and a patient, and make us worse at being friends, parents, husbands, and wives. . . .
>
> The argument against empathy isn't that we should be selfish and immoral. It's the opposite. It's that if we want to be good and caring people, if we want to make the world a better place, then we are better off without empathy. (Bloom, 2016, pp. 2–3)

Philosopher Peter Singer made a similar argument in his 2015 book, *The Most Good You Can Do*.

These criticisms haven't gone unchallenged. Empathy advocates have called the Prinz-Bloom conception of empathy either wrong (e.g., Persson & Savulescu, 2018) or too narrow (e.g., Zaki, 2016)—then touted the virtues of "true" empathy.

A Different Meaning of Empathy

As the Obama and Bloom quotes illustrate, both sides in this controversy use empathy to mean (a) seeing the world through another person's eyes and/or (b) feeling as another feels. But there is another common way to think about empathy—as an emotional step in a process of caring for another. People who think this way, and I'm one of them, define empathy neither as taking the other's perspective nor as feeling as the other feels, but as feeling *for* the other. Across the centuries, feeling for another in need has been given various names—names that are often translated into English as *compassion* or *pity*. Seeking a less value-laden label, some of us have called this emotional state *empathic concern*.

The purpose of the present book isn't to add to the recent controversy about empathy by trying to tell you that what I and others call empathic concern is true empathy. Nor will I claim that this other-oriented emotion is a panacea or, conversely, that we'd be better off without it. Rather, my purpose is to present an empirically based scientific analysis of the nature and function of empathic concern. I'm interested in this emotional state not because feeling for another has played an important role in the recent empathy controversy, which it hasn't, but because it has for centuries been thought to motivate care for the welfare of those for whom it's felt. And if it does this, then empathic concern plays a central role in our social relations, both one-to-one and in society—which makes it something we need to know as much about as possible.

Avoiding Terminological Tangles

Before going further, let me say a few words about terminology. I've already noted that there are psychological phenomena other than the emotional state I'm calling empathic concern that also have been called empathy, including but not only the phenomena referred to in the recent controversy. Some of these other phenomena have at least as much right to be called empathy as does feeling for another. So, if you want to call one (or more) of them empathy, I can't object. But I hope you won't then simply toss this book aside as irrelevant to your interest. No matter what you mean by the word empathy, feeling for another in need is still an important emotional state. In fact, most people who use empathy to refer to a different phenomenon assume that their phenomenon will lead us to feel for the person who is its target. Thus, empathic concern remains relevant as a downstream consequence.

Of course, there's a danger if you and I use the word empathy to mean different things. You might think I'm talking about what you mean when I'm not. To avoid this, you'll need to find some other term for the emotional state I'm calling empathic concern: *Sympathy* and *compassion* are currently popular alternatives. And, in the pages that follow, you'll need to make a mental substitution of your chosen term for mine. If you do this, and if you use your

4 • EMPATHIC CONCERN

chosen term to refer to nothing more (or less) than what I call empathic concern, then we should be able to get on without confusion and unproductive verbal squabbles.

What's Ahead

Looking ahead to the rest of the book, Part I details what empathic concern is: Chapter 1 provides examples of this emotional state and a formal definition, then describes the development of a brief self-report measure. Chapter 2 reviews empirical evidence that indicates the need to distinguish empathic concern from a different but not mutually exclusive emotional reaction to another's need—self-oriented personal distress. Chapter 3 specifies how empathic concern differs from, but also relates to, seven other psychological phenomena that have been called empathy—and it offers my labels for each of the other phenomena. Again, it's fine if you prefer to use different labels, but if so, you'll need to make mental substitutions.

The last three chapters of Part I build on the first three to expand our understanding of empathic concern. Chapter 4 specifies the situational conditions necessary to feel this other-oriented emotion; Chapter 5 addresses its evolutionary roots; and Chapter 6 describes some of its variations. Together, the six chapters of Part I provide an up-to-date conceptual and empirical analysis of what empathic concern is.

Part II shifts attention from empathic concern itself to examination of its role in our lives. Chapter 7 explores the motivational consequences of this emotional state, focusing on the empathy–altruism hypothesis. The next four chapters consider behavioral consequences. Rather than simply lauding or castigating its effects, existing empirical research supports a more nuanced view—that empathic concern offers important benefits at both the interpersonal and intergroup levels (Chapters 8 and 10) but also has important liabilities (Chapters 9 and 11), including the liabilities that have troubled Jesse Prinz and Paul Bloom. The benefits can be gained only if we recognize and address its liabilities. Chapter 12 provides examples of how the potential of empathic concern has been and can be realized. An Epilogue reviews the argument and suggests needed next steps.

The last half century of theory and research has taught us quite a lot about the nature and importance of empathic concern. My hope is that the present compilation of this knowledge will be of use to readers of at least four types: First and foremost, to other empathy researchers in psychology, philosophy, neuroscience, and compassion science. Second, to students in these fields as well as in other behavioral sciences—both graduate students and advanced undergraduates. Third, to writers and journalists reporting on empathy research. And fourth, to policymakers and program designers interested in realistically tapping the potential of empathy to improve interpersonal and intergroup relations in education, business, politics, and more. By taking stock of where we are, I hope this compilation will move us forward— stimulating not only more theory-based research on the nature and function of empathic concern but also more theory-based applications.

WHAT EMPATHIC CONCERN IS

1 A DEFINITION—AND A MEASURE

To understand what empathic concern is, we first need a definition. Working toward that end, let's start with some examples:

1. A man was going down from Jerusalem to Jericho and fell among robbers, who stripped him and beat him and departed leaving him half dead. Now by chance a priest was going down the road; and when he saw him he passed by on the other side. So likewise a Levite, when he came to the place and saw him, passed by on the other side. But a Samaritan, as he journeyed, came to where he was; and when he saw him, he had compassion. (Luke 10: 30–33 RSV)

   The Samaritan's compassion is a classic case of empathic concern.

2. There are many contemporary cases as well. In *Empathy and Moral Development*, Martin Hoffman presented a number, including this one from a student:

   > My cousin's mom died. He was too young to understand, and he just kept playing with his toys. I tried to smile and play with him, but I kept on thinking about how not having his mother would affect him. He wouldn't have the sweet hugs when he bumped his knee. Especially since his father was strict and very much a disciplinarian. And all I could think of was that the softness of his mother was gone and he'd miss that. But he wasn't recognizing it. He thought everything was great. (Hoffman, 2000, p. 82)

3. In October 1987, millions of Americans watched and worried as rescuers worked around the clock for over two days to save "Baby Jessica" McClure, an 18-month-old toddler who had fallen into a deep, narrow well.
4. At the start of his book *Against Empathy*, Paul Bloom not only reflected on public response to the mass shooting at Sandy Hook Elementary. He also shared his personal reaction:

> I watched videos of frantic parents running to the crime scene and imagined what that must feel like. Even thinking about it now, my stomach churns. Later that afternoon I was in a coffeehouse near my office, and a woman at a table next to me was sniffling and hoarse, being consoled by a friend, and I heard enough to learn that although she knew nobody at Sandy Hook, she had a child of the same age as those who were murdered. (Bloom, 2016, pp. 1–2)

Most of us, like Paul and this woman, have felt sympathy for the loved ones of the dead in the latest school shooting, terrorist bombing, hurricane, wildfire, flood, or earthquake. And most of us have felt sorry for homeless refugees and unwanted immigrants.
5. Early on a spring morning, my wife Judy was driving in the Great Smoky Mountains on her way to join friends for a hike. Rounding a curve, she came on a tiny bear cub stumbling in confused circles at the side of the road, with no momma bear in sight. The cub seemed near death. Deeply concerned, Judy was relieved to learn that someone had already called the National Park Service. The cub was picked up within an hour, taken to a bear-rescue center nearby, and, over several months, nursed back to health.
6. I, and likely you, have felt sorry for a friend distressed by a romantic breakup or after the death of a parent—or of a beloved pet.
7. We've also felt our hearts melt at seeing the round face, big soft eyes, and snub nose of harp-seal pups or baby pandas in ads seeking contributions for their protection.

Each of these examples involves feeling for another in need—feeling sorrow, concern, sympathy, compassion, and the like. And, as I said in the Introduction, this feeling-for is the essence of what I mean by empathic concern.

In contrast, here are two emotional reactions to another's state that aren't cases of empathic concern:

A Definition—and a Measure • 11

1. On an airplane in rough weather, I sense the nervousness and fear of passengers around me and become nervous and afraid, too. Over the past few decades, feeling the same distress that another person feels has often been called empathy (by, for example, Bloom, 2016; Decety & Lamm, 2009; de Vignemont & Singer, 2006; Eisenberg & Strayer, 1987). But, as I also said in the Introduction, to feel as another feels isn't the same as feeling-for. So, if Paul Bloom in Example 4 felt only the same desperation and panic that the Sandy Hook parents felt—and didn't also feel for them—he wasn't experiencing empathic concern. (Knowing Paul, I strongly suspect he also felt for them.)

2. You feel elated for your friend who just learned that her cancer screening was clear. Such elation has been called *empathic joy* (Smith, Keating, & Stotland, 1989; Stotland, 1969). Your elation is an other-oriented response to the perceived welfare of another, so I think it qualifies as an empathic emotion. But because the other is relieved instead of in need, your emotion is positive not negative. It's empathic joy not empathic concern.

Defining Empathic Concern

With these examples before us, let me offer a more formal definition: *Empathic concern is an other-oriented emotional state elicited by and congruent with the perceived welfare of another in need.* Like most definitions, this one needs some elaboration.

First, empathic concern as defined isn't a single, discrete emotion but encompasses a host of other-oriented emotions. It includes feelings that people may report as sympathy, compassion, softheartedness, tenderness, sorrow, sadness, upset, distress, concern, grief, and more. These emotional states are other-oriented in the sense that they involve feeling for the other—feeling sympathy for, compassion for, sorrow for, distress for, and so on. (The "for" here specifies the target of our empathic concern, the person in need, not that we feel as a proxy for or "in the place of" this person.)

Second, to say that empathic emotion is "congruent with the perceived welfare of another in need" refers to a congruence of valence. Empathic concern has a negative valence because the perceived welfare of another in need is negative—it wants improving. But, again, this doesn't mean that you feel the same negative emotion the person in need feels. It would be congruent to feel sad or sorry for someone who is upset and distressed—like the friend in Example 6. Or, as in Example 2, to grieve for a young cousin who is happy and unaware of the need you perceive. Or, like the good Samaritan, to feel compassion for the victim of a mugging, who may be unconscious and feeling nothing at all. On the other hand, to feel *schadenfreude* (malicious glee) at seeing a rival suffer is an emotional response elicited by the perceived welfare of another in need, but not a congruent response. Feeling glee (a positive emotion) at the rival's suffering (a negative state) is the antithesis of empathy.

Third, although feelings of sympathy and compassion are inherently other-oriented, we can feel sorrow, distress, concern, and grief when something bad happens directly to us. Both the other-oriented and self-oriented versions of these emotions may be described as feeling sorry or sad, upset or distressed, concerned or grieved. This double use has led some psychologists to blur the distinction between the two versions, but I think doing so is a mistake. When speaking of empathic concern, it's crucial to know whose welfare is the focus of the emotion. Are we feeling sad, distressed, concerned for the other? If so, we're feeling empathic concern. If we're feeling these emotions because of what has befallen us—including, perhaps, the experience of seeing the other suffer—we're feeling a form of what has been called *personal distress*, which I'll discuss in Chapter 2.

Fourth, the range of others for whom we can feel empathic concern is wide. It includes not only family and friends (Examples 2 and 6) but also strangers near and far (Examples 1, 3, and 4). It even includes members of other species—especially members who are young, cute, and vulnerable (Examples 5 and 7).

Fifth, as noted in the Introduction, some people prefer to use a term other than empathic concern to label the general class of congruent, other-oriented emotions just described. They speak instead of *sympathy* (Decety & Lamm, 2009; Eisenberg & Strayer, 1987; Maibom, 2018; Roughley & Schramm, 2018; Stueber, 2018; Wispé, 1991), *sympathetic distress* (Hoffman, 2000), or *compassion* (DeSteno, 2015; Goetz, Keltner, & Simon-Thomas, 2010; Nussbaum, 2001; Singer & Klimecki, 2014). As long as it's clear that we're talking about the same other-oriented emotional state, then to use a different label is fine. Social psychologists like me settled on *empathic concern*—and on *empathy* for short—back in the 1970s when *sympathy* seemed patronizing, and *compassion* carried connotations of religion. Because these connotations linger, I still prefer *empathic concern* to these alternatives.

Developing a Valid Measure

To know whether a person is feeling empathic concern for another in need—and, if so, how much—we must be able to measure this emotional state. The sine qua non of any measure is its validity: Does it measure what it's supposed to?

By far the most common strategy for assessing the validity of a psychological measure is to look for *convergent validity*. That is, to see whether the measure correlates at least moderately positively with existing measures of the same psychological phenomenon. But there's a problem with this strategy. All too often, we can't be confident of the existing measures' validity because their validity was determined in the same way, by checking those measures' convergent validity. And, if you trace the lineage of an existing measure back through its association with other existing measures to association of these measures with previous measures and so on, you almost always come to a point where convergent validity is replaced by *face validity*. That is, you come to a point where the only basis for the validity of the measure is that it looks like it would measure what it's supposed to. Face validity is often desirable, but it's not enough. We need empirical evidence that our measure is valid.

To avoid reliance on this regress to face validity, colleagues and I used a different strategy to establish the validity of a brief self-report measure of empathic concern, a strategy that might be called *induced-state validity*. This strategy involved identifying other-oriented emotions that people who were experimentally induced to feel a lot of empathic concern for a person in need reported feeling more strongly than did people induced to feel only a little empathy for the person.

Pursuing this strategy, we randomly assigned research participants to two groups and treated the groups identically except for an empathy induction. Such a procedure ensured that any difference in other-oriented emotion reported by the two groups was due to the empathy induction rather than to (a) some difference between the people in the two groups (within the limits of chance, random assignment equated the groups), (b) features of the person in need whom the two groups encountered (the person was exactly the same), or (c) any other difference in what the two groups experienced (except for the induction, the two groups were treated identically).

To provide concrete examples of how we employed this validation strategy, let me describe two experiments. The first was conducted around 1975 and produced an initial five-item measure of empathic concern. The second,

14 • EMPATHIC CONCERN

conducted several decades later, used the then current and still popular six-item version of this measure. The two experiments employed very different techniques to induce empathy, providing evidence that the measure isn't limited to one specific empathy-induction procedure.

Inducing Empathy with False Physiological Feedback (Coke, Batson, & McDavis, 1978, Experiment 2)

The first experiment used an elaborate, indirect procedure involving false physiological feedback to induce empathic concern. Participants were female introductory psychology students. When each arrived for her individual appointment, a male experimenter seated her in a small research room at a desk with headphones, two skin-conductance electrodes, and a Galvanic Skin Response (GSR) monitor. A written introduction explained that the purpose of the research was to assess students' evaluative and emotional (GSR) reactions to pilot broadcasts for two programs being considered for adoption by the local university radio station. The first program, Bulletin Board, announced upcoming campus events. The second, Campus Concerns, allowed students to make appeals for help with various campus projects.

The Campus Concerns broadcast that each participant heard was an appeal for help from Katherine McDavis, a graduate student in the School of Education. Unable to afford to pay participants needed for her master's thesis research, Katherine was asking for volunteers. We assumed that—by itself—Katherine's appeal would arouse little empathic concern. But, by providing the participants randomly assigned to two experimental conditions different readings on the GSR monitor while listening to the appeal, we led those in one condition to believe that they were feeling considerable concern (high-empathy condition) and those in a second condition that they were feeling very little (low-empathy condition).

As had been true following the announcement, the first questionnaire that participants completed after listening to Katherine's appeal assessed their emotional state. For each of 23 emotion adjectives, participants circled a number from 1 (*not at all*) to 7 (*extremely*) to indicate the degree to which they had experienced that emotion while listening. Among the 23 were eight adjectives that we thought might reflect empathic concern—*empathic, concerned, softhearted, warm, sorrowed, touched, compassionate*, and *moved*. Our goal was to identify which, if any, actually did.

We used principal-component analysis to determine which emotion adjectives were measuring empathic concern. (Principal-component analysis is a statistical procedure that is able to detect which measures in a set are measuring the same underlying dimension or component.) Our component analysis revealed that five adjectives were measuring the same component: *empathic, concerned, softhearted, warm,* and *compassionate.* Therefore, we created an empathic-concern index by averaging responses to these five adjectives.

Providing evidence of the induced-state validity of this five-item index, participants in the high-empathy condition scored significantly higher on the index than did participants in the low-empathy condition. At least in this experiment, the five items seemed to provide a valid measure of empathic concern.

Switching to a Six-Item Index

By 1987, Jim Fultz, Pat Schoenrade, and I were able to analyze data from five more studies in which empathic concern had been measured in response to various need situations (Batson, Fultz, & Schoenrade, 1987). Three of the five studies employed an experimental induction of empathic concern; the other two assessed naturally occurring individual differences in response to an empathy-inducing situation. Principal-component analyses of data from each study revealed that, across the five studies, responses to six adjectives— *sympathetic, tender, softhearted, warm, compassionate,* and *moved*— consistently measured the same component. So, based on these component analyses, we created an index that averaged participants' responses to these six adjectives. This measure, which has come to be called the Empathic Concern Index, has been used to measure empathic concern in many studies since 1987 (see Batson, 2011, for a review and references).

Why aren't *empathic* and *concerned* on the Empathic Concern Index? You probably noticed that neither *empathic* nor *concerned* is on this six-item index. That's because in the new studies, each of these adjectives proved problematic.

Some participants in the new studies failed to rate *empathic.* When asked about the missing response, these participants said either that they weren't sure what the word meant or they weren't sure what we meant by it. Then, when we explained what we meant, they almost always said, "Oh, you mean like sympathetic!"

In recent years, a number of scholars have made a conceptual distinction between empathy and sympathy (e.g., Decety & Lamm, 2009; de Waal, 2009; Eisenberg & Strayer, 1987; Wispé, 1986)—although historical justification for drawing a distinction is questionable (see Ilyes, 2017; Jahoda, 2005). Unlike these scholars, our research participants seemed to treat empathy and sympathy as synonyms. And because our participants were more familiar with the term sympathy, we replaced *empathic* with *sympathetic* to avoid having missing data.

Concerned proved ambiguous. Some participants interpreted it to mean feeling concerned for the person in need, which is what we intended. But, reflecting the second use of adjectives such as concerned noted earlier, others interpreted it to mean a self-focused, disturbed feeling prompted by hearing of the person's need, which wasn't our intent. So we eliminated *concerned* from our measure.

With neither *empathic* nor *concerned* on the six-item index, did this index still measure empathic concern? We believed it did. Substituting *sympathetic* for *empathic* allowed us to measure the same other-oriented emotional state while circumventing the problem of missing data. Omitting *concerned* avoided its ambiguity.

Turning to the other five adjectives on the six-item index, three had been on the original five-item index—*softhearted, warm,* and *compassionate.* Only *tender* (which we borrowed from William McDougall, 1908) and *moved* were new. Given the item overlap on the two indexes and the cohesion of items on each index, we felt confident that both were measuring the same underlying dimension. Moreover, in retrospect, we felt that not having *empathic* and *concerned* on our measure was a benefit. Their absence emphasized that we weren't using empathic concern to specify a single emotion but as an umbrella term to cover a variety of congruent emotions felt for another in need.

Range of applicability of the Empathic Concern Index. Research before and after 1987 has shown that the range of need situations for which the six-item Empathic Concern Index can tap empathic concern is wide, including (a) men as well as women in need, (b) chronic as well as acute needs, (c) mild as well as severe needs, (d) remote as well as immediate needs, and (e) mental distress (adjustment, coping) as well as physical pain. Turning from the range of need situations to the range of those feeling empathy, the Index has been found appropriate to assess empathic concern felt by men as well as women, and by people in whom empathic concern is experimentally induced as well as people in whom it occurs naturally (see Batson, 2011, Appendices B–G, for summaries of this research).

A Definition—and a Measure • 17

Inducing Empathy with Perspective Instructions (Batson, Sager, Garst, Kang, Rubchinsky, & Dawson, 1997, Experiment 2)

To provide an example of evidence for the induced-state validity of the six-item Empathic Concern Index, let me describe the procedure and results of one of the many experiments that have used perspective instructions to induce empathic concern. In this experiment, male and female introductory psychology students listened and reacted to a pilot broadcast for a campus public radio program, News from the Personal Side, that ostensibly reported the effect of local news stories on the lives of those involved. Before listening, each participant received instructions for one of two possible listening perspectives. (To prevent hypothesis guessing, all participants were led to believe that everyone else received the same perspective instructions they did.)

Participants in the low-empathy condition read instructions designed to inhibit empathic concern:

> Try to be as objective as possible about what has happened to the person interviewed and how it has affected his or her life. To remain objective, do not let yourself get caught up in imagining what the person has been through and how he or she feels as a result. Just try to remain detached as you listen to the broadcast.

Those in the high-empathy condition read instructions designed to increase empathic concern:

> Try to imagine how the person being interviewed feels about what has happened and how it has affected his or her life. Try not to concern yourself with attending to all the information presented. Just concentrate on trying to imagine how the person interviewed in the broadcast feels.

This perspective manipulation may seem straightforward, but like most experimental manipulations of psychological states, it's not. More is required than simply giving research participants an instruction sheet. Colleagues and I found it important that experimenters ask participants to (a) read over the instructions several times to make sure they had the perspective clearly in mind before listening to the broadcast, (b) be sure to maintain the perspective while listening, and (c) after listening, take a few minutes to think about what was said. At the same time, we cautioned experimenters not to go overboard, lest participants dismiss any empathic feelings they had (or didn't have) as an artifact of the instructions. We found that the best way for experimenters to convey all this was to run participants in person, one at a time. Once a participant understood what to do, he or she was left alone to read and adopt the assigned perspective, listen to the broadcast tape, and complete reaction questionnaires—all without any interaction with the experimenter. (To prevent experimenters treating participants in the two perspective conditions differently, experimenters were kept unaware of which perspective instructions each participant received until after all measures had been taken.)

Katie Banks, a young woman in need. The News from the Personal Side broadcast that each participant heard presented the plight of Katie Banks, a senior at the university struggling to provide for her younger brother and sister after their parents were killed in an automobile accident. Katie described her situation in these words:

> It's, it's just such a nightmare. (pause) I guess I'm still numb. I know life has to go on. The most important thing for me now is to graduate on time. I need to be able to get a good job and support my little brother and sister.
>
> You know, the help we've gotten so far has really been wonderful. But we've got a long way to go. If we don't get more help, I'm afraid I'll have to drop out of school and find a job. And that's going to make things worse, I think, because everybody knows that without a college degree you can't make much money. If I do have to drop out, I—I'm afraid I'll have to give up the children. I just—I won't make enough to support them! (See Batson, 2019, pp. 3–4, for a complete transcript of this pilot broadcast.)

Measuring empathic concern for Katie. After listening to the broadcast, participants completed an Emotional Response Scale (see Figure 1.1). On it, participants indicated by circling a number from 1 (*not at all*) to 7 (*extremely*) the degree to which they had experienced each of 26 emotions while listening. (Colleagues and I have used longer or shorter Emotional Response Scales in other studies—ranging from 10 to 28 adjectives—and, when needed, we have slightly altered the title of and instructions for the Scale to fit the cover story of each study.) Among the 26 emotion adjectives were the six on the Empathic Concern Index: *sympathetic, softhearted, warm, compassionate, tender*, and *moved* (for ease of recognition, these adjectives are printed in bold type in the figure, but not when the scale is administered to participants).

Emotional Response Scale

Please indicate by circling a number the degree to which you experienced each of these emotional reactions while listening to the broadcast. Do not worry if you were not feeling many of these emotions; only a few may apply to a particular broadcast. Be sure to circle a response for each item.

	not at all			moderately			extremely
1. alarmed	1	2	3	4	5	6	7
2. grieved	1	2	3	4	5	6	7
3. **sympathetic**	1	2	3	4	5	6	7
4. intent	1	2	3	4	5	6	7
5. **softhearted**	1	2	3	4	5	6	7
6. troubled	1	2	3	4	5	6	7
7. **warm**	1	2	3	4	5	6	7
8. concerned	1	2	3	4	5	6	7
9. distressed	1	2	3	4	5	6	7
10. low-spirited	1	2	3	4	5	6	7
11. intrigued	1	2	3	4	5	6	7
12. **compassionate**	1	2	3	4	5	6	7
13. upset	1	2	3	4	5	6	7
14. disturbed	1	2	3	4	5	6	7
15. **tender**	1	2	3	4	5	6	7
16. worried	1	2	3	4	5	6	7
17. **moved**	1	2	3	4	5	6	7
18. disconcerted	1	2	3	4	5	6	7
19. feeling low	1	2	3	4	5	6	7
20. perturbed	1	2	3	4	5	6	7
21. heavy-hearted	1	2	3	4	5	6	7
22. sorrowful	1	2	3	4	5	6	7
23. bothered	1	2	3	4	5	6	7
24. kind	1	2	3	4	5	6	7
25. sad	1	2	3	4	5	6	7
26. touched	1	2	3	4	5	6	7

FIGURE 1.1. Version of the Emotional Response Scale used by Batson, Sager et al. (1997). The six adjectives that comprise the Empathic Concern Index are printed in boldface.

Cronbach's alpha, which is an indicator of the degree to which the items on an index form an internally consistent measure, was .86 for the six-item index, indicating good internal consistency.

Evidence of induced-state validity of the Empathic Concern Index. Demonstrating the ability of the Empathic Concern Index to detect the difference in empathic concern for Katie induced by the perspective instructions, participants in the high-empathy condition scored significantly higher ($p < .001$) on the Index than did participants in the low-empathy condition. Similar results supporting the induced-state validity of the Empathic Concern Index have been found in many other experiments (see Batson, 2011).

Effect of gender on responses to the Index. In each condition of this experiment, we found that women reported significantly more empathic concern for Katie than did men. In other experiments, we've sometimes found no reliable gender difference on the Empathic Concern Index. (We've never found a reliable difference in the opposite direction, with men reporting more empathic concern than women.) Whether a gender difference is or isn't found may depend on the particular need situation to which participants are responding, or it may be due to chance. Whatever the cause, the gender difference in this experiment didn't cast doubt on the induced-state validity of the Empathic Concern Index for either sex. The difference between the low- and high-empathy conditions was statistically significant both for men and for women, with no Gender x Experimental-Condition interaction.

A limitation of using perspective instructions to induce empathic concern. Before leaving this experiment, I should mention one known circumstance in which perspective instructions such as those used here don't produce a statistically significant difference on the Empathic Concern Index. That's when participants instructed to remain objective can't keep from imagining how the other feels. This can happen when, for example, undergraduate research participants see a fellow student react with clear discomfort to a series of electric shocks (as in Cialdini, Schaller, Houlihan, Arps, Fultz, & Beaman, 1987, Experiment 1). Note that the failure in such a circumstance is a failure in the ability of perspective instructions to induce different levels of empathic concern, not in the ability of the Index to detect a difference that exists. So this limitation isn't cause to question the validity of the Index as a measure. Rather, it suggests that a different manipulation of empathic concern may be required when studying highly impactful need situations (see Batson, Duncan, Ackerman, Bolen, & Birch, 1981, Experiments 1 & 2, for two such manipulations).

Conclusion

Empathic concern, as I define it, refers to an other-oriented emotional state elicited by and congruent with the perceived welfare of another in need. Rather than feeling as the other feels, empathic concern involves feeling *for* the other. Moreover, it doesn't refer to a single emotion but is an umbrella term that includes feelings described not only as empathy and concern but also as sympathy, compassion, tenderness, sorrow, sadness, distress, and grief. Colleagues and I have developed a brief six-item self-report Empathic Concern Index to measure empathic concern, and we've used experiments to establish the Index's induced-state validity.

Yet despite the evidence of validity, this measure isn't problem free. To use self-reports assumes that respondents are able and willing to report their level of empathy. But sometimes, social norms or role expectations for how we should respond to various need situations may lead us to think and/or say we're feeling more (or less) empathic concern than we really are. Think, for example, of the different expectations when the person in need is one's father, sister, or friend—or one's superior or subordinate. Think also of expectations when the potential empathizer is each of these people.

When strong norms or expectations exist, a self-report measure shouldn't be trusted to be valid. But in response to a range of strangers' needs (such as the needs of Katherine McDavis and Katie Banks), the Empathic Concern Index has shown itself to be an effective measure of the difference between experimental groups induced to feel high empathic concern and groups induced to feel low. Because the high- and low-empathy groups have been equated (within the limits of chance) by random assignment, the observed difference between these groups can't be explained by individual differences in desire to be or to appear concerned. The difference must be due either to the empathy manipulation or to chance. And the probability that it's due to chance is infinitesimally small—less than one in a thousand (i.e., $p < .001$)—in study after study.

Still, in such experiments, it's likely that some of the *within-group variance* in self-reports of empathic concern (that is, the variance in the amount of empathy reported by different people within the same experimental condition) is due to the desire of some respondents to be seen or see themselves as concerned for the welfare of others in need. This within-group variance weakens our measure by making it harder to detect reliable between-group differences in empathic concern. Yet for adults fluent in the language, I think self-reports are at present the best way to assess empathic concern—and to distinguish

22 • EMPATHIC CONCERN

such concern from other emotional responses to encountering another in need. The six-item Empathic Concern Index is the measure I recommend for most research purposes, especially for research using between-group experimental designs.

I make this recommendation despite recent promising steps toward development of physiological measures of empathic concern. For example, "loving-kindness" meditation, which is based on a Buddhist view of compassion, has been found to reliably activate certain positive-affect brain regions when the meditator focuses loving, kind thoughts on another person (see Bloom, 2016; Klimecki, Leiberg, Ricard, & Singer, 2014; Lamm & Singer, 2010; Singer & Klimecki, 2014). Loving-kindness meditation may have this effect because it increases the meditator's valuing of others' welfare, which, as will be discussed in Chapter 4, seems to be a necessary condition for feeling empathic concern. So, although not a physiological marker for empathic concern itself, the neural activation produced by such meditation may provide a marker for one of its necessary antecedents.

Another neural possibility: Partial overlap has been found between the regions in the anterior insula (AI) and anterior cingulate cortex (ACC) that are activated when we experience pain ourselves and the regions activated when we believe someone we care for is experiencing pain (see Hein, Morishima, Leiberg, Sul, & Fehr, 2016; Lamm, Decety, & Singer, 2011; Singer, Seymour, O'Dougherty, Kaube, Dolan, & Frith, 2004; Singer, Seymour, O'Dougherty, Stephan, Dolan, & Frith, 2006; Tusche, Böckler, Kanske, Trautwein, & Singer, 2016; Zaki, Wager, Singer, Keysers, & Gazzola, 2016). But, as discussed in the next two chapters, it's not clear at this point whether this overlap reflects (a) other-oriented empathic concern, (b) self-oriented personal distress felt because it's upsetting to us to know this other is in pain, or (c) "catching" the other's pain so that we feel the same pain he or she feels. Neuroimaging techniques may someday be able to distinguish among these various emotional responses to another's need (for an ambitious attempt, see Ashar, Andrews-Hanna, Dimidjian, & Wager, 2017), but I don't believe we're there yet (see Mauss & Robinson, 2009). And distinguishing among these possibilities is necessary if we're to have a valid measure of empathic concern.

Third, a possible extracranial physiological measure also deserves mention. Respiratory sinus arrhythmia (RSA)—the variation of heart rate when breathing in and breathing out—has shown encouraging signs of being able to track feelings of empathic concern distinct from other emotional responses to another's need (see Stellar, Cohen, Oveis, & Keltner, 2015). Unfortunately, RSA is subject to a potential confound. Stellar and colleagues (2015) found, as have others, that RSA is associated with heart-rate decrease, which has in turn been found to be associated with increased outward attention of the sort that occurs not only under conditions evoking other-oriented empathic concern but also when attending to people or objects without necessarily feeling for them (Eisenberg, Fabes, Miller, Fultz, Shell, Mathy, & Reno, 1989; Eisenberg, Fabes, Schaller, Miller, Carlo, Poulin, Shea, & Shell, 1991). So, greater RSA may simply be an indicator of outward attention, not of empathic concern. These limitations of existent physiological measures lead me to conclude that the Empathic Concern Index, despite relying on self-reports, is the best measure we currently have.

Having specified what empathic concern is and how it can be measured, we need to differentiate it from other psychological states with which it's often confused. Most immediately, we need to distinguish this other-oriented emotional response from self-oriented personal distress produced by seeing another in need. The next chapter considers how to do that—both conceptually and empirically.

2 DISTINGUISHING EMPATHIC CONCERN FROM PERSONAL DISTRESS

Imagine being out for a run along a quiet country road. Rounding a curve, you're shocked to see a sports car overturned, half in and half out of the ditch. The driver, a young woman, lies on the pavement—face bloody and bruised, eyes closed, barely moving. Her left leg is twisted at a grotesque angle. You experience a cascade of emotions: fear, confusion, anxiety, upset, distress, sympathy, compassion, worry.

As discussed in Chapter 1, some of these emotions—your sympathy and compassion—are forms of empathic concern. But others are more self-oriented—your fear, confusion, anxiety, upset, and distress. To distinguish these self-oriented feelings evoked by encountering another in need from other-oriented empathic concern, they've been called personal distress.

How Important Is This Distinction? Two Answers

Is the distinction between empathic concern and personal distress important? Psychologists have offered two very different answers to this question.

1. It's Unimportant

One answer is based on a tension-reduction view of motivation. It claims that feelings of empathic concern and personal distress aren't distinct in any psychologically important way. Feelings of both types combine to produce an overall level of aversive arousal

Empathic Concern. C. Daniel Batson, Oxford University Press. © Oxford University Press 2023.
DOI: 10.1093/oso/9780197610923.003.0003

26 • EMPATHIC CONCERN

which, in turn, produces motivation to reduce this arousal as effectively and efficiently as possible.

The best-known tension-reduction analysis of our emotional response when encountering someone in need—someone like the young woman just described—is the *arousal: cost-reward model*. This model was originally proposed in 1969 by Irv Piliavin, Judy Rodin, and Jane Piliavin, and was then developed over the next two decades by Jane Piliavin, Jack Dovidio, Sam Gaertner, and Russ Clark. Focusing on response to emergencies, Jane and her colleagues summarized the model's core in two propositions:

(1) In general, the arousal occasioned by observation of an emergency and attributed to the emergency becomes more unpleasant as it increases, and the bystander is therefore motivated to reduce it.

(2) The bystander will choose that response to an emergency that will most rapidly and most completely reduce the arousal, incurring in the process as few net costs (costs minus rewards) as possible. (Piliavin, Dovidio, Gaertner, & Clark, 1982, p. 281)

According to this model, not only are feelings of personal distress part of the aversive arousal we're motivated to reduce, so are feelings of empathic concern:

> Despite apparent variations in emotional content, the process by which another's need promotes helping seems dynamically similar across a variety of situations . . . . Empathy costs involve internalizing the need or suffering of the victim and produce a continued and perhaps increased level of unpleasant arousal. (Piliavin, Dovidio, Gaertner, & Clark, 1981, p. 236; also see pp. 7, 80–82, and 235)

Or, as Martin Hoffman put it, "Empathic distress is unpleasant and helping the victim is usually the best way to get rid of the source" (1981a, p. 52).

The arousal: cost-reward model highlighted two ways to reduce aversive arousal caused by seeing another person in need. One way is to flee the scene, as did the priest and Levite in the parable of the good Samaritan. Escape allows us to get away from the stimulus causing our arousal. The other way is to help. Relieving the other's distress by helping turns off the stimulus causing our distress. In sum,

The arousal: cost-reward model is a tension-reduction model that assumes that the victim's need produces an arousal state in the potential benefactor and that the goal of helping is to alleviate one's own aversive state. (Dovidio, Piliavin, Schroeder, & Penner, 2006, pp. 130–131)

2. It's Crucial

The second answer to the question of importance of the distinction between empathic concern and personal distress is that it's crucial. This answer maintains that even though both can be felt in response to the same need situation, empathic concern and personal distress don't just tumble together into one seething cauldron of aversive arousal that motivates behavior to reduce the arousal. Instead, whereas feelings of personal distress produce motivation to remove our own distress, empathic concern produces motivation to remove the distress of the person in need.

Although never dominant, this second answer has been around in psychology since the early 1900s. At that time, William McDougall described two emotional responses to encountering another in need that are essentially the same as what I'm calling empathic concern and personal distress—"the tender emotion" and "sympathetic pain."

McDougall used the parable of the good Samaritan to highlight the difference between these two emotions, contrasting the tenderness felt by the Samaritan with what he imagined to be the sympathetic pain of the priest and Levite:

No doubt the spectacle of the poor man who fell among thieves was just as distressing to the priest and the Levite, who passed by on the other side, as to the good Samaritan who tenderly cared for him. They may well have been exquisitely sensitive souls, who would have fainted away if they had been compelled to gaze upon his wounds. The great difference between them and the Samaritan was that in him the tender emotion and its impulse were evoked, and that this impulse overcame, or prevented, the aversion naturally induced by the painful and, perhaps, disgusting spectacle. (McDougall, 1908, p. 65)

McDougall's armchair analysis of the parable is intriguing, but it can't be considered evidence for his—or my—distinction between these emotions.

28 • EMPATHIC CONCERN

Both popularity and parsimony favor the claim that empathy and distress combine to produce an overall level of aversive arousal. Before doubting this claim, we need evidence that empathic concern and personal distress are distinct.

Initial Evidence of Distinctiveness: Back to Katherine McDavis

As you may recall, participants in the Katherine McDavis experiment described in Chapter 1 (Coke et al., 1978, Experiment 2) heard Katherine's audiotaped appeal for volunteers to take part in her master's thesis research. Participants' level of empathic concern while listening to the appeal was manipulated by providing false Galvanic Skin Response (GSR) feedback. After listening, all participants rated the degree to which they felt a number of emotions, five of which measured empathic concern.

What I didn't report in Chapter 1 is that empathic concern wasn't the only emotional response measured in this experiment. Feelings of personal distress caused by learning of Katherine's need were also assessed.

Predictions from the Two Answers

If empathic concern and personal distress are functionally equivalent sources of aversive arousal, then the arousal shown on the GSR meter in the high-arousal condition should produce reports not only of greater empathy but also of greater distress. And, reflecting this general aversive arousal, participants' ratings of the empathic concern and personal distress adjectives should measure the same underlying dimension or component in the principal-component analysis described in Chapter 1. Finally, ratings on both the empathy and distress adjectives should be higher in the high-arousal condition than in the low.

On the other hand, if empathic concern and personal distress are distinct emotional states with different motivational consequences, then because Katherine's need for research participants was not upsetting or disturbing, reports of personal distress should be unaffected by the arousal manipulation. Further, ratings of the empathy and distress adjectives should measure two distinct, orthogonal (i.e., uncorrelated) components. And, finally, only ratings of empathic concern should be higher in the high-arousal condition.

A First Measure of Personal Distress

To measure personal distress in the Katherine McDavis experiment, 13 adjectives thought likely to reflect distress were included among the 23 on the questionnaire assessing participants' emotional state—*alarmed, anxious, grieved, troubled, distressed, upset, uneasy, disturbed, worried, perturbed, disconcerted, bothered,* and *irritated*. The principal-component analysis of responses to all 23 adjectives revealed that eight of the 13 were measuring the same component—*alarmed, troubled, upset, disturbed, perturbed, disconcerted, bothered,* and *irritated*. So, ratings of these eight adjectives were averaged to form an index of personal distress.

Indicating distinctiveness rather than equivalence, the component measured by these eight distress adjectives was orthogonal to (i.e., uncorrelated with) the component described in Chapter 1 that was measured by the five empathic-concern adjectives. Further, the empathy adjectives were minimally related to the personal-distress component, and the distress adjectives were minimally related to the empathic-concern component. And, unlike the strong effect of the GSR feedback on empathic concern that was reported in Chapter 1, this feedback had no significant effect on responses to the index created by averaging the eight distress adjectives. Both high- and low-feedback participants reported feeling little distress. Further, those in the high-feedback condition reported feeling significantly less distress than empathic concern ($p < .001$). More evidence of distinctiveness of the two emotional states.

A Revised Eight-Item Index of Personal Distress

The analyses that Jim Fultz, Pat Schoenrade, and I did on data from the five additional studies conducted by 1987 (discussed in Chapter 1) produced a closely related but more conceptually coherent set of eight adjectives to measure personal distress in response to another's need—*alarmed, grieved, troubled, distressed, upset, disturbed, worried,* and *perturbed*. Accordingly, we created a revised Personal Distress Index by averaging ratings of these eight. As had the principal-component analysis of data from the Katherine McDavis experiment, component analyses of data from each of the five studies produced a personal-distress component orthogonal to the empathic-concern component described in Chapter 1.

The statistic that was used to assess how much an adjective contributed to each of these components is called the *loading* of the adjective on the

30 • EMPATHIC CONCERN

component. Like correlation coefficients, loadings can vary from −1.0 (a perfect negative relationship) through zero (no relationship) to 1.0 (a perfect positive relationship). As is customary, a loading of .60 or higher was used to identify adjectives making a major contribution to a component. (If you're more comfortable thinking in terms of correlation coefficients rather than loadings, you can do so—the loading of each adjective on each of the orthogonal components is equal to the correlation between the adjective and the component.)

Table 2.1 gives the loadings of the six empathic-concern and the eight personal-distress adjectives on the empathic-concern and personal-distress components in each of the five additional studies. Across studies, as you can

Table 2.1 Principal–Component Loadings of Self-Reported Emotional Responses to Another in Need (Five Studies)

	Study[a]									
	1		2		3		4		5	
	E[b]	D	E	D	E	D	E	D	E	D
Empathic-concern adjectives										
Sympathetic	.53	.58	.74*	.23	.69*	.29	.84*	.04	.82*	.20
Tender	.32	.66*	.86*	.18	.78*	.28	.78*	.31	.74*	.36
Softhearted	.73*	.14	.80*	.11	.86*	.17	.83*	.05	.86*	.29
Warm	.71*	.23	.80*	-.03	.80*	.19	.68*	.20	.66*	.15
Compassionate	.82*	.09	.73*	.40	.80*	.24	.86*	.14	.90*	.17
Moved	.78*	.37	.78*	.41	.74*	.42	.67*	.31	.72*	.40
Personal-distress adjectives										
Alarmed	.49	.72*	.15	.63*	.34	.72*	.11	.77*	.19	.80*
Grieved	.48	.65*	.58	.55	.33	.70*	.42	.68*	.30	.72*
Troubled	.54	.58	.22	.80*	.33	.75*	.39	.59	.32	.87*
Distressed	.48	.65*	.32	.81*	.48	.67*	.25	.87*	.28	.86*
Upset	.32	.82*	.38	.74*	.38	.80*	.17	.87*	.28	.89*
Disturbed	.38	.82*	.20	.76*	.38	.76*	.18	.89*	.24	.90*
Worried	.18	.87*	.35	.67*	.34	.72*	.18	.78*	.39	.81*
Perturbed	-.11	.59	-.18	.76*	-.13	.69*	-.02	.82*	.11	.68*

[a]Studies are as follows: 1. Batson, Cowles, & Coke (1979). 2. Coke (1980). 3. Toi & Batson (1982). 4. Fultz (1982). 5. Batson, O'Quin et al. (1983).

[b]E = Empathic-concern component; D = Personal-distress component. The two components are orthogonal (i.e., uncorrelated).

Asterisk (*) denotes loading above .60.

see, the empathy adjectives almost always loaded highly on the empathic-concern component, and the distress adjectives almost always loaded highly on the personal-distress component.

Still, to find that the six empathic-concern adjectives and the eight personal-distress adjectives loaded on distinct, orthogonal components didn't mean that the two indexes created by averaging ratings of the adjectives loading highly were uncorrelated. To the contrary, scores on the empathy and distress indexes were positively correlated in each of the five studies, with correlations ranging from .44 to .75.

These positive correlations may seem to suggest that the two indexes were measuring a single emotional state after all. But, although the positive correlations are consistent with this possibility, they don't clearly support it. There are at least three other reasons to expect the two indexes to be correlated when the two components aren't: First, given that both empathic concern and personal distress are emotions, they should be similarly affected by individual differences in general emotionality and in readiness to report emotions. Second, because both are evoked by perception of someone in need, individual differences in judgments about whether the target in a given study is in need—and, if so, the severity of the need—should have parallel effects on each. Third, in each of the five studies, all adjectives were rated on the same response scale, with adjectives on the two indexes intermixed. As a result, individual differences in response-set bias (the tendency to use the lower or higher end of a response scale) should produce a positive correlation between the two indexes.

In contrast to the correlations of the indexes, which can be affected by these individual-difference factors, the principal-component analyses compared each participant's rating of each adjective to his or her rating of each of the 13 other adjectives comprising the two indexes. And, by producing two uncor-related (orthogonal) components, the analyses made it clear that participants consistently responded similarly to the six empathy adjectives, responded similarly to the eight distress adjectives, and responded differently to the adjectives in the two sets.

Since 1987, the revised eight-item Personal Distress Index has been used along with the six-item Empathic Concern Index described in Chapter 1 in much research (again, see Batson, 2011, for a review and references). In this re-search, adjectives on the two indexes have been intermixed on the Emotional Response Scale described in Chapter 1. Figure 2.1 shows the placement of the eight personal distress adjectives on the 26-item version of that scale presented in Figure 1.1. (For ease of recognition, the eight distress adjectives

Emotional Response Scale

Please indicate by circling a number the degree to which you experienced each of these emotional reactions while listening to the broadcast. Do not worry if you were not feeling many of these emotions; only a few may apply to a particular broadcast. Be sure to circle a response for each item.

	not at all			moderately			extremely
1. **alarmed**	1	2	3	4	5	6	7
2. **grieved**	1	2	3	4	5	6	7
3. sympathetic	1	2	3	4	5	6	7
4. intent	1	2	3	4	5	6	7
5. softhearted	1	2	3	4	5	6	7
6. **troubled**	1	2	3	4	5	6	7
7. warm	1	2	3	4	5	6	7
8. concerned	1	2	3	4	5	6	7
9. **distressed**	1	2	3	4	5	6	7
10. low-spirited	1	2	3	4	5	6	7
11. intrigued	1	2	3	4	5	6	7
12. compassionate	1	2	3	4	5	6	7
13. **upset**	1	2	3	4	5	6	7
14. **disturbed**	1	2	3	4	5	6	7
15. tender	1	2	3	4	5	6	7
16. **worried**	1	2	3	4	5	6	7
17. moved	1	2	3	4	5	6	7
18. disconcerted	1	2	3	4	5	6	7
19. feeling low	1	2	3	4	5	6	7
20. **perturbed**	1	2	3	4	5	6	7
21. heavy-hearted	1	2	3	4	5	6	7
22. sorrowful	1	2	3	4	5	6	7
23. bothered	1	2	3	4	5	6	7
24. kind	1	2	3	4	5	6	7
25. sad	1	2	3	4	5	6	7
26. touched	1	2	3	4	5	6	7

FIGURE 2.1. Version of the Emotional Response Scale Used by Batson, Sager et al. (1997). The eight items that comprise the Personal Distress Index are printed boldface.

are printed in bold type in Figure 2.1, but aren't when the scale is administered to participants.)

Is the Distinction between Empathic Concern and Personal Distress Qualitative or Quantitative?

In the Katherine McDavis experiment—and in each of the five additional studies analyzed in 1987—empathic concern and personal distress were found to be distinct emotional responses to another's need. But what's the nature of this distinction? The second answer to the question of distinctiveness assumes it's qualitative—that the two emotional states are different in kind. But Jane Piliavin and her colleagues, reflecting their adoption of the first answer, suggested that the distinction is quantitative. They claimed personal distress is evoked by immediately present, high-impact needs that produce high arousal, such as "severe, life-threatening situations," whereas empathic concern is evoked by less immediate and lower impact needs—"less critical, less intense problem situations" (Piliavin et al., 1981, p. 235). Martin Hoffman offered a similar argument, suggesting that immediate, high-impact needs (e.g., when another person is in physical pain) can produce "empathic over-arousal," which transforms the empathy into personal distress (Hoffman, 2000, pp. 198–205; also see Eisenberg, 2000).

Although not noted at the time, data from the five studies analyzed in 1987 spoke to the question of whether the distinction between empathic concern and personal distress is qualitative or quantitative. Immediacy and impact of the needs that participants encountered varied across the studies, so it was possible to examine whether, when immediacy and impact are high, reports of personal distress replace reports of empathic concern.

Studies 1–3 in Table 2.1 didn't involve immediate, high-impact discomfort. Instead, participants listened to an audiotape of a radio broadcast in which a young woman, who had been in an auto accident several weeks earlier, described dealing with bad scars on her face (Study 1) or on her legs (Study 2), or she described being in a wheelchair and possibly having to give up her career aspirations (Study 3). Studies 4 and 5 did involve immediate, high-impact physical discomfort. Participants watched over closed-circuit TV (actually a videotape) while an introductory psychology student like themselves unexpectedly reacted with obvious pain to a series of random electric shocks.

Participants in the first three studies reported significantly more empathic concern than personal distress ($p < .001$)—as had participants in the Katherine McDavis experiment. Given that these studies involved

34 • EMPATHIC CONCERN

less-immediate, chronic need rather than acute physical discomfort, this difference is entirely consistent with the quantitative claim that lower impact need situations evoke empathic concern, not personal distress. Further, the last two studies in the table, which involved immediate high-impact discomfort, produced reports of personal distress that were significantly higher than in the first three studies. This increase is consistent with the quantitative claim that high-impact physical discomfort evokes high personal distress.

But, contrary to the quantitative claim, there was no evidence that personal distress replaced empathic concern in the last two studies. Instead, reported empathic concern was high—if anything, higher than in the first three studies. This pattern contradicted not only the claim that high-impact physical discomfort produces personal distress and not empathic concern (Piliavin et al.) but also the claim that when empathic arousal becomes high, it turns into personal distress (Hoffman; Eisenberg).

Apparently, empathic concern isn't limited to less-immediate chronic needs, nor is it replaced by personal distress when the need is immediate and high-impact. Instead, both empathic concern and personal distress can be felt in response to high-impact needs. And, as the principal-component analyses reported in the last two columns of Table 2.1 show, the empathic concern and personal distress evoked by such needs are felt as two qualitatively distinct emotional states (for further evidence, see Fabi, Weber, & Leuthold, 2019). We shall see in Chapter 7 that these emotional states also have qualitatively distinct effects on motivation.

A Complication: Is the Reported Distress Self-Oriented Personal Distress or Other-Oriented Empathic Distress?

In Chapter 1, I noted that adjectives such as the eight on the Personal Distress Index can be used to describe both self-oriented distress evoked by encountering another person's need and other-oriented distress felt for the person in need—the latter being a form of empathic concern. To find that the adjectives on the Personal Distress Index load highly on a component orthogonal to the component on which empathic-concern adjectives load indicates that participants in the five studies in Table 2.1 responded to the distress adjectives in terms of self-oriented personal distress, not empathic distress. But experiments using a different need situation—the plight of Katie Banks (described in Chapter 1)—highlight a complication. In response to her need, distress reported by research participants seems to reflect empathic distress for Katie rather than personal distress.

The first clear evidence that the distress for Katie is empathic rather than personal came from an experiment conducted by Batson, Batson, Slingsby, Harrell, Peekna, and Todd (1991, Experiment 1) in which all participants listened to the News from the Personal Side broadcast about Katie. (As you may recall, Katie was struggling to finish her final year of college while caring for her younger brother and sister after their parents died in a car crash.) Following the broadcast, participants completed the Emotional Response Scale that included the six adjectives comprising the Empathic Concern Index and the eight adjectives comprising the Personal Distress Index. A principal-component analysis revealed that in response to Katie's need, participants' ratings of the empathy and distress adjectives didn't load on two orthogonal components as they had in each of the five studies analyzed in 1987. Instead, except for "perturbed," all adjectives of both types loaded highly (above .60) on a single component, indicating that the distress adjectives were measuring empathic distress. (Four sadness adjectives—*low-spirited*, *feeling low*, *heavyhearted*, and *sad*—also loaded above .60 on this component, indicating that they reflected empathic sadness felt for Katie rather than personal sadness.)

Comparing the single-component structure in response to Katie's need with the two-component structure in each of the five studies in Table 2.1, Batson, Batson et al. (1991) proposed:

> When people observe another's physical discomfort, reports of distress are likely to reflect the degree to which they are distressed by this spectacle; when people hear about someone's struggles adjusting to a difficult situation, reports of distress are likely to reflect the degree to which they are distressed for this person. This latter form of distress reflects empathy rather than personal distress as these terms have been defined in the empathy-altruism literature. (p. 415)

Supporting this proposal, it had been found that when people are faced with another's physical suffering, response to the adjectives *concerned* and *grieved* are strongly associated with responses to adjectives such as *alarmed, disturbed*, and *perturbed* and not with adjectives such as *sympathetic, compassionate*, and *tender* (Batson, O'Quin, Fultz, Vanderplas, & Isen, 1983). In contrast, when responding to another's adjustment/coping problems, *concerned* and *grieved* strongly associate with *sympathetic, compassionate*, and *tender* (Batson, Batson, Griffittt, Barrientos, Brandt, Sprengelmeyer, & Bayly, 1989; Batson, Dyck, Brandt, Batson, Powell, McMaster, & Griffitt, 1988). Results of subsequent experiments have continued to support the idea that others' physical suffering and others' adjustment/coping problems typically cue the two different uses of the distress adjectives. The former cues self-oriented personal distress; the latter, other-oriented empathic distress. (For a possible neurological basis for this distinction, see Bruneau, Dufour, & Saxe, 2013.)

Batson, Batson et al. (1991) concluded:

> These observations caution against reifying the empathy and distress indexes used in past research, assuming that they measure the same psychological state in response to every need situation. These observations also underscore the importance of having converging evidence from experimental manipulations of empathy when interpreting results that are based on self-reports, especially self-reports of empathy relative to distress. (p. 415)

Relation of Two Forms of Perspective Taking to the Two Forms of Distress

Shannon Early, Giovanni Salvarani, and I used two forms of perspective taking to further test the proposed distinction between personal and empathic distress (Batson, Early, & Salvarani, 1997). There are two different ways to imagine the effects of another's need situation: You can imagine how the person in need is affected by his or her situation (an imagine-other perspective). Or you can imagine how you would be affected were you in the other's situation (an imagine-self perspective).

In his pioneering research on empathy, Ezra Stotland (1969) found that each of these perspectives led to more physiological arousal and self-reported emotion than did trying to remain objective (an objective perspective). He also found that the physiological and self-report effects of the imagine-other and imagine-self perspectives weren't the same. When his participants observed a young man undergo what they thought was a painful diathermy experience (an electrically induced hot sensation in his hand), those asked to adopt an imagine-other perspective showed more vasoconstriction (constriction of the capillaries in the thumb of their nondominant hand) and, at the end of the diathermy experience, reported feeling relieved. Stotland (1969) interpreted these responses as evidence that the imagine-other participants "were reacting to the feelings they perceived the model as having at a given moment" (p. 296). In contrast, those asked to adopt an imagine-self perspective showed more palmar sweat and reported feeling more tension and nervousness both before and during the experience—responses Stotland interpreted as evidence of a more self-oriented emotional reaction that was "not quite so tied to the experience of the model" (p. 297).

Building on Stotland's research, Shannon, Giovanni, and I predicted different emotional consequences for the imagine-other and imagine-self perspectives among participants confronted with the Katie Banks need situation. Given that Katie was struggling to cope with a difficult situation rather than experiencing immediate physical pain (as was Stotland's young man), our predictions were more complex than Stotland's. First, we predicted that imagining Katie's feelings would produce an increase in empathic concern, whereas imagining how you would feel in her situation would produce an increase in both empathic concern and distress. Symmetry might suggest that an imagine-self perspective should increase only distress, but we didn't expect so neat a pattern. Imagining yourself in Katie's situation may lead you to feel personal distress, as Stotland's imagine-self participants seemed to do. But it may also be an important source of information about what she's going through and, as a result, evoke other-oriented empathic concern. To test this possibility, we added a measure of the nature of any distress experienced in the different perspective conditions. We predicted that distress reported by participants instructed to adopt an imagine-other perspective would be predominantly empathic distress felt for Katie, whereas distress reported by participants instructed to adopt an imagine-self perspective would include both direct (personal) distress and empathic distress.

Perspective Instructions

In our experiment, we randomly assigned male and female undergraduates to one of three perspective conditions prior to listening to the broadcast with Katie's interview. Participants in the objective and imagine-other conditions read the same instructions used in the Katie Banks experiment described in Chapter 1. Those in the imagine-self condition read:

> Try to *imagine how you yourself would feel if you were experiencing what has happened to the person being interviewed and how this experience would affect your life.* Try not to concern yourself with attending to all the information presented. Just concentrate on trying to imagine how you yourself would feel. (Batson, Early, & Salvarani, 1997, p. 752, italics in the original)

38 • EMPATHIC CONCERN

Measuring Emotional Response to Katie's Need

The reaction questionnaire that participants completed to assess their emotional response had two parts. Part 1 was the 26-item Emotional Response Scale shown in Figures 1.1 and 2.1. For each adjective, participants indicated how much they had experienced that emotion while listening to the pilot broadcast. Part 2 measured the degree to which any distress that participants experienced was direct personal distress or empathic distress felt for the person in need.

Responses to Part 1 revealed that the two imagine perspectives (imagine-other, imagine-self) evoked greater empathic concern for Katie than did the objective perspective ($p < .01$), and the imagine-self perspective evoked greater distress than either the objective or the imagine-other perspective (both $ps < .01$). Moreover, as predicted, empathic concern was significantly higher than distress in the imagine-other condition ($p < .001$), whereas both empathic concern and distress were high in the imagine-self condition, with no reliable difference. From these data, however, we don't know the nature of the reported distress.

Nature of the Reported Distress in Each Perspective Condition

Responses to Part 2 permitted us to test the prediction that participants in the imagine-other condition would report feeling empathic distress for Katie, whereas participants in the imagine-self condition would report feeling both direct (personal) and empathic distress. Instructions for Part 2 explained that some of the emotions rated in Part 1 could be experienced in different ways. For example,

> You can feel *directly distressed*, as you might when you have a bad experience . . . . You can be *distressed for* someone else who has a bad experience, as when a person suffers a broken relationship or fails to succeed on a task. Each of these emotions may be described as distress, but they are different types of distress. (Batson, Early, & Salvarani, 1997, p. 753, italics in the original)

Participants were then asked to indicate the degree to which they experienced each type of response for four of the adjectives rated in Part 1: *distressed, upset, troubled,* and *grieved*. That is, they rated the degree to which they felt "*directly distressed,* as you might when you have a bad experience" and the degree to which they felt "*distressed for* the person being interviewed." Next, they rated the degree they felt "*directly upset*, as you might when you have a bad experience" and the degree they felt "*upset for* the person being interviewed." And so on.

We created a Direct-Distress Index (Cronbach's alpha = .97) by averaging the directly distressed ratings for the four emotions asked about and an Empathic-Distress Index (alpha = .95) by averaging the four distressed-for ratings. As predicted, participants in the imagine-self condition reported feeling more direct distress than did participants in the objective and imagine-other conditions ($p < .005$), with no reliable difference between the objective and imagine-other conditions. Also as predicted, participants in the two imagine conditions reported feeling more empathic distress than did participants in the objective condition ($p < .005$), with no reliable difference between the two imagine conditions.

Correlations between scores on the Distress Index from Part 1 of the questionnaire and the two type-of-distress indexes from Part 2 provided further evidence of the different nature of the distress reported in the two imagine conditions. In the imagine-other condition, the Distress Index from Part 1 was highly correlated with the Empathic-Distress Index from Part 2, $r = .76$, but only moderately correlated with the Direct-Distress Index, $r = .40$, suggesting that participants in this condition interpreted the distress adjectives as referring primarily to empathic distress. In the imagine-self condition, the Distress Index from Part 1 was highly correlated with the Direct-Distress Index from Part 2, $r = .77$, and weakly correlated with the Empathic-Distress Index, $r = .25$, suggesting that in this condition the distress adjectives were interpreted as referring primarily to direct personal distress. In contrast, the Empathic Concern Index from Part 1 was highly correlated with the Empathic-Distress Index from Part 2 in each imagine condition (other, self), $rs = .52$ and .74 respectively, and only weakly correlated with the Direct-Distress Index, both $rs = .23$.

To summarize the rather complicated results of this experiment, two different imagine perspectives—imagining how another is affected by his or her situation and imagining how you would be affected by that situation—produced different emotional consequences. Participants instructed to imagine how Katie felt reported more empathic concern than distress. And when asked about the nature of their distress, these participants said it was predominantly empathic distress for Katie, not direct distress. In contrast, participants instructed to imagine how they would feel in Katie's situation

40 • EMPATHIC CONCERN

reported high levels of both empathic concern and distress. When asked about the nature of their distress, these participants said they felt both direct and empathic distress.

Might These Results Be Due to Experimental Demand?

But perhaps the results of this experiment are simply a product of demand characteristics—that is, of pressure that the experimental procedure put on participants to respond in a particular way (Orne, 1962). After all, in order to compare the effects of the two imagine perspectives, participants in the different conditions were instructed to adopt a particular perspective while listening to the interview with Katie, and afterward all participants were asked about particular emotional reactions. Perhaps after being told what perspective to adopt, participants simply reported the emotional reactions they thought we wanted them to report.

One common source of experimental demand can immediately be ruled out—different cues from the experimenter in different experimental conditions. The experimenters (whose gender was matched to each participant's) were kept unaware of participants' perspective condition until after all measures were taken, making it impossible for experimenters to know what cues to provide. The three perspective conditions differed only in their typewritten instructions, so if there were cues about how to respond, the instructions must be the source.

But that seemed unlikely. The objective and imagine-other instructions made no mention of participants' feelings, only the feelings of the person interviewed. The imagine-self instructions did mention the participant's feelings, but with no cues as to what those feelings should be. Further, participants received only one set of perspective instructions and thought all other participants received this set too, leaving participants with no basis for guessing how we expected them to respond relative to participants given other instructions—indeed, leaving them with no basis for thinking there were other instructions. Thus, the instructions provided little direction about how participants should feel, almost certainly not enough to produce the complex pattern of differences and correlations observed.

Finally, the parallels between results of this experiment using self-reports and results of the earlier experiment by Stotland (1969) using physiological measures provided additional assurance that the results of this experiment weren't simply a product of self-reports made in the absence of true feeling. Buffone, Poulin, DeLury, Ministero, Morrison, and Scalco (2017) also found similar results using physiological measures. In combination, these considerations lead me to have far more doubt about a demand explanation of the results than doubt about the results themselves.

Conclusion

Empathic concern and personal distress are two possible emotional responses when we encounter another in need. The former is other-oriented, a response to how the need affects the other's welfare. The latter is self-oriented, a response to how the other's need affects our own welfare. The distinction between these two emotional states isn't just quantitative, with low-impact needs producing empathy and high-impact needs producing distress. Although low-impact needs are less likely to produce personal distress, high-impact needs can produce high levels of both empathic concern and personal distress. And when these two emotional states co-occur, they're experienced as qualitatively distinct, with reports of each falling on orthogonal components in principal-component analyses. Moreover, as we shall see in Chapter 7, the two states also have qualitatively distinct motivational consequences.

At the end of Chapter 1, I noted that use of a self-report scale to measure empathic concern involves a danger: Respondents' claims to feel other-oriented concern can be inflated by a desire to present themselves as caring and kind. Because personal distress is a less socially desirable response, use of a self-report scale to measure it seems less vulnerable to this danger. But, as we discovered, self-report measures of personal distress sometimes have another problem. Adjectives used to report self-oriented personal distress can also be used to report other-oriented empathic distress, a form of empathic concern. In the need situations studied to date, this second use is most apparent when respondents are faced with a person confronting an adjustment/coping problem. In such situations, ratings of the distress adjectives are likely to indicate empathic rather than personal distress. However, when faced with a person experiencing physical pain—such as the driver on the pavement at the start of this chapter—ratings of the distress adjectives seem to provide a valid measure of personal distress.

3 DISTINGUISHING IT FROM OTHER THINGS CALLED EMPATHY

Because I'm using "empathy" as shorthand for empathic concern, I not only need to distinguish such concern from personal distress but also from other psychological phenomena that have been called empathy, noting evidence and issues related to each. Further, I need to specify both how I'll refer in subsequent chapters to each of these other phenomena—and to specify how each relates to empathic concern. An imagination exercise I first used over a decade ago (Batson, 2009) may help make the distinctions clear:

> You meet a friend for lunch. She seems distracted, staring into space. Gradually, she begins to cry, then to explain that she just learned she's losing her job because of layoffs. She says she's not angry but hurt and scared. Near tears yourself, you feel very sorry for her and say so. What you don't say is that you're reminded of the talk about job cuts where you work. Seeing your friend so upset makes you anxious and uneasy. You even feel a brief flash of relief: "Thank God it wasn't me!"

Empathic concern, defined in Chapter 1 as an other-oriented emotional state elicited by and congruent with the perceived welfare of someone in need, appears in only one aspect of this example—feeling sorry for your friend. Your anxiety and uneasiness are forms of personal distress. But the example also contains seven other phenomena that have been called empathy, each of which is distinct from empathic concern.

Empathic Concern. C. Daniel Batson, Oxford University Press. © Oxford University Press 2023.
DOI: 10.1093/oso/9780197610923.003.0004

Knowing What Another Person is Thinking and Feeling

A number of scholars, researchers, and clinicians have referred to knowing another person's internal state—his or her thoughts and feelings—as empathy (e.g., Brothers, 1989; Damasio, 2002; de Waal, 1996; Dymond, 1950; Freud, 1922; Ickes, 1993; Kohler, 1929; Levenson & Ruef, 1992; Wispé, 1986; Zahavi & Overgaard, 2012). Such knowledge has also been the focus of research on "theory of mind" in humans and other primates (e.g., Adams, 2001; Goldman, 1993; Gordon, 1995; Meltzoff & Decety, 2003; O'Connell, 1995; Povinelli, Bering, & Giambrone, 2000; Premack & Woodruff, 1978; Ravenscroft, 1998; Tomasello & Call, 1997).

Sometimes, to know what someone else is thinking and feeling can pose quite a challenge, especially if you have limited clues—for example, think of seeing a stranger sitting alone on a park bench, slumped forward, head down. But it's relatively easy to know what your friend at lunch is thinking and feeling. Once she explains, you can be confident what's on her mind: Losing her job. From what she says and how she acts, you may think you also know how she feels: Hurt and scared. Of course, you might be wrong, at least about some nuances.

Accurate knowledge of another person's thoughts and feelings may seem necessary if we're to experience other-oriented empathic concern. But it's not. We can experience true concern based on a false perception of another's state. Even if you're quite wrong about what your friend is thinking and feeling (not likely in this example), to feel sorry for her is to experience empathic concern. Feeling such concern requires that we perceive the other to be in need, not that our perception be accurate. Nor does it require that our perception match the other's perception of his or her thoughts and feelings, which is the standard used to determine accuracy in the research by Bill Ickes (1993) and colleagues on *empathic accuracy*. (The possibility that the other might fail to correctly identify his or her own thoughts and feelings tends to be ignored in that research, as noted by Thomas and Fletcher, 1997.) Despite what your friend says, perhaps she really is angry.

Of course, any attempt to help a person in need is more likely to be beneficial if we have an accurate perception of the need. So it's not surprising that clinicians, whose primary concern is to help their clients, tend to emphasize accurate perception of a client's state rather than other-oriented feeling for the client (Kohut, 1959; Rogers, 1975; Wiesenfeld, Whitman, & Malatesta, 1984). Physicians do, too (MacLean, 1967).

Matching the Posture or Expression—or the Neural State—of an Observed Other

Automatically matching the posture or expression of another person is a definition of empathy in many dictionaries. Psychologists are more likely to call such matching either *mimicry* (Bavelas, Black, Lemery, & Mullet, 1987; Chartrand & Bargh, 1999; Dimberg, Thunberg, & Elmehed, 2000; Hoffman, 2000) or *imitation* (Meltzoff & Moore, 1997).

Mimicry and Imitation

The role of mimicry and imitation in social perception—including perception of another person's emotional state—has received considerable attention over the last half-century (see, for example, Chartrand & Bargh, 1999; Dimberg et al., 2000; Hoffman, 2000; Niedenthal, 2007; Öhman, 2002; Vaughan & Lanzetta, 1981). But in recent years, doubts have arisen about whether matching another's posture or expression is as automatic as had been assumed. Neither humans nor members of other species mimic or imitate all actions of others. It may be hard to resist tensing and twisting when watching someone balance on a tightrope; yet I can watch someone file papers with no inclination to act similarly. Something more than automatic matching must be involved to select those actions we copy and those we don't (see Lakin & Chartrand, 2003; Tamir, Robinson, Clore, Martin, & Whitaker, 2004; Zentall, 2003, for suggestions). To mention just one possibility, rather than automatically copying the tightrope walker's action, I may be trying, however futilely, to control or correct it—much as I twist my body to bring an errant putt back on line.

Meltzoff and Moore (1997) presented evidence that even in infants, imitation is an active goal-directed process. And in adults, behavior matching often serves a higher-order communicative function. In the words of Bavelas, Black, Lemery, and Mullett (1986), "I show how you feel" in order to convey "fellow feeling" and support (also see Buck & Ginsburg, 1991). Rather than examples of automatic mimicry, parallel bodily expression of emotion may be part of a more controlled higher-level cognitive process of recognizing, labeling, and sharing another's emotion (Niedenthal, 2007; Niedenthal, Winkielman, Mondillon, & Vermeulen, 2009).

Response matching may at times provide clues to the internal states of others, but we humans also use both memory and general knowledge to infer what others think and feel in various situations (Singer, Seymour, O'Doherty,

Kaube, Dolan, & Frith, 2004; Tomasello, 1999). Indeed, the problem of anthropomorphism arises precisely because we have the ability and inclination to make such inferences not only about other humans but also about other species—and even about our cars. Moreover, with humans we can also rely on direct communication: Your friend told you what she was thinking and feeling.

Neural Matching

In 2002, Stephanie Preston and Frans de Waal sought to provide a unified theory of empathy by focusing on matched neural states rather than matched behavior. They viewed empathy as *"any process where the attended perception of the object's state* [i.e., the perceived state of the individual empathized with] *generates a state in the subject* [the individual empathizing] *that is more applicable to the object's state or situation than to the subject's own prior state or situation"* (Preston & de Waal, 2002, p. 4, italics in the original).

Preston and de Waal based their theory on a perception-action model (PAM). According to this model, perceiving another's emotional reaction in a given situation leads us to automatically match his or her neural state because our perception of another's behavior and our perception of our own behavior activate some of the same neural circuits. In their words:

> According to the perception-action hypothesis, perception of a behavior in another automatically activates one's own representations for the behavior, and output from this shared representation automatically proceeds to motor areas of the brain where responses are prepared and executed. (Preston & de Waal, 2002, pp. 9–10)

Thus, when we see another person in an emotional state, we come to feel what the other feels. (The PAM was based on the work of Wolfgang Prinz, 1987, 1997, but Prinz's original depiction of the link between perception and action referred to physical action rather than emotional responses, and it was far less automatic than Preston and de Waal's depiction.)

Over the years, de Waal (2006, 2008, 2009) has embellished the PAM with a Russian-doll metaphor. As with a set of Russian dolls—where the smallest lies at the core of each increasingly larger one—de Waal has claimed that matching another's neural activation and emotional state through the perception-action link lies at the core of and is the basis for all more complex empathic processes, including empathic concern.

Perception of the emotional state of another automatically activates shared representations causing a matching emotional state in the observer. With increasing cognition, state-matching evolved into more complex forms, including concern for the other and perspective taking. (de Waal, 2008, p. 279)

I must confess that I doubt this claim. To suggest that shared neural representations provide the unifying source of all empathic feelings seems to considerably overestimate the role of matched emotional states, at least among humans. As with mimicked action, perception of another's emotional state doesn't always and automatically lead to an emotional state, whether matched or unmatched (de Vignemont & Singer, 2006; Singer & Lamm, 2009), nor do emotional reactions to the state of another always require direct perceptual cues or shared neural activation (Danziger, Faillenot, & Peyron, 2009; Lamm, Decety, & Singer, 2011; Lamm, Meltzoff, & Decety, 2010).

Moreover, evidence is growing that the neural activity associated with our response to the emotional experiences of others only partially overlaps the neural activity associated with our own emotion-arousing experiences (e.g., Morrison & Downing, 2007; Zaki, Ochsner, Hanelin, Wager, & Mackey, 2007; Zaki et al., 2016). And, although Preston and de Waal cited neural "mirroring" as important evidence for their PAM (2002, pp. 10, 14), increasing doubt has been cast on the extent to which such mirroring is unlearned and automatic, and on the role it plays in understanding and responding to another's plight (see Decety, 2010; Gallese, Gernsbacher, Heyes, Hickok, & Iacoboni, 2011; Glenberg, 2011; Hickok, 2014; Jacob, 2008).

Perhaps in response to these issues, Preston and de Waal have come to speak less of perception of another's state automatically generating a matching state in the perceiver and to speak more of the perceiver activating a representation by employing his or her own experience and knowledge of the other's state, situation, and person (e.g., de Waal & Preston, 2017). Cognitive processes now seem to play a far more prominent role than in the 2002 PAM.

Matching another's behavior or neural representation may at times facilitate feeling empathic concern, but neither behavioral nor neural matching seems necessary or sufficient to experience such concern. Your friend's tears may have caused you to tear up, too. Still, it's unlikely that sharing her tears or matching her neural state was necessary for you to feel sorry for her. More likely, her tears made it clear how upset she was, and you felt like crying because you were sorry about what she was going through.

Coming to Feel as Another Person Feels

Coming to feel the same emotion that someone else feels is another common dictionary definition of empathy. And it's a definition used by some philosophers (Darwall, 1998; Goldman, 1992; Nichols, 2001; Sober & Wilson, 1998), neuroscientists (Damasio, 2003; Decety & Lamm, 2009; de Vignemont & Singer, 2006), and psychologists (Berger, 1962; Eisenberg & Strayer, 1987; Englis, Vaughan, & Lanzetta, 1982; Feshbach & Roe, 1968; Gruen & Mendelsohn, 1986; Wondra & Ellsworth, 2015). Alternatively, many psychologists call coming to feel as the other feels *emotional contagion* (e.g., de Waal, 2009; Hatfield, Cacioppo, & Rapson, 1994). As noted in the Introduction, feeling as another feels is what recent critics of empathy like Jesse Prinz and Paul Bloom mean by the term. The idea of feeling-as raises several issues.

Bottom Up or Top Down?

This third phenomenon called empathy has often been seen as the link between the previous two: Mimicry, imitation, or neural-state matching (Phenomenon 2) leads us to feel as the other feels (Phenomenon 3), and our feeling reveals to us what the other is feeling (Phenomenon 1)—a *bottom-up* account of how we come to know the internal states of others. But there's another possibility. Feeling as another feels may be the product of a *top-down* inferential process in which knowing how the other feels precedes feeling as he or she feels.

Long ago, the Scottish Enlightenment philosopher David Hume began his great classic, *A Treatise of Human Nature* (1739–1740/1896), by distinguishing two forms of perception that he thought comprised all mental content—impressions and ideas:

> Those perceptions, which enter with most force and violence, we may name *impressions*; and under this name I comprehend all our sensations, passions, and emotions, as they make their first appearance in the soul. By *ideas* I mean the faint images of these in thinking and reasoning. (Hume, 1739–1740/1896, p. 1, italics in original)

After dealing with ideas and reasoning in Book I of the *Treatise*, Hume turned to the passions in Book II—and to the role of sympathy in coming to feel as another feels. (He used the term sympathy not empathy because the latter term didn't exist in his day.) Hume thought sympathy was remarkable. Indeed,

> No quality of human nature is more remarkable, both in itself and in its consequences, than the propensity we have to sympathize with others, and to receive by communication their inclinations and sentiments, however different from, or even contrary to our own. . . . A cheerful countenance infuses a sensible complacency and serenity into my mind; as an angry or sorrowful one throws a sudden damp upon me. . . .
>
> When any affection is infus'd by sympathy, it is at first known only by its effects, and by those external signs in the countenance and conversation, which convey an idea of it. This idea is presently converted into an impression, and acquires such a degree of force and vivacity, as to become the very passion itself, and produce an equal emotion, as any original affection. (pp. 316–317)

Hume thought that being similar to the other facilitated this conversion from idea to impression, as did proximity, familiarity, kinship, and friendship—all features that enliven our perception of the other's sentiments and passions.

In today's terms, we might say that Hume's is a cognitively mediated, top-down analysis of how we come to feel as others feel. First, we form an idea of their thoughts and feelings from observing what they say and do: "When we sympathize with the passion and sentiments of others, these movements appear at first in *our* mind as mere ideas, and are conceiv'd to belong to another person, as we conceive any other matter of fact" (p. 319, italics in original). Second, the idea, if sufficiently forceful and vivid, is then "converted into an impression" and becomes "the very passion itself." Hume's top-down view is thus quite different from the bottom-up account in which perception of the other's state leads us to automatically match that state either behaviorally or neurologically, thereby coming to feel as the other feels, which enables us to know what he or she is feeling.

How Similar is the Same?

Those who employ a feeling-as conception of empathy often qualify it by saying that the empathizer need not feel exactly the same emotion, only a similar one (e.g., Eisenberg, 2000; Hoffman, 2000). But it's unclear how similar is similar enough to be considered feeling as. If you feel sorry for your friend because she's hurt and afraid, is that feeling as she feels? Not really—sorrow

50 • EMPATHIC CONCERN

and fear are qualitatively different emotions. Indeed, even if you feel sorry for her because she's sorry she lost her job, her sorrow and yours aren't really the same. Hers is over losing her job whereas yours is over her sorrow.

Beyond Matching to Catching

Sometimes one person feels the same emotion as another, yet we wouldn't call it empathy. Think of two basketball fans sitting rows apart who both feel sad after the home team loses in overtime. They have the same emotional response to the same event, but their responses are parallel rather than empathic.

To rule out parallel responses like this one, many who use a feeling-as conception say that empathy involves not only emotion matching but also emotion catching (e.g., Hatfield et al., 1994). And they say that to have evidence of catching, more is required than that one person has a physiological response of roughly the same magnitude at roughly the same time as another—what Levenson and Ruef (1992) called "shared physiology." The emotion must also be received (caught) from the other—hence the term contagion.

Catching another's emotion can be hard to determine. To illustrate the difficulty, consider one of the research findings most frequently cited as support for a feeling-as conception of empathy. Abraham Sagi and Martin Hoffman (1976) presented one- to two-day-old infants with either (a) tape-recorded sounds of another infant crying, (b) recorded sounds of a synthetic nonhuman cry, or (c) no sounds. Infants who were presented with another infant's cry cried significantly more than those presented with a synthetic cry or with silence. Sagi and Hoffman claimed that this difference provided evidence of one newborn infant matching and catching another's affective state, thus displaying an inborn "rudimentary empathic distress reaction" (1976, p. 176). Grace Martin and Russ Clark (1982) reported much the same difference but with even more specificity—they found that infants increased their crying to another infant's recorded cry and not to recordings of (a) their own cry, (b) an older child's cry, or (c) the cry of an infant chimpanzee.

Following Sagi and Hoffman, many scholars have interpreted these findings as evidence of a rudimentary feeling–as form of empathy. There are, however, alternative explanations for an infant crying in response to another infant's cry—alternatives that have rarely been recognized in the empathy literature (as noted by Dondi, Simion, & Caltran, 1999). One alternative is that the crying is a competitive response that increases the chances of getting food or comfort (Soltis, 2004; Zahn-Waxler, Schoen, & Decety, 2018; Zeifman, 2001). Imagine that we did a parallel study with baby birds in the nest. We would likely interpret the rapid spread of peeping and open-mouth straining once one baby bird starts peeping and straining as parallel and competitive rather than as a rudimentary empathic response. Another alternative: The other infant's distress cry may serve as a signal of danger, danger that then induces distress and crying—again, a parallel response. And another: Perhaps crying in response to another infant's cry reflects an innate inclination to imitate certain actions of others (Meltzoff & Moore, 1997). If so, it wouldn't be catching the other's feeling of distress but copying the other's behavior of crying. Given these alternatives, I think that a feeling-as interpretation of infants' reactive cries has been accepted too quickly.

Feeling-With; Compassion

Feeling with a person in need is a variant of feeling as the other feels, at least if feeling with means feeling alongside. To illustrate, you may feel sad because you wish to let your friend know that you recognize she's feeling sad and that you commiserate. Some scholars have called such a feeling *compassion* because compassion literally means "feeling with." But compassion is more often used to mean feeling *for* a person in need—what I'm calling empathic concern. Remember the description of the good Samaritan's reaction to the beaten, half-dead man who fell among thieves: "And when he saw him, he had compassion" (Luke 10:33). It seems clear that the Samaritan was feeling for, not with, this man (who was likely unconscious and so not feeling anything). When I use the term compassion, I mean feeling for.

Is Feeling-As a Source of Empathic Concern?

Coming to feel as another person feels, whether parallel or caught, may at times enable you to better understand how the other feels, which may in turn lead you to feel empathic concern. But it's important to recognize that feeling as the other feels is neither necessary nor sufficient to experience such concern. Regarding necessity, return again to your friend. To feel sorry for her, you didn't need to feel hurt and afraid, too, only to know that she was hurt and afraid. Regarding sufficiency, remember the example from Chapter 1 of flying in rough weather. Sensing the nervousness of other passengers on the plane, I became nervous too—a form of personal distress, not empathic concern.

Intuiting or Projecting Yourself into Another's Situation

Listening to your friend, you may have asked yourself what it would be like to be a young woman just told she's losing her job. German philosopher Theodor Lipps, whose primary interest was aesthetics (i.e., appreciation of art), used *Einfühlung* ("feeling into") to describe the act of imaginatively projecting yourself into another person's situation—or projecting yourself into the situation of an inanimate object such as a gnarled, dead tree on a bleak, windswept hillside (Lipps, 1903). It was to translate Lipps's *Einfühlung* that psychologist Edward Titchener (1909) created the English word "empathy."

This original conception of empathy as aesthetic projection often appears as a definition in dictionaries, and it has appeared in recent philosophical discussions of simulation (imagining yourself in the other's situation) as a way to understand another's internal state (e.g., Stueber, 2006). But aesthetic projection is rarely what's meant by empathy in contemporary psychology or neuroscience—although Lauren Wispé did include this use in his 1968 analysis of sympathy and empathy, calling it *aesthetic empathy*.

Intuiting or projecting ourselves into another's situation may give us a lively sense of what the other is thinking and feeling, which may in turn facilitate other-oriented empathic concern. But when another person's need is obvious because of what has happened or been said, such projection isn't necessary. And when the other's need isn't obvious, projection runs the risk of producing an inaccurate understanding of the other's state—especially if we don't have a clear sense of relevant self-other differences (as noted by Neyer, Banse, & Asendorpf, 1999).

Imagining How Another Is Affected by His or Her Situation

Rather than imagining how it would feel to be a young woman just told she's losing her job, you more likely imagined how your friend in particular is affected by losing her job. Doing so could be based not only on what she says and does but also on your knowledge of her character, values, and desires. Wispé (1968) called imagining how another is affected by events *psychological empathy* to differentiate it from his aesthetic empathy. Dennis Regan and Judith Totten (1975), and Martha Nussbaum (2001), simply called it empathy. When Ezra Stotland (1969) reported his experiments in which participants watched the young man undergo a painful diathermy treatment, he spoke of this form of perspective taking as an imagine-him perspective. More generally, it's been called an imagine-other perspective (see Chapter 2).

G.T. Barrett-Lennard (1981) offered helpful elaboration on what an imagine-other perspective involves, describing it as a process "in which Person A opens him- or herself in a deeply responsive way to Person B's feelings and experiencing but without losing awareness that B is a distinct other self" (p. 92). This process of responsively knowing requires sensitivity to the way the other is affected by his or her situation. Rather than projection, it involves active reception (also see Rogers, 1961, Chapter 17, and Rogers, 1975).

As discussed in Chapter 2, instructions to imagine how another person is affected by his or her situation have often been used to induce empathic concern in laboratory experiments. However, this imagine-other perspective shouldn't be confused with or equated to the empathic concern it evokes. There is clear evidence from the Katie Banks experiments described in Chapters 1 and 2—and from many other experiments (see especially Coke et al., 1978, Experiment 1)—that an imagine-other perspective and empathic concern are different psychological states. Imagining how another is affected is a perceptual/cognitive state (Barrett-Lennard called it an "empathic attentional set"), whereas empathic concern is an emotional state. Returning to your friend, you likely imagined how she felt about losing her job, and doing so likely intensified your feelings of sorrow for her. Still, this act of imagination and your resulting sorrow were distinct.

Imagining How You Would Think and Feel in the Other's Place

Adam Smith (1759/1976) colorfully referred to the act of imagining how you would think and feel in another person's situation as "changing places in fancy." George Herbert Mead (1934) sometimes called it role taking and sometimes empathy. In the Piagetian tradition, it has been called perspective taking, role taking, and decentering (Piaget, 1932/1965; also see Epley, Keysar, Van Boven, & Gilovich, 2004; Galinsky, Ku, & Wang, 2005; Galinsky & Moskowitz, 2000; Galinsky, Wang, & Ku, 2008; Krebs & Russell, 1981; Steins & Wicklund, 1996). Stotland (1969) called it an imagine-self perspective, as have I (Chapter 2).

54 • EMPATHIC CONCERN

Distinguishing an Imagine-Self Perspective from Projection and from an Imagine-Other Perspective

To adopt an imagine-self perspective is similar to the act of projecting yourself into another's situation (Phenomenon 4). However, these two concepts were developed independently in very different contexts, one aesthetic and the other interpersonal, so it seems best to keep them separate. An imagine-self perspective focuses on imagining your own thoughts and feelings were you in the other's situation—not on imagining what you would feel were you the other in that situation.

The imagine-self and imagine-other perspectives have often been treated as equivalent (e.g., Aderman, Brehm, & Katz, 1974; Davis, 1994; Davis, Conklin, Smith, & Luce, 1996; Lerner, 1980). Yet there is considerable evidence that they shouldn't be (for some of the evidence, see Batson, Early, & Salvarani, 1997; Batson, Lishner et al., 2003; Majdandžić, Amaschaufer, Hummer, Windischberger, & Lamm, 2016; Myers, Laurent, & Hodges, 2014; Stotland, 1969). As documented in Chapter 2, although both an imagine-other and an imagine-self perspective can stimulate empathic concern, an imagine-self perspective is also likely to evoke self-oriented feelings of distress whereas an imagine-other perspective is not. What wasn't described in Chapter 2 is evidence that the two perspectives produce cognitive and neurophysiological differences as well:

Cognitive differences. Mark Davis and several colleagues used a thought-listing procedure to assess cognitive effects of these two forms of perspective taking (Davis, Soderlund, Cole, Gadol, Kute, Myers, & Weihing, 2004). They had participants watch a 150-second video segment of a talk-show interview with a woman named Jackie who had serious kidney problems. In the segment, Jackie tried unsuccessfully to fight back tears as she spoke about her physical weakness and experience with dialysis. Davis and colleagues found that participants in the imagine-other condition reported both more target-related thoughts and fewer self-related thoughts than did participants in the imagine-self condition ($p < .01$ for each comparison). It seems that in response to Jackie, who presented clear information about her situation and reaction to it, an imagine-self perspective wasn't required to recognize and care about her need. Instead, an imagine-self perspective inhibited other-oriented thoughts and feelings.

Interestingly, Davis and colleagues (2004) found different results in a second experiment, likely due to an important procedural change. In that experiment, participants watched a relatively bland video interview in which

Lisa, an average student with no apparent need, talked about her experiences at college. Results revealed that participants in both an imagine-other and an imagine-self condition reported more self-related thoughts than did participants instructed to remain objective. It seemed that with no clear need or strong reactions, participants who were instructed to imagine Lisa's feelings found they had to imagine themselves in her situation as a stepping-stone, which produced more self-related thoughts (as in an earlier experiment that used the Lisa tape—Davis, Conklin, Smith, & Luce, 1996, Experiment 1).

Neurophysiological differences. The research by Davis and colleagues (2004) suggested that when confronted with a person in clear distress, an imagine-other perspective increases other-related thoughts whereas an imagine-self perspective increases self-related thoughts. Extending this suggestion, if an imagine-other perspective involves sensitive attention to the plight of the other and maintenance of clear self-other differentiation, whereas an imagine-self perspective involves thinking of oneself in the other's situation, then the two perspectives should lead to differences in hemodynamic (blood flow) activity in areas of the brain associated with self-other differentiation (e.g., the right inferior parietal cortex/temporoparietal junction—TPJ). Three neuroimaging studies by Jean Decety and his colleagues provided data consistent with this prediction (Jackson, Brunet, Meltzoff, & Decety, 2006; Lamm, Batson, & Decety, 2007; Ruby & Decety, 2004).

Once More, Bottom Up or Top Down?

In *The Theory of Moral Sentiments* (1759/1976), Adam Smith built on David Hume's cognitively mediated, top-down analysis of sympathy to present his own account of how we come to feel as another person feels. Smith's account differed from Hume's in two important ways: First, rather than beginning with the sympathizer's attention to behavioral manifestation of the other's sentiments, passions, and emotions, as did Hume, Smith began with attention to the other's situation that produced the behavioral response. Second, Smith added a perceptual/cognitive step—imagining yourself in the other's situation (i.e., an imagine-self perspective)—which he thought was necessary for us to appreciate the other's internal state:

> As we have no immediate experience of what other men feel, we can form no idea of the manner in which they are affected, but by conceiving what we ourselves should feel in the like situation. Though our brother is upon the rack, as long as we ourselves are at our ease, our senses will

never inform us of what he suffers.... It is by the imagination only that we can form any conception of what are his sensations.... By the imagination we place ourselves in his situation, we conceive ourselves enduring all the same torments, we enter as it were into his body.... His agonies, when they are thus brought home to ourselves, when we have thus adopted them as our own, begin at last to affect us, and we then tremble and shudder at the thought of what he feels. (Smith, 1759/1976, p. 9)

Paralleling Hume, Smith believed that the likelihood of imagining yourself in the other's situation depends on similarity, proximity, familiarity, kinship, and friendship. (For more detail on sympathy in Hume and Smith, see Ilyes, 2017, and the Introduction to Smith's *The Theory of Moral Sentiments* by the editors, Raphael and Macfie; Smith, 1759/1976, especially pp. 11–13.)

I noted earlier that, rather than the cognitively mediated top-down analyses of Hume and Smith, automatic bottom-up processes—such as Preston and de Waal's original PAM—are often invoked today to explain how we come to feel as others feel. Bottom-up explanations are, as you might expect, especially popular among those wanting to make a case for empathy in human infants (e.g., Bloom, 2016) or in species lacking a well-developed prefrontal cortex (e.g., de Waal, 2009).

An Imagine-Self Perspective as a Source of Empathic Concern

If the other's situation is unfamiliar or unclear, then imagining how you would feel in this situation may provide a useful—possibly essential—basis for understanding his or her plight. In such a case, an imagine-self perspective may serve as a stepping-stone to perceiving the other as in need and to feeling empathic concern.

But this stepping-stone can be slippery. When the other person differs from me, then for me to imagine how I would think and feel in his or her place may prove misleading, especially if I lack a clear sense of how we differ (Hygge, 1976; Jarymowicz, 1992; Kameda, Murata, Sasaki, Higuchi, & Inukai, 2012; Van Boven, Leowenstein, Dunning, & Nordgren, 2013). Prior similar experience may increase my empathic concern (Hodges, Kiel, Kramer, Veach, & Villanueva, 2010). Yet even if I think the other is similar and his or her situation familiar, for me to imagine my own experience may inhibit my empathy. I may become wrapped up in how I would or did react and lose sight of the other person and his or her need (Israelashvili, Sauter, & Fischer, 2020;

Nickerson, 1999; Ruttan, McDonnell, & Nordgren, 2015). While listening to your friend, your thoughts about how you would feel if you were laid off led you to become self-concerned—to feel anxious, uneasy, and lucky by comparison. These self-oriented feelings likely dampened your empathic concern.

Having a General Disposition, or Trait, to Feel for Others

Taking a step back from the specifics of lunch with your friend, you may have a general disposition to think about and/or feel for others when they're in need. This disposition, often called empathy by individual-difference researchers, may have intensified your empathic concern for your friend. (Someone who lacks this disposition may feel little for a friend in need.) But—paralleling the effect of an imagine-other perspective discussed earlier—even though this disposition may have intensified your empathic concern, the two are distinct. As defined in Chapter 1, empathic concern is a response to the plight of a specific individual or individuals in a specific situation. It's an emotional state, not a trait.

There doubtless are individual differences in the ability and inclination to experience empathic concern—as well as in the ability and inclination to experience the other psychological states that have been called empathy. But, except for being able to identify individuals at the extreme low end of an ability-and-inclination continuum (e.g., psychopaths), I don't think we yet have a good way to assess these individual differences. Many researchers believe we can get an accurate measure of such differences by having people fill out self-report questionnaires that ask them how much they care about others in need, questionnaires such as the Empathic Concern Scale of Mark Davis's (1983) Interpersonal Reactivity Index. I don't. I fear that these self-report questionnaires are more likely to tap a desire to *appear* caring than to provide an accurate indicator of a person's readiness to care for someone in need. (For evidence supporting this fear, see Batson, Bolen, Cross, & Neuringer-Benefiel, 1986.)

Conclusion

I've described these seven other psychological phenomena that have been called empathy for two reasons. First, I hope to reduce confusion by recognizing distinctions. Distinctions wouldn't be necessary if the term empathy referred to just one thing and everyone agreed on what that thing is.

58 • EMPATHIC CONCERN

But, as with many psychological terms, it doesn't. Empathy has been used in a variety of ways. And despite claims from Wispé in 1986 and Cuff, Brown, Taylor, and Howat in 2016—and many others in between—that their concept of empathy is the right one, I know of no clear historical or logical basis for such claims.

In such a situation, the best we can do is recognize the different phenomena, specify the labels we're adopting, and use them consistently. Accordingly, I shall use the term empathic concern—and empathy for short—to refer only to the other-oriented emotion described in Chapter 1. I shall refer to the seven other phenomena as in the various section headings of this chapter:

—Knowing another's thoughts and feelings
—Matching the behavior or neural state of another
—Feeling as another feels
—Projecting yourself into another's situation
—Imagining how another feels (an imagine-other perspective)
—Imagining how you would feel in another's situation (an imagine-self
  perspective)
—A disposition to feel for others.

My second reason for describing the other phenomena is to specify how each relates to empathic concern. Four are cognitive or perceptual states that can, at times, promote such concern—knowing another's thoughts and feelings, intuiting your way into another's situation, imagining how another is affected by his or her situation, and imagining how you would be affected by his or her situation. One is an alternative emotional state that can at times promote empathic concern—feeling as the other feels. Another is a physiological state that may enable us to feel as the other feels and so, at times, lead to empathic concern—matching the other's behavior or neural activation. Finally, a personal disposition to feel for others can, at times, facilitate empathic concern. Thus, all seven can facilitate feeling empathic concern, but none always does.

Given the prominence and popularity of claims that empathic concern is a source of sensitive response to the suffering of others, I've focused this book on it. In doing so, I don't deny that several of the other phenomena called empathy have also been proposed as sources of sensitive response, independent of their effect on empathic concern. For example, it has been suggested by Preston and de Waal (2002), among others, that coming to feel as another person feels can lead us to respond to the other's suffering as we would to our own. It has also been suggested that imagining how we would think and feel in the other's place can lead, via increased cognitive understanding, to a more sensitive response to the plight of members of stereotyped out-groups (e.g., Galinsky et al., 2005, 2008; Galinsky & Moskowitz, 2000). However, whether either phenomenon can have these effects independent of its effect on empathic concern currently remains an open question—as is true for pro-social effects of each of the other phenomena.

Although distinctions among the various things called empathy are some-times subtle, there seems little doubt that each of these things exists. Indeed, most are familiar experiences. But their familiarity shouldn't lead us to over-look their significance. The processes whereby we can come to know the in-ternal states of others—and by which we can be motivated to respond with sensitive care to others' distress—are of enormous importance for our life to-gether. Some great thinkers, including David Hume and Adam Smith, have suggested that these processes are the basis for all social perception and inter-action. Personally, I suspect that's going too far. Yet there's little doubt that the processes called empathy are key elements of our nature.

4 NECESSARY CONDITIONS FOR FEELING EMPATHIC CONCERN

With some understanding of what empathic concern is and isn't, we can turn attention to the conditions necessary to experience it. Having defined empathic concern as an other-oriented emotional state elicited by and congruent with the perceived welfare of a person in need (Chapter 1), one necessary condition is obvious: *perceiving the other as in need*. But at least one more condition must be necessary because we don't feel empathic concern in response to every need we perceive. I believe that *valuing the other's welfare* is the second necessary condition. When these two conditions are met—and when we're not inhibited by some more pressing matter—I think we'll experience empathic concern. When either condition is not met, we won't.

The relationship between these two conditions is specified in Figure 4.1, which shows that the two join to form a shared causal path. The multiplication sign between the conditions indicates that they combine multiplicatively. That is, some level of each is necessary, and beyond this threshold level, the magnitude of empathic concern is a product of the strength of each. Although the present chapter focuses on these two necessary conditions, it also considers two other conditions—one or both of which have often been thought necessary for empathic concern. For each, I'll explain why I don't think it is.

Condition 1: Perceiving the Other as in Need

In preceding chapters, I've often spoken of perceiving another as in need yet haven't said exactly what that means. It's time to be more

---

Empathic Concern. C. Daniel Batson, Oxford University Press. © Oxford University Press 2023.
DOI: 10.1093/oso/9780197610923.003.0005

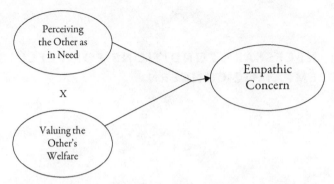

FIGURE 4.1. Two Necessary Conditions for Feeling Empathic Concern.

precise. Formally, *perceiving another as in need involves perception of a discrepancy between the other's current state and what you think is desirable for him or her on one or more dimensions of well-being.* Dimensions of well-being include not only the presence of physical pleasure, positive affect, satisfaction, and security but also the absence of physical pain, stress, anxiety, negative affect, danger, and disease.

A perceived need can vary in magnitude as a function of three factors: (1) The number of dimensions of well-being on which discrepancies are perceived. (2) The size of each discrepancy (how far the current state is from the desired). And (3) the perceived importance of each discrepant dimension for the well-being of the person in need. In combination, these three factors define the magnitude of the perceived need.

The discrepancy in well-being that's at issue is for the person in need not the person feeling empathic concern. But the perception at issue is that of the person feeling empathy not the person in need. There are times when people perceive themselves to be in need, yet others don't. When this happens, these others won't experience empathic concern (unless they consider the person's false perception of need to be a need). There are also times when people don't perceive themselves to be in need yet others do. These others may well feel empathic concern.

Perception of need seems to be a threshold function of two situational factors: First, the discrepancy (real or apparent) between what is and what is desirable must be noticed (Clark & Word, 1972, 1974; Latané & Darley, 1970). Second, attention must be focused on the person in need, not on the self or some other aspect of the situation (Aderman & Berkowitz, 1983; Gibbons & Wicklund, 1982; Milgram, 1970; Weiner, 1976; Wicklund, 1975). Both of these factors must simultaneously be present to perceive another's need.

Complicating matters, other cognitive and situational factors may lead a perceiver to minimize or even deny an apparent need, factors such as being led by the reactions of other bystanders to misinterpret the situation ("No one else seems upset, so I guess that scream wasn't a cry of distress, only play."—Latané & Darley, 1970). There are also factors that may facilitate perception of need in ambiguous situations, such as the imagine-other and imagine-self perspectives discussed in Chapters 2 and 3. Either perspective may make you more likely to perceive the other as in need (although imagining yourself in another's situation may do the opposite if you don't think you would experience need in that situation).

By these criteria, the bloody and broken driver at the start of Chapter 2 was clearly in need. So were the targets in all of the examples at the start of Chapter 1: The physical condition of the man attacked on the road to Jericho, Baby Jessica in the well, and the circling bear cub were far from what was desirable for each on important dimensions of well-being, as were the states of the frantic parents of Sandy Hook children and the friend suffering a romantic breakup or loss of parent or pet. The young cousin whose mother had died, the harp-seal pups, and baby pandas were also in clear need even though they weren't aware of it. Again, it's the perception of discrepancy by the individual feeling empathy that's at issue, not the perception by the individual in need.

Is Innocence Necessary for Empathic Concern?

Philosopher Martha Nussbaum claimed that in addition to perceiving a person as in need, we must perceive him or her to be free from responsibility for causing the need before we can feel empathic concern—or, using her term, before we can feel compassion (Nussbaum, 2001). Nussbaum thought perception of need and perception of innocence were two separate necessary conditions. She also noted that we readily feel concern for our children even when they bring suffering on themselves. She reasoned that this is because we see children as too young to be held responsible. Such reasoning, however, doesn't explain the concern we feel for adults we especially care about—close friends, lovers, spouses, siblings, parents—when they bring suffering on themselves. This omission leads me to offer a different account.

Rather than two separate necessary conditions, I think freedom from responsibility contributes to perception of need. We often feel that people who bring suffering on themselves get what they deserve. If so—and if we also believe that people *should* get what they deserve (as Mel Lerner's, 1980, just-world hypothesis suggests many of us do)—then there's no discrepancy between our perception of their current state and the state we deem desirable for them. So we perceive no need. (For evidence that this is true, see Decety, Echols, & Correll, 2010.) But deservedness isn't the only dimension of well-being on which we assess the state of others, especially cared-for others. Discrepancies on another dimension, such as freedom from suffering, may lead to perception of need and to empathic concern when there's no discrepancy on deservedness. I think this is why we can feel concern for close others even when they cause their need.

Vulnerability as a Form of Need

Vulnerability is another special case. At times, there's no current discrepancy between another's state and what we think is good for him or her—that is, there's no immediate need—yet we perceive the person to be vulnerable to need in the future. This vulnerability is itself a form of need. As with the case of the young cousin at the start of Chapter 1, perception of vulnerability is likely when the other is viewed as defenseless or unaware of potential danger. Imagine your reaction at seeing a young child happily running across a grassy meadow or seeing this child safely asleep in bed—or at seeing a puppy in similar situations. There's no immediate need. Still, as we shall find in Chapter 6, research indicates that the child's—or puppy's—vulnerability is apt to trigger empathic feelings of tenderness, warmth, and softheartedness.

Evidence That Empathic Concern Requires Perception of Need

Not wanting to take anything for granted, several psychologists in the 1960s conducted research to test whether empathic concern requires perception of need. Most notably, Seymour Berger (1962) had research participants believe that at the onset of a visual signal a young man they were watching perform a task either received an electric shock (electric-shock condition) or did not (no-shock condition). Then, immediately following the visual signal, the young man either jerked his arm (movement condition) or didn't (no-movement condition). Participants knew that they themselves wouldn't be shocked during the experiment.

Berger reasoned, first, that both a painful stimulus in the environment (shock) and a distress response (arm jerk) were necessary for an observer to perceive the young man to be in need (i.e., experiencing pain). He reasoned, second, that if his participants were feeling empathic concern for the young man as opposed to feeling fear or anxiety about the shock itself, they should display no physiological reaction to watching the task performance unless they perceived the young man to be in need. Accordingly, Berger predicted that only in the shock/movement cell of his 2 x 2 design would participants show increased physiological arousal because only these participants would perceive need. For participants in each of the other three cells, some information necessary for perception of need was missing.

Results followed the predicted pattern. Participants in the shock/movement cell were more physiologically aroused (as assessed by electrodermal skin conductance) when observing the young man than were participants in the other three cells. Berger concluded that empathic arousal occurs only in response to perceived need. Subsequent research also supported this conclusion (e.g., Bandura & Rosenthal, 1966; Craig & Lowery, 1969; Craig & Wood, 1969). And, a few years later, Staffan Hygge (1976) demonstrated that the evoked physiological arousal (again assessed by skin conductance) was a response to what observers believed the other person was experiencing, not a response to what they believed they would experience in the other's situation (also see Kameda et al., 2012; Lamm et al., 2010).

Who Can Perceive Another as in Need?

Surprisingly perhaps, perception of another as in need may be a uniquely human skill. If so—and if perception of need is a necessary condition for empathic concern—then feeling empathic concern must be uniquely human also. Could this be true? Like most claims about uniquely human skills, this one merits skepticism. But unlike some, it also merits consideration.

Necessary cognitive abilities. Think about the cognitive abilities necessary to perceive another to be in need. First, we must recognize that the other is an *animate being*, qualitatively different from physical objects and distinct from other animate beings. This recognition typically occurs in the child's first year of life. It also occurs early in the development of nonhuman primates and many other mammals.

Second, it's necessary to recognize that the other has desires and feelings—the internal states necessary to experience pleasure and pain, good and bad. Developmental psychologist and primatologist Michael Tomasello spoke of this recognition as understanding that the other is a *sentient intentional agent*, not merely an animate being (Tomasello, 1999). He presented evidence that such understanding emerges in normal children around the end of their first year, when they begin to recognize that they have desires and feelings—and that other people do, too. Tomasello suggested that this second recognition may be the result of a uniquely human attribute that allows the child to understand that other intentional agents are beings "like me yet distinct from me." With this recognition, the child begins to see others as having needs, and to see them as acting with purpose when they circumvent barriers and use alternative behavioral routes to reach desired states (also see Hrdy & Burkhart, 2020; Tomasello, 2014, 2020). Young children frequently extend these perceptions too far, applying them not only to people and animals but also to toys and machines. Over time, experience hones the application.

Who has these abilities? By age two, most normally developing children have the cognitive abilities necessary to perceive need (Köster, Ohmer, Nguyen, & Kärtner, 2016; Warneken, 2015). Do our close primate relatives, such as chimpanzees and bonobos, have these skills too? What about other higher mammals, such as elephants, whales, dolphins, and dogs?

A number of examples seem to show evidence of perception of need in other species. Consider one offered by Franz de Waal that involved two chimpanzees at the Arnhem Zoo—Krom and Jakie (de Waal, 1996, p. 83). Krom, an elderly female, had spent over 10 minutes pulling and pushing on a rubber tire, which held some water, that was hanging on a horizontal log extending from a climbing frame. Unfortunately for her, there were a half-dozen tires, all heavy, hanging in front of the tire with the water, and she made no progress getting it off the log. Jakie, a seven-year-old male whom Krom had cared for as a juvenile, watched her struggle unsuccessfully with the tire and finally give up. When she walked away, he went over and pushed the tires off the log one by one until he got to the tire with the water. He then carried it straight to Krom, who began scooping out water with her hand and drinking. Jakie's behavior seems hard to explain without making the assumption that he perceived Krom's need—what she wanted but didn't have—and acted to meet that need.

A second de Waal example seems to show anticipation of need on the part of Kakowet, an old and experienced male bonobo (de Waal, 2006, p. 71). At the San Diego Zoo where Kakowet lived, the moat around the bonobo enclosure was routinely drained for cleaning. One day, unnoticed by the keepers, several young bonobos had gotten into the dry moat and couldn't get out. When the keepers went to open the valve and refill the moat, Kakowet appeared at the window waving his arms and screaming. His action alerted the keepers, preventing a tragedy.

A third example comes from Jane Goodall. She reported anticipation of infant distress by a chimpanzee mother, Gremlin:

> Gremlin's concern for Gimble went way beyond merely responding to his appeals for help; like a good mother she would anticipate trouble. Thus when Gimble played with young baboons Gremlin often watched closely and, if the game got the least bit rough, and long before Gimble himself seemed worried, she firmly took him away. Once, as she was carrying him along a trail, she saw a small snake ahead. Carefully she pushed Gimble off her back and kept him behind her as she shook branches at the snake until it glided away. (Goodall, 1990, p. 169)

These examples are certainly suggestive. But without knowledge of context and history, I hesitate to place on them the heavy weight of a claim that chimpanzees and bonobos can perceive need. I also hesitate to place that weight on the observations of consolation in chimpanzees (one chimp calming another who has been harmed by a third—Romero, Castellanos, & de Waal, 2010) or on the research of Yamamoto and colleagues, who claimed to provide clear experimental evidence of perception of need in chimps (Yamamoto, Humle, & Tanaka, 2012). And I hesitate to place such weight on examples in other species that might be cited, including elephants who help a wounded or sick member of the herd to rise (Moss, 2000; Poole, 1997), dolphins and whales who rescue pod-mates and even humans (Caldwell & Caldwell, 1966; Connor & Norris, 1982), dogs that sniff, nuzzle, and lick a human stranger who pretends to cry (Custance & Mayer, 2012) or that lead rescue workers to their injured masters (Medina, 2022; Patel, 2022), or rats who act to free a cage-mate from a restraint (Bartal, Decety, & Mason, 2011). Why am I so hesitant? Frans de Waal taught me to be.

In his delightful book *Good Natured* (1996), de Waal provided a nice illustration of how hard it is to resist the assumption that when other animals display behavior similar to the behavior humans might display in a given situation, their behavior is the product of equally complex cognitive abilities. Most dog lovers and owners, including myself, are quite familiar with canine guilt after doing wrong—the drooped head and tail, the slinking. Mango, a Siberian husky, displayed such guilt after she shredded newspapers, magazines, and books despite being scolded and punished for doing so. Her owner thought Mango knew the shredding was wrong and did it out of spite for having been left alone, then felt guilty afterward.

Animal-behavior consultant Peter Vollmer used a simple demonstration to show that although Mango behaved *as if* she felt guilt, her behavior was the product of a learned stimulus-response relation (Vollmer, 1977). With Mango out of the house, Vollmer had her owner shred some newspapers. Mango was then let back in, and her owner left for fifteen minutes. On the owner's return, Mango acted as "guilty" as when she shredded things herself. In de Waal's words, "The only thing she seemed to understand was: Evidence + Owner = Trouble" (de Waal, 1996, pp. 107–108). We can easily be misled about the thoughts and feelings underlying a behavior when it's taken out of the context of situational cues and learning history (see Call & Tomasello, 2008; Custance & Mayer, 2012; Penn, Holyoak, & Povenilli, 2008, Povenelli & Vonk, 2004; Tomasello, Call, & Hare, 2003).

Even the most touching and tantalizing examples of nonhuman response to another in need fail to show unequivocal awareness of the need. Consider the famous 1996 case of Binti Jua, the eight-year-old female gorilla at the Brookfield Zoo outside Chicago who rescued and gently held an unconscious three-year-old boy after he fell into the primate enclosure. She eventually turned the boy over to the zoo staff unharmed. Evidence of perception of need? Of empathic concern? Anthropologist and primatologist Joan Silk shed further light:

> Some have cited this incident as evidence for empathy and sympathy in apes, arguing that Binti Jua was motivated by compassion and concern for the welfare of the child (Preston & de Waal, 2002). However, other facts need to be considered. Binti Jua was hand-reared by humans, after being rejected by her own mother. Concerned that Binti Jua might become a neglectful mother herself, the zoo staff used operant training methods to guide the development of appropriate maternal skills. One of the things that she was trained to do was to retrieve a doll-like object and bring it to the front of the enclosure, where the zoo personnel could inspect it. (Silk, 2009, pp. 275–276)

Did Binti Jua perceive the boy's need and act to meet it? Or was her response generalized from prior stimulus-response learning? I don't think we know. As with Mango, behavior taken out of context can easily be misread. (For similar doubts about empathic concern in other species, see Custance & Mayer, 2012, and Panksepp, 2011.) We can hope to soon have clearer evidence, but for now, I'll limit my claims about the ability to perceive need—and to experience empathic concern—to humans. There's little doubt that by two years of age, most normal human children are capable of perceiving need.

Condition 2: Valuing the Other's Welfare

The two cognitive abilities that Tomasello emphasized—recognize others as animate beings and recognize them as sentient intentional agents—enable us to perceive need. But to feel empathic concern requires more: We need to care whether the other is in need. In normal humans, the capacity to value (care about) another's welfare emerges somewhere between one and three years of age (Hepach, Vaish, & Tomasello, 2013). When it fails to develop, we speak of psychopathy (Blair, 2007).

One often hears lip service paid to valuing all human life or to valuing the welfare of all humanity. But most of us place different value on the welfare of different others. We value the welfare of some highly, others very little. We may even negatively value the welfare of a person we don't like, such as a rival or enemy.

If we place little value on the welfare of someone we perceive to be in need, we aren't likely to think about how this person is affected by the need—except perhaps as a clue to how we might control his or her behavior. We may understand what this person needs, but we don't care. It provides no basis for feeling empathic concern.

If we place negative value on a person's welfare, as we might if we dislike the person or are in competition, then perceiving need is likely to produce emotions quite different from empathic concern. Events in the person's life are likely to evoke feelings antithetical to rather than congruent with his or her welfare—feelings of pleasure at the person's suffering (the malicious glee called schadenfreude) and pain at his or her success.

If we place positive value, we make a congruent assessment. We value events that we think will bring the person pleasure, satisfaction, safety, or relief. We devalue events that will bring him or her pain, sorrow, discontent, danger, or disappointment. Such valuing not only produces a lively response to events that affect the person's welfare—much like our response to events that affect our own welfare—but it also produces vigilance. We're on the lookout for events that might benefit or harm, and we adopt an imagine-other perspective toward such events. If the other's welfare is or could be diminished, we feel empathic concern.

Evidence of the Link Between Valuing and Empathic Concern

Cindy Turk, Laura Shaw, Tricia Klein, and I (Batson, Turk, Shaw, & Klein, 1995) found evidence of a link between valuing the other's welfare and feeling empathic concern in an experiment in which we adapted the campus radio pilot-testing procedure developed by Coke and others (1978), described in Chapter 1. As in their Experiment 2, our participants received false physiological feedback leading them to believe they either were or weren't empathically aroused by Katherine McDavis's Campus Concerns appeal for volunteers to take part in her master's thesis research. Crosscutting this empathy manipulation, we added a status-of-need manipulation, creating a 2 x 2 design. After listening to Katherine's appeal and reporting their emotional response including empathic concern (six-item scale), half of the participants in each empathy condition (low, high) learned that she was no longer in need of volunteers (need-removed condition); the other half weren't given this information (still-in-need condition).

For participants in the need-removed condition, empathic concern was measured twice—first, right after listening to Katherine's broadcast (to check comparability at that point with empathy felt by participants in the still-in-need condition) and a second time after learning that Kathrine no longer needed volunteers for her research. Finally, valuing of Katherine's welfare was measured both for those who thought she was still in need and for those who knew she was no longer in need.

Participants led to believe both that they were empathically aroused by Katherine's appeal and that she was still in need (high-empathy/still-in-need cell) rated their empathic concern and their valuing of her welfare higher on average than did participants led to believe they weren't empathically aroused by her need. It seemed that the high-empathy/still-in-need participants made a backward inference from their induced empathic feelings to valuing ("If I feel like this for Kathy, I must value her welfare."), indicating that they considered valuing necessary for empathic concern.

Importantly, when those induced to feel high empathy learned that Katherine was no longer in need, their empathic concern dropped but their valuing of her welfare remained. This pattern of responses showed, first, the cross-situational durability of valuing and, second, the independence of valuing, once established, from perception of need.

Intrinsic Not Extrinsic Valuing

As the experiment just described suggests, the valuing that evokes empathic concern seems to be intrinsic not extrinsic. That is, the other's welfare is valued as an end-in-itself, not simply as a means to some other end. If someone whose welfare I value extrinsically is in need, I may feel concerned, upset, anxious, or sorry. But these emotions are apt to be self-oriented—evoked by the implications of the other's plight for my own welfare. For example, I may be sorry to hear that the mechanic who promised to have my car fixed by Tuesday has come down with the flu and the car won't be ready for another week. However, if honest, I must admit that my sorrow is almost entirely over not getting the car. I have little feeling for the mechanic's discomfort and difficulties.

In contrast, if my good friend Rebecca, whose welfare I value intrinsically has the flu, I'm likely to feel sorry for *her*. I've incorporated her welfare into my own value structure, so I spontaneously imagine how she's affected. Hearing of her need, I feel other-oriented empathic concern. It's the threat to her welfare, not mine, that evokes my emotional response.

There seems little doubt that we can value another's welfare extrinsically, even someone quite close. A young child may be upset that his mother is sick because of the implications for his own welfare (Knafo, Zahn-Waxler, Van Hulle, Robinson, & Rhee, 2008; Zahn-Waxler, Radke-Yarrow, Wagner, & Chapman, 1992). So may an adult faced with the illness or injury of a spouse. Extrinsic valuing of this sort underlies interdependence-theory analyses of close relationships. This theory assumes that we value a close relationship to the extent that our partner is necessary for our own well-being (Berscheid, 1983; Kelley, 1979).

At times, extrinsic valuing can lead to intrinsic valuing: What was once valued extrinsically may become functionally autonomous and valued in its own right (Allport, 1937). But it's also true that perceptions of extrinsic valuing can undermine perceptions of intrinsic valuing (see Aronson & Carlsmith, 1963; Lepper, 1983). Reflecting such undermining, I probably would have felt more empathic concern on hearing my mechanic had the flu were my car *not* in the shop at the time.

Everyday terms for what I'm calling intrinsic valuing of another's welfare are *caring* or *loving*. Love is often thought to be an emotion, but I believe it's more appropriate to think of love as a form of valuing that can evoke a variety of emotions. When one person loves another—for example, when a mother loves her child—there are likely to be feelings of heartache and

EMPATHIC CONCERN

sadness at prolonged separation and feelings of warmth and joy at reuniting. Cognitive processes such as perceived similarity, familiarity, and attractiveness can facilitate love. However, its basic character seems to be affective and evaluative—like the related but more general concepts of *attitude* and *sentiment*. Like them, love involves relatively enduring value placed on the target (even though love can, of course, end).

Other Proposed Necessary Conditions Instead of Valuing

Rather than claiming that valuing the other's welfare is a necessary condition for feeling empathic concern (alongside perceived need), one of two other conditions has often been thought necessary—perceived similarity or adopting an imagine-other perspective.

Perceived Similarity

Many scholars have considered perceived similarity necessary to feel empathic concern. Indeed, for me not to do so may seem surprising, given that I and other social psychologists (e.g., Dennis Krebs, 1975) have used experimental manipulations of similarity to induce empathic concern.

The reason I don't consider similarity necessary is because evidence indicates that similarity's effect on empathic concern isn't due to the similarity itself but to its consequences, such as liking and care, that reflect valuing of the other's welfare. Most relevant is the evidence from two small experiments explicitly designed to tease apart the direct and indirect effects of similarity on empathic concern (Batson, Turk et al., 1995, Experiments 1 and 2). In these experiments, colleagues and I provided female research participants with information that "Lynn" (ostensibly one of the other female participants in the research session) had interests that were quite similar to their own—or that Lynn's interests were quite dissimilar. We then measured (a) valuing of Lynn's welfare and (b) empathic concern felt for her. Importantly, empathy was measured either when Lynn was to receive positive consequences—raffle tickets for correct responses on a task (no-need condition)—or when she was to receive negative consequences—electric shocks for incorrect responses (need condition).

Consistent with the idea that valuing is a target-specific disposition that is independent of perceived need, we predicted that learning Lynn's interests were similar would lead to greater valuing of her welfare whether or not she was in need. Consistent with the idea that valuing leads to increased empathic concern when the valued other is perceived to be in need, we predicted that this greater valuing of the similar Lynn's welfare would be associated with increased empathic concern only when she was perceived to be in need. Finally, we predicted that any association of similarity with empathic concern when Lynn was in need would be mediated by valuing of Lynn's welfare.

Results supported each of these predictions. The experimental manipulation of similarity led to greater valuing of Lynn's welfare whether or not she was in need, but this greater valuing led to increased empathic concern only when she was in need. Moreover, when Lynn was in need, the empathic concern felt for her was more closely associated with the increased valuing than with perceived similarity. The effect of similarity was indirect, through valuing.

Adopting an Imagine-Other Perspective

Even more surprising may be my focus on valuing rather than on adopting an imagine-other perspective. In previous chapters, you've seen much evidence that imagining how another person is affected by being in need can increase empathic concern. It's the technique most frequently used to induce empathy in laboratory research. Outside the lab as well, empathy is often induced by imagine-other instructions, including self-instructions. We say to others or to ourselves, "Just think what she's going through!" Surely, adopting an imagine-other perspective is a necessary condition for feeling empathic concern.

For a long time, I thought it was. I named perceiving another as in need and adopting his or her perspective as the two necessary conditions for empathic concern (see Batson, 1987, 1991; Batson & Shaw, 1991). But subsequent research convinced me that an imagine-other perspective isn't necessary.

It's now clear that we can feel empathic concern for someone in need without being instructed to adopt his or her perspective. Most of us naturally place at least moderate positive value on the welfare of other people (including total strangers) as long as we don't have grounds for antipathy. (Psychopaths seem to be a conspicuous exception, but they comprise only a small percentage of the population.) Indicative of this value, when research participants learn about a stranger in clear need, those not given any perspective instructions report levels of empathic concern that are, on average, not significantly different from the levels reported by those instructed to imagine how the stranger is affected by his or her situation (Batson, Eklund, Chermok, Hoyt, & Ortiz, 2007, Experiment 2; Davis et al., 2004; McAuliffe, Carter, Berhane, Snihur, & McCullough, 2020; McAuliffe, Forster, Philippe,

& McCullough, 2018; Morelli & Lieberman, 2013). In these studies, an objective perspective seems to reduce empathic concern rather than an imagine-other perspective increasing it. (On the other hand, if there are grounds for antipathy—e.g., the person in need has attributes we dislike or is a member of a group we stigmatize—our natural response may be to remain detached and objective. But insofar as I know, this possibility has never been explicitly tested.)

Research has also shown that when we place either little value or negative value on another person's welfare, we can imagine how this person is affected by his or her need and still feel relatively little empathic concern. For example, colleagues and I found that even though research participants who imagined the thoughts and feelings of a convicted murderer serving a life sentence reported feeling more empathic concern for him than did participants who remained objective, they still reported far less empathy than is typical when participants imagine the thoughts and feelings of a stranger in need (Batson, Polycarpou, Harmon-Jones, Imhoff, Mitchener, Bednar, Klein, & Highberger, 1997).

Similarly, another set of colleagues and I found that participants reported feeling less empathic concern for Bryan Banks—an undergraduate badly hurt when hit by a car—if they knew he had previously been nasty rather than nice to a lost and frightened elderly woman. If Bryan had been nasty, participants liked him less, placed less value on his welfare, and, in turn, reported less empathic concern. This was true even for those led to adopt an imagine-other perspective, who were thinking about how the accident affected his life (Batson, Eklund et al., 2007, Experiment 1).

The results of these lines of research are the reason I now believe the two necessary conditions for empathic concern are perceiving another as in need and valuing his or her welfare. As depicted in Figure 4.2, adopting an imagine-other perspective seems to lie downstream from valuing—on the diagonal line to the junction where valuing combines with perception of need to evoke empathic concern. Valuing the other's welfare, not perspective taking, seems to be what's necessary to induce empathy.

That said, when inducing empathic concern in laboratory experiments, I've continued to use perspective instructions (and sometimes similarity) to manipulate valuing, rather than trying to manipulate valuing itself. Valuing another's welfare is most apparent in close and enduring relationships with family and friends. These relationships have a past and future, creating obligations and expectations for how we should feel and act. Such obligations

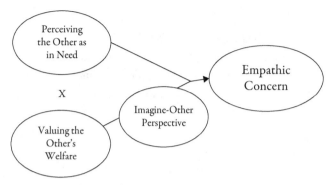

FIGURE 4.2. Location of Imagine-Other Perspective in Relation to the Two Necessary Conditions for Feeling Empathic Concern.

and expectations can, in turn, lead us to report feeling what we think we should, introducing serious experimental confounds. To avoid the confounds associated with relationship-based valuing, random assignment to perspective instructions (imagine-other vs. objective) often provides the most effective manipulation of empathic concern.

Still, it's important to recognize that when positive valuing exists, perspective instructions aren't necessary. Valuing leads us to imagine how the target feels about events. And if we perceive him or her to be in need, valuing the other's welfare leads us to feel empathic concern.

Conclusion

I've suggested that empathic concern is the product of two necessary conditions—perception of another as in need and intrinsic valuing of that other's welfare. *Perception of need* can be formally defined as perceiving some discrepancy between a person's current state and what's desired for him or her on one or more dimensions of well-being. Such discrepancies may involve the absence of happiness, success, security, and so on, the presence of suffering, failure, vulnerability, and so on, or both. The magnitude of a person's need is a function of the number of discrepancies and the perceived size and importance of each. Although the needs that evoke empathic concern belong to other people, the relevant perception of these needs is by the person who feels empathy. Despite suggestive evidence, I don't think we yet know whether any species other than humans has the cognitive skills necessary to infer others' internal states—that is, the skills necessary to perceive others as in need.

Intrinsic valuing of the other's welfare involves wanting the other to experience as much well-being and as little need as possible. Moreover, it involves wanting this as an end-in-itself, not as a means to some other end.

Empathic concern seems to be a multiplicative function of these two necessary conditions (Figure 4.1). Some threshold amount of each is necessary to experience any empathic concern at all, and, beyond this threshold, the amount experienced is a product of the magnitude of the perceived need and the strength of the intrinsic valuing.

One or both of two other conditions are frequently thought to be a necessary condition for feeling empathic concern—perceived similarity and adopting an imagine-other perspective. I don't think either is necessary. Research indicates, first, that perceived similarity affects empathic concern through its effect on valuing (and, as we shall see in the next chapter, that it's quite possible to value the welfare of, and to feel empathic concern for, quite dissimilar others). Second, research indicates that adopting an imagine-other perspective affects empathic concern because it increases valuing. Third, in the normal stream of behavior, valuing the other's welfare spontaneously evokes this perspective. Valuing seems to be the causative condition.

This analysis of the necessary conditions to feel empathic concern highlights two issues. First, although research has provided data consistent with the analysis, the most direct evidence for naming intrinsic valuing of the other's welfare as a necessary condition comes from several sets of experiments done by colleagues and me. Until there are tests of the relevant hypotheses by other researchers, the present analysis should be considered only suggestive.

Second, the focus on intrinsic valuing of the other's welfare begs the question of whether such valuing is even possible. After all, doesn't the idea that we can intrinsically value the welfare of at least some others—valuing their welfare for their sakes and not ours—violate the theory of natural selection? If it does, then either the claim that such valuing is a necessary condition for feeling empathic concern is wrong or the theory of natural selection is wrong, and the latter seems most unlikely. Chapter 5 addresses this question.

5 EMPATHIC CONCERN'S EVOLUTIONARY ROOTS

Valuing the welfare of our children is almost certainly genetically based. Less certain, but certainly intriguing, is the thought that parental care provides the genetic basis for all intrinsic valuing of another's welfare and, thereby, for all cases of empathic concern.

This thought was common a century ago. Psychologists then were strongly influenced by Darwin's ideas about instinctive love based on "parental and filial affections," which he linked to "the all-important emotion of sympathy" (Darwin, 1871, p. 308). It does seem clear that if mammalian parents didn't care for their vulnerable and dependent offspring—putting up with endless hassles, exhaustion, and risks to personal safety—these species would quickly die out. Might our empathic feelings of sympathy, tenderness, and compassion for those who *aren't* our children also be grounded in this strong impulse of mammalian parents to care for their young? I think it's possible.

William McDougall's Parental Instinct and Tender Emotion

Shortly after the start of the 20th century, William McDougall provided an argument for parental care as the basis for empathy (McDougall, 1908). He described the *parental instinct*—which he considered to be the most powerful of all instincts—and associated *tender emotion*. McDougall didn't think of instincts as automatic or reflexive, as we often do today. For him, each instinct included a cognitive, an affective (emotional), and a conative (motivational) component. He thought that the cognitive and conative

---

Empathic Concern. C. Daniel Batson, Oxford University Press. © Oxford University Press 2023.
DOI: 10.1093/oso/9780197610923.003.0006

78 • EMPATHIC CONCERN

components were modifiable by experience and learning but the affective component wasn't. Further, he thought that a unique emotion was at the core of each instinct and defined its character—and that the tender emotion defined the character of the parental instinct. According to McDougall, this instinct

> is primarily to afford physical protection to the child, especially by throwing the arms about it; and that fundamental impulse persists in spite of the immense extension of the range of application of the impulse . . . . . Tender emotion and the protective impulse are, no doubt, evoked more readily and intensely by one's own offspring, because about them a strongly organized and complex sentiment [i.e., an intrinsic positive value] grows up. But the distress of any child will evoke this response in a very intense degree in those in whom the instinct is strong . . . . . By a further extension of the same kind the emotion may be evoked by the sight of any very young animal, especially if in distress . . . . . In a similar direct fashion the distress of any adult (towards whom we harbor no hostile sentiment) evokes the emotion. (McDougall, 1908, pp. 61–63)

McDougall's tender emotion is essentially the same as what I'm calling empathic concern. And, as you can see, McDougall claimed that the tender, empathic feelings at the core of the human parental instinct can be felt not only for other children but also for adults in need, and even for members of other species.

Of course, we shouldn't accept such claims too quickly. As discussed in Chapter 4, many mammalian species lack the prefrontal cortical structures and cognitive abilities necessary to experience empathic feelings. Yet they still display parental care. If McDougall's claims are right, the human parental instinct must go well beyond nursing, providing other kinds of food, offering protection, and keeping the young close—the activities that characterize parental care in most mammalian species.

The Human Parental Instinct

We humans have doubtless inherited key aspects of our parental instinct from ancestors we share with other mammalian species, as Stephanie Preston has documented (Preston, 2013, 2022; also see Marsh, 2016, 2019). But in humans, this instinct has become considerably less automatic and more flexible (Dixon

Evolutionary Roots · 79

& Dweck, 2022; Feldman, 2017; Hrdy & Burkhart, 2020). It includes other-oriented, tender feelings for the child that are based on inferences about his or her needs and desires ("Is that a hungry cry or a wet cry?" "She won't like the fireworks; they'll be too loud."). It also involves clear recognition of the distinctiveness—even dissimilarity—of self and other. Parents must recognize that their child's needs are often quite different from their own, as is their child's capacity to address needs. And it involves intrinsic valuing of the child's welfare, producing, as McDougall suggested, tender empathic concern when the child is in need.

Parental care based on empathic concern didn't supplant the more primitive cue-based responses of our ancient ancestors. Rather, it supplemented them and increased the flexibility with which they are employed (as argued by, for example, Bell, 2001; Damasio, 2002; Hoffman, 1981b; MacLean, 1990; Sober, 1991; Sober & Wilson, 1998; Taylor, 2002; and Zahn-Waxler & Radke-Yarrow, 1990). The added flexibility permitted anticipation and prevention of needs, even evolutionarily quite novel ones such as the need to avoid sticking a pin in an electrical outlet.

Note that McDougall's focus on the tender emotion, which involves feeling *for* the other, is different from Frans de Waal's grounding of the parental instinct in emotional contagion and affective resonance, which involve feeling *as* the other (de Waal, 2009; Preston & de Waal, 2002—see Chapter 3). McDougall's emotional focus is also different from the processes thought to lie at the core of what attachment theorists, following John Bowlby (1969), have called "the caregiving behavioral system."

Attachment theorists rely on an ethological perspective, which originally focused on innate behaviors as biologically programmed response sequences ("fixed action patterns") to specific stimuli ("innate releasing mechanisms") of the sort found in imprinting (see Eibl-Eibesfeldt, 1970; Lorenz, 1981). However, to apply this perspective to human parental care, attachment theorists deemphasized automatic responses to specific stimuli and instead focused on cognitively complex and flexible care that is, ideally, sensitive to both the child's immediate needs and his or her long-term needs for protection and security. This shift in focus allowed the caregiving system to incorporate not only anticipation and prevention of needs but also sensitivity to the unique demands of various need situations (Bowlby, 1969; George & Solomon, 1999). Thus, attachment theory's analysis of human parenting overlaps with the cognitive and conative components of McDougall's parenting instinct. But its analysis gives little attention to McDougall's tender emotion, which he considered to be the instinct's core. (However, for a version of attachment

80 • EMPATHIC CONCERN

theory that does place emotion in a central role in human parenting, see Bell, 2001, discussed later.)

Extending This Instinct

McDougall claimed more than that the human parental instinct is complex and flexible, need-based not just cue-based, proactive not just reactive. As noted, he also claimed that the tender feelings lying at the heart of this instinct have a range of applicability that extends well beyond parent-child relations. He claimed that through cognitive generalization based on learning and experience, we can come to care about the welfare of non-kin—including strangers and at least some members of other species—in the same way if not to the same degree that we care about the welfare of our children. So for him, the parental instinct and tender emotion come into play in many if not all cases both of intrinsically valuing another's welfare and of empathic concern when the other is in need. Further, McDougall thought the parental instinct and tender emotion aren't limited to those who have children. It's part of our genetic nature from birth.

As suggested at the end of Chapter 4, the prospect of such generalization may seem implausible and at odds with the theory of natural selection. Christopher Boehm (1999), for one, has argued this. But consider the evidence.

Evidence Relating Parental Care and Empathic Concern

First, there's research suggesting links between the brain regions and neurochemistry related to parental care and the regions and chemistry related to empathic concern.

Brain Regions

Much of the relevant brain-region research builds on the ideas of three luminaries of modern neurophysiology, Paul MacLean and Antonio and Hanna Damasio. MacLean described the human brain as *triune*, consisting of a hierarchy of "three-brains-in-one." Oldest is the evolutionarily ancient reptilian (or protoreptilian) brain that we share with reptiles and mammals. Next is the paleomammalian brain that we share with all mammals and which includes the limbic system. Most recent is the neomammalian brain (the frontal and prefrontal cortex) that is found only in "higher" mammals and reaches its greatest proportional size in humans. According to MacLean, each of these brains has "its own special intelligence, its own subjectivity, its own sense of time and space, and its own memory, motor, and other functions" (MacLean, 1990, p. 9). Each operates somewhat independently but not autonomously—the three intermesh and function together. MacLean thought that parental care, play, and social bonding, which he considered to be the "functions that would seem to have favored the evolution of the human sense of empathy and altruism" (1990, p. 520), all arise from the interrelationship of areas of the neomammalian frontal and prefrontal cortex with a subdivision of the paleomammalian limbic system.

Antonio and Hanna Damasio sketched the empathy implications of their research with patients who have brain lesions. In addition to the limbic areas involved in the expression of emotion, Antonio Damasio proposed that "the brain regions in the metarepresentation of mental states are critical for the process of empathy, and they include . . . regions of parietal association cortex and of prefrontal cortex" (2002, p. 269; also see Decety & Chaminade, 2003; Eslinger, 1998; Immordino-Yang, McColl, Damasio, & Damasio, 2009; Kim, Kim, Kim, Jeong, Park, Son, Song, & Ki, 2009; Lamm et al., 2007; Masten, Morelli, & Eisenberger; 2011; and Ruby & Decety, 2004).

Hanna Damasio summarized:

> There is a system in certain sectors of the prefrontal cortex that is critical for the learning and maintenance of certain aspects of social behavior that pertain to interpersonal relationships. After damage to this system, empathy, as well as emotions such as embarrassment, guilt, pride, and altruism, are not evoked, and personal and social decisions become defective. (2002, p. 281)

Behavioral observations seem quite consistent with these suggestions about the neurophysiology of empathic concern. Observations are also consistent with the neurophysiological evidence that for normal operation of the human parental instinct, cortical processes involved in the perception of the internal state and needs of the child interact with midbrain-based pleasure centers and reaction tendencies to produce goal-directed motivation (MacLean, 1990). Antonio Damasio (1994, 1999, 2003) has repeatedly pointed out that one of the virtues of relying on emotions and goal-directed motives to guide action rather than on more automatic stimulus-response patterns and "regulatory mechanisms" is that emotions and their associated goal-directed motives can be adaptive under a wide range of environmental

82 • EMPATHIC CONCERN

conditions, including novel ones. As noted earlier, such flexibility is a key feature of care for human offspring.

To illustrate the flexibility that emotions can introduce, consider an emotion quite different from empathic concern—anger. Aggressive responses occur in many species that likely don't experience anything like the emotion we call anger. Among humans, however, aggressive responses are stimulated, tempered, and generalized by feelings of anger that are a product of complex cognitive assessment of the situation, especially assessment of the intentions of others. In parallel fashion, tender empathic feelings permit more flexible and adaptive parental care, care that isn't simply reflexive or reactive to distress cues but is directed toward the goal of enhancing the child's welfare as needed in the specific situation.

Arguing similarly, David Bell (2001) described the human parental caregiving system as "directed toward the needs of the infant" (p. 220) and therefore based on relatively sophisticated cognitive processes. Bell recognized that this system also involves "some emotional processes located in older parts of the brain that appear to follow a different, emotional logic" (p. 216). And he assumed that this sophisticated and flexible caregiving system is present not only in humans but also in other primates. Kim Bard's (1995) review of evidence that at least some forms of proactive, flexible parental care exist in chimpanzees and other great apes is consistent with this assumption. So, too, is evidence indicating the importance of practice and observational learning for effective expression of parental care in these primates. However, as suggested in Chapter 4, it may be best at this point to reserve judgment on whether parental care by primates other than humans is based on inferences about the infant's needs and desires rather than on operant conditioning, imitation, and cue-based responses.

Consistent with a depiction of human parental care as need and value based—and as having other-oriented emotion at its core—Bartels and Zeki (2004) found that mothers looking at photos of their own child and at photos of another child (aged-matched) not only showed more activation of the periaqueductal gray (PAG) region in the midbrain, which is known to be involved in maternal behavior in mammals, to photos of their own child but that the mothers also showed more activation of regions in the cortex associated with higher cognition and emotion (especially positive, tender feelings) as well as with goal-directed activity. These regions included the medial insula, dorsal and ventral anterior cingulate cortex, lateral orbito-frontal cortex, and lateral prefrontal cortex. The first three of these cortical regions are associated with emotion and motivation—and are known to have direct connections

Evolutionary Roots • 83

with the PAG. (For informative descriptions of the relevant neuroanatomy, see Allman, Watson, Tetreault, & Hakeem, 2005, and Craig, 2005, 2009.) Finally, as would be expected, Bartels and Zeki's mothers reported feeling more "love," "wanting to protect," and "tender" toward their own child (also see Leibenluft, Gobbini, Harrison, & Haxby, 2004).

Neurochemistry

In recent years, much research on the neurochemistry of parental care has focused on the neuropeptide hormone oxytocin (OT)—and on the role of oxytocin in birth, lactation, and maternal care (see Carter 1998, 2014, for reviews). Here, I'll simply note three findings from the extensive research program of Ruth Feldman and her colleagues on the role of oxytocin in human parental behavior.

1. Feldman, Weller, Zagoory-Sharon, and Levine (2007) reported an association between mothers' levels of plasma oxytocin and the cognitive as well as behavioral aspects of mother-infant bonding, including the mother's thoughts about the infant and her vigilance for the infant's welfare. Based on this study, and on related research that included neurophysiological data (e.g., Atzil, Hendler, & Feldman, 2011), Feldman suggested that

> the neural basis of mothering integrates OT-rich subcortical motivational limbic areas with higher-level networks implicated in emotional modulation, social cognition, and empathy, that allow the mother to read her infant's signals and plan adequate parenting. (Feldman, 2012, p. 384)

2. Gordon, Zagoory-Sharon, Leckman, and Feldman (2010) looked at parents' interactions with their first-born child during the month after birth and again six months later. Gordon and colleagues found that plasma oxytocin increased in both mothers and fathers across this time period. They also found that the oxytocin levels of the mother and father in a given couple were comparable and correlated at both points in time. Finally, they found that the oxytocin-behavior association differed for the two parents. In mothers, oxytocin levels correlated with "affectionate parenting" (e.g., "motherese" vocalizations, experience of positive affect, and affectionate

touch), but in fathers, with "stimulatory parenting" (e.g., moving the child's limbs, tactile stimulation, and object presentation—Gordon et al., 2010, p. 377; also see Feldman, Zagoory-Sharon, Weisman, Schneiderman, Gordon, Maoz, Shalev, & Ebstein, 2012).

3. Weisman, Zagoory-Sharon, and Feldman (2011) found that the play with their six-month old infant by fathers who inhaled oxytocin (compared to fathers who inhaled a placebo) involved more frequent touch and longer engagement. The fathers who inhaled oxytocin also showed greater respiratory sinus arrhythmia (RSA)—which, as noted in Chapter 1, may be associated with empathic concern and/or outward attention. In addition, the infant's salivary oxytocin level, RSA, time of social gaze, and toy exploration all rose in the oxytocin condition, even though the infant had inhaled no oxytocin.

Evidence of Generalization of Tender Feelings and Nurturant Care

What about evidence of generalization of tender feelings and nurturant care beyond progeny? McDougall (1908) claimed that we can extend the tender feelings that evolved as part of the human parental instinct to a wide range of others, including adult strangers and members of other species. The idea is that through cognitive generalization we "adopt" these non-progeny, and, as a result, their needs evoke our empathic concern. Is this at all plausible?

Well, first, it's important to recognize that parental care in many species isn't limited to offspring. As Tom Insel, a leader in mammalian neuroscience, explained: "Rat mothers will show intense devotion and defense of their young, but they are not selective in their maternal behavior, offering the same level of care to unrelated young in the nest" (Insel, 2002, p. 255). Apparently, the occurrence of unrelated young in a rat's nest is sufficiently rare that there hasn't been strong selection pressure for a more discriminating maternal response. And rats aren't unique. Adoption of non-kin has been observed in many mammalian species. But parental care by nonparents—what's currently discussed as *alloparenting* and *cooperative breeding*—is far more extensive, other-regarding, and emotionally and cognitively based in humans (Hrdy, 2009; Hrdy & Burkhart, 2020; Tomasello, 2020).

Second, in a highly interdependent and cooperative species like our own, natural selection may not simply have tolerated generalization of parental care. There may have been reproductive benefit for extending a genetically

Evolutionary Roots • 85

transmitted nurturant impulse beyond offspring. Due to selection pressure on the small, closely knit hunter-gatherer communities in which our genetic predispositions for social behavior are thought to have evolved, generalization of nurturant care to siblings, to the offspring of other community members, and even to other adults in the community, may have increased the likelihood of a person's genes surviving (Caporeal, Dawes, Orbell, & van de Kragt, 1989; Hrdy 2009; Sober & Wilson, 1998). If it's true that the human parental instinct relies less on cue-based stimulus-response patterns and more on the complex and flexible cognitive processes of intrinsic valuing, perception of need, and empathic concern, this instinct would be easier to generalize.

Third, within contemporary society, the prospect of such generalization appears more plausible when one thinks of the tender care typically provided by nannies and workers in day-care centers, as well as by adoptive parents and pet owners. Moreover, tender, nurturant feelings are experienced not only by adults. As early as the second year of life, children of both genders can display tender care toward people, pets, stuffed animals, and dolls (Davidov, Paz, Roth-Hanania, Uzefovsky, Orlitsky, Mankuta, & Zahn-Waxler, 2021; Davidov, Zahn-Waxler, Roth-Hanania, & Knafo, 2013; Hepach et al., 2013; Zahn-Waxler & Radke-Yarrow, 1990). Pets, too, at least dogs, can provide care to family members (Batson, 1983). But, although the human parental instinct seems to have a broad reach, *receipt* of nurturance during childhood may be necessary for its normal expression (Harlow, Harlow, Dodsworth, & Arling, 1966; Hrdy, 2009).

Oxytocin as a Neurochemical Basis for Generalization?

Suggesting its contribution to generalization, there is evidence that oxytocin may not only play a role in parental nurturance but also in adult friendships and love relationships. The evidence ranges from research on the role of oxytocin in pair bonding of monogamous prairie voles (in contrast to nonmonogamous meadow voles) to research on human romantic relations. Reflecting on the former, Curtis and Wang (2003) suggested:

> One possibility for the origin of pair bonding is that pair-bonding species have co-opted the mechanism (or mechanisms) by which maternal bonds are formed. This possibility is further supported by observations that even sexually naïve male prairie voles display maternal-type behaviors when exposed to pups, and that prairie vole

86 • EMPATHIC CONCERN

mothers display considerably more maternal care than do meadow vole mothers. (p. 51)

Regarding human romantic relations, Grewen, Girdler, Amico, and Light (2005) reported an association between relationship closeness (reflected in partner support) and level of plasma oxytocin before and after warm contact with the partner. This association was found for both men and women.

More generally, Shelley Taylor (2002) proposed the existence of a "tending instinct" that is quite similar to McDougall's parental instinct (although she made no reference to his work). Taylor suggested that the instinct to nurture offspring and to establish attachment bonds—the instinct to "tend and befriend"—underlies "various forms of tending throughout society" (Taylor, 2002, p. 158). She also suggested that this instinct may have its neurochemical base in oxytocin and the endogenous opioid peptides (EOPs). In line with this suggestion, Taylor cited evidence that oxytocin may be released not only during sexual intercourse, at birth, and during nursing, but also in other affiliative experiences (e.g., the evidence provided by Turner, Altemus, Enos, Cooper, & McGuinness, 1999; also see Bell, 2001, and Panksepp, 1998).

Four lines of research speak to oxytocin's role in empathic concern felt for strangers. (1) Zak, Stanton, and Ahmadi (2007) found that a nasal oxytocin infusion increased generosity toward strangers among men in a competitive situation—an Ultimatum Game. These researchers speculated that the increase in generosity was mediated by the effect of oxytocin on empathic emotion. (2) Barraza and Zak (2009) had a randomly assigned group of UCLA undergraduates (male and female) watch a video interview in which a father described the plight of his two-year-old son who had a terminal brain tumor. The video also showed scenes of the child in the hospital. A second group watched an interview in which the father described visiting the zoo with his son without mentioning anything about the son's illness. After watching, those undergraduates who saw the hospital video both reported more empathic concern and showed increased plasma oxytocin compared to those who saw the zoo video. The empathy-oxytocin association in this study was especially strong among women. (3) Evidence of plasma oxytocin increase has also been found in both men and women after affiliative experiences with dogs (Odendaal & Meintjes, 2003). (4) Using a different research technique, Liu, Gong, Li, and Zhou (2017) provided evidence that the positive effect of the oxytocin pathway gene CD38 on research participants' contributions to a fundraiser to help a teacher buy medicine to survive kidney disease was mediated by the participants' self-reported empathic concern felt for the teacher. Specifically, Liu and colleagues found that participants with CD38 genotypes that led to higher oxytocin levels (AA/AC genotypes) reported feeling more empathic concern for the teacher and donated more money to the fundraiser than did participants with the CC genotype (also see Buffone & Poulin, 2014).

This research on oxytocin is intriguing. It has led some researchers to suggest that oxytocin provides the neurochemical basis not only for parental care but also for other forms of care, including empathy-based care for non-kin. But oxytocin research is also complex and not always consistent. Oxytocin has been found to be highly associated with maternal care and social attachment in some mammalian species and not in other, even closely related ones. For example, an association has been found in rats but not in mice (Carter, 1998; Insel, 2000; Kendrick, 2000; Nelson & Panksepp, 1998; Olazábal & Young, 2006). And vasopressin, not oxytocin, may underlie paternal care and pair-bonding in at least some mammalian species (Curtis & Wang, 2003; Insel, 1997, 2002).

Those most knowledgeable about research on oxytocin suggest that it's still too soon to make any strong claims about its role in parental care and other forms of nurturant care in humans (e.g., Carter, 1998; Donaldson & Young, 2008; Insel, 2000, 2002; Panksepp, 1998). As Insel (2000) summarized:

> The available data support the hypothesis that oxytocin is critical for maternal behavior and pair-bond formation in select nonhuman animals. Humans have oxytocin and brain oxytocin receptors, but the role of this neuropeptide system in human attachment remains highly speculative. (p. 176)

Evidence from human oxytocin studies since 2000 may have tipped the scales from "highly speculative" to tantalizing, but it still seems too soon to reach a verdict. After reviewing this evidence, Churchland and Winkielman (2012) raised a number of key interpretational issues, then counseled caution.

Brain Regions That May Be Involved in Generalization of Empathic Concern

Turning from neurochemistry to brain activity, Singer and colleagues (2004) found increased activation in the anterior insula (AI) and rostral anterior cingulate cortex (ACC) among women who thought their romantic partner was receiving painful (vs. not painful) electrical stimulation. Bartels and Zeki

88 • EMPATHIC CONCERN

(2000) found increased activation in the middle insula (mainly on the left side) and in the ACC (ventral and bilateral) when participants looked at a photo of their romantic partner compared to when looking at photos of friends. Jackson and colleagues (2006) found AI and ACC activation among participants imagining an unfamiliar other in a painful (vs. not painful) situation. And Lamm and colleagues (2007) found that activation of the anterior medial cingulate cortex (aMCC) correlated positively with self-reported empathic concern among participants watching patients undergo a painful therapeutic treatment. Thus, several of the same (or closely associated) brain regions that are activated in mothers looking at photos of their own child (Bartels & Zeki, 2004) are activated not only when cued to a loved one's distress but also when seeing—or even imagining—an unknown other in distress (also see Immordino-Yang et al., 2009; Kim et al., 2009; Morelli & Lieberman, 2013). Once again, this evidence is consistent with the idea that empathic concern for non-kin is an expression of generalized parental nurturance. Consistent, but not conclusive.

Infant-Like Features Can Increase Empathic Concern

There is also psychological research consistent with the idea that empathic concern for non-kin may be linked to parental care. David Lishner and colleagues found in a series of three experiments that both men and women reported more empathic concern when an adult stranger in need had a more infant-like face or voice (Lishner, Oceja, Stocks, & Zaspel, 2008). In the first two experiments (one run in the U.S.; one in Spain), participants read a news article about a female university student struggling to take care of her younger brother and sister after their parents were killed in an automobile accident. (The article, actually fictitious, was based on the Katie Banks broadcast described in Chapter 1.) Embedded in the article was one of two color photos, ostensibly of the university student. One photo showed the face of a young adult woman; the second was a morphed version of the first photo that made the young woman look more infant-like. This was done by changing the spacing of her facial features in the direction of a baby-face template.

Half of the participants in each experiment were randomly assigned to read the article with the first photo (adult-face condition); the other half, to read the article with the morphed photo (infant-like-face condition). After reading, all participants rated a list of emotion adjectives, including the adjectives on the Empathic Concern Index: *sympathetic, tender, softhearted, warm, compassionate,* and *moved* (although *sympathetic* was omitted in Spain because research by Oceja & Jiménez, 2007, had indicated that this English adjective can't be accurately translated into Spanish with a single word). In both experiments, participants who saw the more infant-like face reported feeling significantly more empathic concern for the young woman than did participants who saw the adult face.

Lishner and colleagues' third experiment was a generalized replication of the first two. In it, male and female undergraduates listened to a pilot radio broadcast in which a male newscaster interviewed a female undergraduate struggling to cope with a genetic heart defect. Participants then rated emotion adjectives to indicate how much they experienced various emotions while listening. Among the adjectives were five of the six empathic-concern adjectives (in this experiment, *softhearted* was excluded given that the young woman's need involved a heart problem). The young woman's voice during the interview was either unaltered (adult-voice condition) or was digitally modified to have a 12% higher pitch, which produced a younger sounding voice (infant-like-voice condition). Paralleling the results of Experiments 1 and 2, participants randomly assigned to hear the more infant-like voice reported feeling significantly more empathic concern than participants who heard the young woman's normal voice.

Testing for Extended Parental Nurturance

To further test the idea that extended parental nurturance underlies empathic concern for strangers, David Lishner, Jennifer Cook, Stacey Sawyer, and I ran two experiments (Batson, Lishner, Cook, & Sawyer, 2005). Results were quite similar, so I'll describe only the second, which provided the more stringent test. In this experiment, undergraduate participants read and responded to one of four versions of a campus newspaper article for a planned feature reporting experiences of students volunteering in the community. The article described helping "Kayla" with rehabilitation exercises after surgery on her severely broken leg. In the four versions, Kayla was either an undergraduate at the university, a child, an adult dog, or a puppy. Each version included exactly the same description of Kayla's struggle with the exercises (the description was constructed to be plausible for all four Kaylas):

> Kayla's rehabilitation exercises sounded like a real ordeal, but when I went to get her she was more than ready. Soon she was hobbling around the therapy room as best she could with that bulky cast. She would try to walk without assistance, but the pain was so great that

she could only take three or four steps. Yet she kept trying. Once she slipped and fell, and let out a cry of pain. Still, she got up and tried again. Kayla just wouldn't quit.

After reading the article, participants indicated how much they experienced various emotions, including the six comprising the Empathic Concern Index.

We reasoned that if extended parental nurturance underlies empathic concern, then less empathy should be reported for the undergraduate Kayla, who was a young adult and not a typical target of nurturant care, than for the other three Kaylas. The child, an obvious target of such care, should evoke strong empathic concern. But so should both the adult dog and the puppy because, regardless of age, dogs are typically in the role of pet and dependent on humans for "parental" care. To use targets in need from a different species was admittedly unusual—yet not without precedent (see, for example, the research of Shelton & Rogers, 1981)—but it provided a strong test of the similarity to progeny claim of extended parental nurturance by juxtaposing it to a claim that similarity to self would determine empathy.

As predicted by extended parental nurturance, reported empathy for Kayla in the Student condition was significantly lower than in the other three conditions, which didn't differ significantly from one another. Of course, a 20-year-old university student differs from a child, dog, and puppy in many ways. I haven't been able to think of a difference other than the difference in need for nurturant care that would produce more empathic concern for them than for the far more similar fellow university student, but maybe you can. Also, I have no evidence that the empathic responses in this experiment were genetically based. For these reasons, I consider the support we found for extended parental nurturance to be only suggestive.

Conclusion

In Chapter 4, I proposed that feeling empathic concern in a given situation is the product of two necessary conditions—perception of another as in need and intrinsic valuing of the other's welfare. The present chapter proposes that the evolutionary basis for this valuing, and for empathic concern, likely lies in parental nurturance and in our ability to extend this nurturance beyond offspring to others. A range of evidence—neurochemical, neurophysiological, and psychological—is consistent with this proposal.

Although not conclusive, this evidence suggests that four evolutionary developments may underlie our capacity to care about the welfare of non-progeny for their sakes, not ours:

1. Evolution of parental nurturance in mammals.
2. Evolution in humans (and perhaps some other higher mammals) of the ability to see others as sentient, intentional agents and, thereby, to perceive them to be in need.
3. Evolution of tender, empathic concern based on perception of need and intrinsic valuing of the child's welfare as a core component of human parental care.
4. Evolution of the cognitive capacity to extend valuing of another's welfare— and therefore empathic concern—beyond offspring.

If it's true that intrinsic valuing and empathic concern have their evolutionary roots in parental care, then we have an answer to the question raised at the end of Chapter 4 about whether the capacity to intrinsically value another's welfare is a violation of the principles of natural selection: It's not. Parental care is entirely consistent with those principles.

6 VARIETIES OF EMPATHIC CONCERN

Appraisal theories of emotion contend that distinct emotions arise in response to different cognitive appraisals of value-relevant situations (Arnold, 1960; Rosenman, 1984; Scherer, 1984; Smith & Ellsworth, 1985; Wondra & Ellsworth, 2015). In Chapter 4, I suggested that the necessary elements of the appraisal producing empathic concern are (a) perception of another person as in need and (b) intrinsic valuing of that person's welfare. Thus, from an appraisal perspective, different types of need should evoke distinct forms of empathic concern for the same valued other. Although it seems unreasonable to expect a distinct form for every difference in need (e.g., a hurt foot vs. a hurt hand), it's reasonable to expect distinct forms for different types of need.

I also suggested in Chapter 4 that perception of need involves perception of a negative discrepancy between a person's current state and what the perceiver thinks is desirable for that person on one or more dimensions of well-being—and I noted two different types of need. The most obvious is *current need*, the perception of an existing discrepancy between what is and what's desirable. Less obvious is *vulnerability*. Even when there isn't an existing discrepancy, a person can be seen as vulnerable to future discrepancies. Here I wish to suggest that these two forms of need evoke two distinct forms of empathic concern—sympathy and tenderness.

Sympathy and Tenderness

Current need is the type of need encountered by participants in the experiments described in preceding chapters, so I assume it requires no elaboration. A cared-for other in current need evokes

Empathic Concern. C. Daniel Batson, Oxford University Press. © Oxford University Press 2023.
DOI: 10.1093/oso/9780197610923.003.0007

a feeling-for that is often reported as sympathy. Vulnerability may need some elaboration. As said in Chapter 4, an appraisal of vulnerability in the absence of current need is likely if the target is viewed as comparatively weak and defenseless—such as a young child or puppy happily playing or safely asleep. The child or puppy's lack of ability to deal with needs that may arise triggers other-oriented feelings often reported as tenderness, warmth, or softheartedness (Dijker, 2001, 2010; Kalawski, 2010; Lishner, Batson, & Huss, 2011; McDougall, 1908; Niezink, Siero, Dijkstra, Buunk, & Barelds, 2012).

Why should we feel anything for vulnerable others when they have no current need? William McDougall's depiction of the human parental instinct, discussed in Chapter 5, suggests an answer. He thought that perceived vulnerability evoked the tender emotion, the defining core of the parental instinct:

> The mere sight or thought of a perfectly happy child; for its feebleness, its delicacy, its obvious incapacity to supply its own needs, its liability to a thousand different ills, suggest to the mind its need for protection . . . . The child, or any other helpless and delicate thing, may call it [the tender emotion] out in the pure form without alloy of sympathetic pain [McDougall's term for what I call personal distress—see Chapter 2]. (McDougall, 1908, p. 63)

Going a step further, McDougall thought that "owing to the subtle working of similarity," we can feel tenderness toward "any and every object that is small and delicate of its kind—a very small cup or chair, or book, or what not" (p. 63). Although I'm not ready to say that we experience empathic concern for every small object, the "Aww; it's so dear!" response evoked by a delicate and fragile teacup does seem to express tenderness.

According to McDougall's analysis then, to see a happily playing or peacefully sleeping child or puppy is likely to evoke tenderness. I doubt, however, that such a sight would evoke sympathy, which seems to require a perception of current need. If the child or puppy were in current need—hurt, frightened, or lonely—I suspect you'd feel sympathy along with tenderness, as did the participants in the Kayla experiment described in Chapter 5 (see Batson, Lishner et al., 2005).

This analysis suggests that we may feel tenderness without feeling sympathy, but not the reverse. Because a person must be vulnerable to a need in order to experience it, current need is evidence of vulnerability. Therefore, the appraisal conditions necessary to evoke sympathy—current need and valuing the other's welfare—should also evoke tenderness.

Explaining an Apparent Empirical Discrepancy Regarding Sympathy and Tenderness

The proposed linkages between current need and sympathy on the one hand, and between vulnerability and tenderness on the other, offer insight into an apparent discrepancy found in the research literature. As documented in previous chapters, colleagues and I have consistently found that research participants exposed to adults in current need report high levels of both sympathy and tenderness. These two empathic emotions tend to co-occur (see Chapter 1; also see Batson, 1987; Batson, Fultz, & Schoenrade, 1987). In their research on emotion prototypes, however, Phil Shaver, Judith Schwartz, Donald Kirson, and Cary O'Connor (1987) found that most respondents placed sympathy and tenderness in different semantic categories—sympathy is in a negatively valenced category along with pity, while tenderness is in a positively valenced category characterized by caring, love, and affection. Only a minority of respondents placed sympathy with tenderness, love, and caring.

Sense can be made of these seemingly discrepant findings in light of the roles of current need and vulnerability in evoking sympathy and tenderness, respectively. If current need implies vulnerability, it's no surprise that colleagues and I find a close association of sympathy and tenderness among people confronted with adults in current need. Nor is it a surprise that, when asked to classify various emotion terms, most of Shaver and colleagues' respondents distinguished between sympathy and tenderness. Thinking abstractly, they probably associated these emotions with current need and vulnerability, respectively.

Testing the Proposed Sympathy-Tenderness Distinction

To test the proposal that perception of current need evokes sympathy whereas perception of vulnerability evokes tenderness, David Lishner, Elizabeth Huss, and I conducted two experiments in which we independently varied these two forms of need and then measured sympathy and tenderness (Lishner, Batson, & Huss, 2011).

In the first experiment, each participant was asked to imagine a particular person in a particular situation. Four different person-situation pairings allowed us to independently manipulate current need and chronic vulnerability. We manipulated current need by varying the situation—participants either imagined the person playing with a Frisbee (low current need) or struggling to walk with a leg in a heavy plaster cast (high current need). We

96 • EMPATHIC CONCERN

manipulated chronic vulnerability by varying the person's age—either a 20-year-old adult (low chronic vulnerability) or a two-year-old child (high chronic vulnerability).

Sympathy was predicted to be higher in the two struggling (high current need) cells than in the two playing (low current need) cells. Tenderness was predicted to be high in the child/playing, child/struggling, and adult/struggling cells, but low in the adult/playing cell. This second prediction was based on the assumption that either chronic vulnerability (as in the case of a child, whether playing or struggling) or acute vulnerability (as in the case of an adult struggling) would produce a perception of vulnerability. To test these predictions, male and female undergraduates were randomly assigned to the four cells of the 2 (current need: low vs. high) × 2 (chronic vulnerability: low vs. high) design.

When participants arrived for the experiment, each received a four-page research packet. The first page described the experiment as a brief survey of feelings when encountering strangers (i.e., "social targets") in various situations. The first page also explained that each participant would be randomly assigned one pairing of a social target and situation from an extensive list. Turning to the next page, all participants read that they had been assigned *Target 4*. For those in the low-chronic-vulnerability condition, Target 4 was "a 20-year-old woman (man)"; for those in the high-chronic-vulnerability condition, "a two-year-old girl (boy)." (Sex of participant and sex of target were always the same.) All participants then read that they had been assigned *Situation 5*. For participants in the low-current-need condition, this assignment meant that they should imagine walking across campus and seeing Target 4 and a young woman playing happily with a Frisbee. For participants in the high-current-need condition, this assignment meant they should imagine seeing Target 4 being helped by a young woman as the target struggles to walk with one leg in a heavy plaster cast. After imagining for about a minute, participants turned to the next page and filled out a feelings questionnaire on which they indicated the extent to which they experienced each of 20 emotions while imagining the target in the situation. Embedded in the list were *sympathetic* and *tender*, as well as the other four adjectives on the Empathic Concern Index.

As expected, participants reported feeling more *sympathetic* in the struggling cells than in the playing cells, and reported feeling more *tender* in the child/playing, child/struggling, and adult/struggling cells than in the adult/playing cell. Moreover, across the three cells in which feelings of sympathy and tenderness were hypothesized to be either both high or both low—adult/playing (low, low), adult/struggling (high/high), and child/ struggling (high, high)—ratings of *sympathetic* and *tender* were positively correlated ($r = .48$), whereas in the one cell in which these feelings were hypothesized to be unrelated—child/playing (low/high)—the correlation was near zero ($r = .06$). Our second experiment provided a generalized replication of these results using a target that participants thought real.

Turning to the other four adjectives on the Empathic Concern Index, in both experiments *softhearted*, *warm*, and *moved* patterned like *tender*, showing sensitivity to perceived vulnerability. Although *compassionate* patterned more like *sympathetic*, it was highly correlated with both *sympathetic* and *tender*, suggesting it was sensitive to both current need and vulnerability. (For additional research on the sympathy-tenderness distinction, see Dijker, 2001, 2010, and Niezink et al., 2012.)

Empathic Distress and Empathic Sadness

In Chapter 2, I noted two other forms of empathic concern—empathic distress and empathic sadness—that, while not measured by items on the Empathic Concern Index, can at times be measured by other adjectives on the Emotional Response Questionnaire shown in Figures 1.1 and 2.1. These other adjectives were included in the Questionnaire to measure self-oriented distress and sadness evoked by encountering another in need. But around 1990, evidence emerged that in response to someone struggling to deal with a difficult adjustment/coping situation, the eight adjectives on the Personal Distress Index discussed in Chapter 2 seem to be a valid measure of other-oriented empathic distress. As quoted in that chapter,

> When people observe another's physical discomfort, reports of distress are likely to reflect the degree to which they are distressed by this spectacle; when people hear about someone's struggles adjusting to a difficult situation, reports of distress are likely to reflect the degree to which they are distressed for this person. This latter form of distress reflects empathy rather than personal distress as these terms have been defined in the empathy-altruism literature. (Batson, Batson et al., 1991, p. 415)

A parallel distinction has been found with sadness. In 1988, Jim Fultz, Mark Schaller, and Bob Cialdini introduced a four-item index of felt sadness that included the adjectives *low-spirited*, *heavyhearted*, *sad*, and *feeling low*

(Fultz, Schaller, & Cialdini, 1988). Using principal-component analysis (see Chapters 1 and 2), Fultz and colleagues demonstrated the independence of this Sadness Index from both the Empathic Concern and Personal Distress Indexes when people are responding to need situations involving physical suffering.

Subsequently, colleagues and I found that in response to the Katie Banks need situation, which involved her struggle to care for her younger brother and sister after the death of their parents, the four adjectives on the Fultz and colleagues' Sadness Index seemed to measure empathic sadness. All four loaded highly (above .60) on a single component that also had high loadings (above .60) from all six empathy adjectives and seven of the eight distress adjectives (only "perturbed" failed to meet this criterion—Batson, Batson et al., 1991, Experiments 1 & 3). Thus, in response to needs involving physical suffering, the four adjectives on the Sadness Index seemed to measure self-oriented personal sadness evoked by witnessing the suffering. But in response to needs involving adjustment/coping, they seemed to measure other-oriented empathic sadness felt for the person in need.

Note that all the evidence indicating that the Distress and Sadness Indexes sometimes measure empathic rather than personal distress and sadness comes from situations involving current need. I suspect that vulnerability alone produces more positive warm, tender feelings rather than either empathic distress or sadness. But, when coupled with current need, vulnerability can intensify feelings of empathic distress and sadness. Think of the university student quoted at the beginning of Chapter 1 who felt sad for her young cousin because he "wouldn't have the sweet hugs [from his mom who had died] when he bumped his knee." This student seems to have experienced empathic sadness evoked by her cousin's current need and vulnerability.

Empathic Anger

Some researchers use the term empathic anger to refer to catching the anger that another person feels after he or she is harmed. Used in this way, empathic anger is a form of emotional contagion, which involves feeling as, not feeling for, the other (see Chapter 3). Other researchers—myself included—use empathic anger to refer to anger felt toward someone who harms a person you care for, regardless of whether the cared-for person feels anger. Recall your friend at lunch in Chapter 3 who felt hurt and afraid, not angry, at being laid off. If you felt anger toward her boss for laying her off, I would call that empathic anger. It's a form of empathic concern—an other-oriented emotion elicited by and congruent with the perceived welfare of another in need.

Martin Hoffman (2000) recognized the difference between these two types of anger, but he called them both empathic. He claimed:

> There are two types of empathic anger. In the first, relatively simple type, the victim is angry at the abuser and the observer picks up that anger through the empathy-arousing mechanisms [such as emotional contagion] and feels empathic anger. In the second, more complex type, the victim feels sad, hurt, or disappointed but *not* angry at the abuser . . . . The two types of empathic anger are combined when the victim feels sad, hurt, disappointed, *and* angry. It should be noted that only the first type involves an affect match between observer and victim. (pp. 97–98, italics in original)

I use the term empathic anger to refer only to Hoffman's second type—although I expand that type to include anger felt toward the harm-doer whether the person who has been harmed feels angry, feels some other emotion (e.g., distress, fear, sadness), or feels nothing at all. For me, the defining feature is whether you feel anger because the harm-doer hurt someone you care about, not whether the cared-for other does or doesn't feel anger. Said another way, I think the appraisal conditions for empathic anger are that you perceive someone to have unjustifiably harmed a person for whom you care.

So defined, empathic anger differs in two important ways from the four forms of empathic concern considered previously. First, although empathic anger is evoked by perception of a cared-for other in need, the need is caused by a person, not by happenstance or natural causes. Second, whereas sympathy, tenderness, empathic distress, and empathic sadness are focused on the cared-for other, empathic anger is focused on and directed toward the harm-doer. As a result, empathic anger is likely to have different motivational and behavioral consequences than the other four forms. (Also note that, using my definition, it's possible to feel empathic anger toward a cared-for other who causes his or her own need through, for example, self-harm or recklessness.)

Guy Vitaglione and Mark Barnett provided evidence of empathic anger as I'm defining it in a study with male and female undergraduate participants (Vitaglione & Barnett, 2003). The study was ostensibly designed to get reactions to public service announcements about drunk driving, and each participant was to listen to one such announcement and then report his or her emotional reactions. In actuality, all participants heard the same announcement, which included an interview with a woman named Susan who had been badly injured when hit by a drunk driver, Robert.

In the interview, Susan described being hit, her current condition, and her feelings. Vitaglione and Barnett (2003) provided this excerpt from Susan's description:

> It hurts so much. Now I have to go to physical therapy to try to get the use back into my leg. It's just not fair. Why did this have to happen to me? I don't even get to see my friends, to talk to them the way I used to. I'm so lonely all the time. (p. 314)

To assess emotional reactions to the interview, participants completed a modified Emotional Response Questionnaire that included, intermixed with other items, the six adjectives on the Empathic Concern Index. It also included eight adjectives to measure anger: *mad, angry, furious, resentful, irritated, enraged, aggravated,* and *outraged.*

Factor analysis—of which principal-component analysis (see Chapters 1 and 2) is a special case—revealed that responses to the empathy and anger adjectives produced a two-factor solution. All six empathic concern adjectives loaded highly (above .60) on one factor, whereas all eight anger adjectives loaded highly (above .60) on a second, orthogonal (i.e., uncorrelated) factor. This factor structure indicated that the empathic-concern and anger adjectives measured two distinct emotional states. At the same time, there was a positive correlation between two indexes created by averaging responses to the six empathic concern adjectives and averaging responses to the eight anger adjectives ($r = .47$). This correlation suggested that the reported anger, which was presumably felt toward the drunk driver, Robert, could be due to concern for Susan.

Consistent with this interpretation, when participants were asked how much they wanted to help Susan and how much they wanted to punish Robert, scores on the empathic-concern index correlated highly ($p < .001$) with desire to help her but not with desire to punish him. In contrast, scores on the anger index correlated highly ($p < .001$) with both desire to punish him and desire to help her. These correlations support the idea that empathic anger is a distinct type of empathic concern with different motivational and behavioral consequences, consequences that include punishing the harmdoer, especially if doing so is likely to benefit the cared-for other who was harmed—or to benefit similar others.

Note, however, it's also possible that the heightened perception of need and valuing of Susan's welfare underlying participants' feelings of empathic concern may have sharpened their awareness of how wrong Robert's behavior was, which led them to feel moral anger—anger at the violation of a moral standard or principle—rather than empathic anger (see Batson, 2016, Chapter 6, for discussion of and evidence for this distinction). Pfattheicher, Sassenrath, and Keller (2019) provided a range of evidence suggesting that, depending on circumstances, either or both of these emotional responses may follow witnessing unjustified harm to a cared-for other.

Empathic Embarrassment

Rowland Miller (1987) defined empathic embarrassment as "embarrassment felt with another even though the other's actions do not reflect upon yourself" (p. 1068). What Miller meant by "felt with another" seems to encompass at least three different psychological states that have been called empathy. Sometimes, he seemed to mean emotional contagion: "Whenever a person suffers the flustered discomfort of embarrassment, observers may recognize and empathically share that embarrassment" (p. 1062). But he also said, "observers may become empathically embarrassed if they are able to imagine themselves in another person's social predicament whether or not the person displays obvious embarrassment" (p. 1062). Here, empathic embarrassment seems to mean that the observers adopt an imagine-self perspective and, as a result, feel the personal embarrassment they would if in the predicament themselves. And, at still another point, Miller spoke of "feeling abashment and chagrin for" the target (p. 1065), which sounds like a form of empathic concern.

Doubt that Empathic Embarrassment is a Form of Empathic Concern

Seeking to provide evidence for one or more of these possibilities, Miller conducted two experiments. In each, undergraduate men and women participated in same-sex pairs, ostensibly as part of an investigation of "physiological changes during impression formation."

Participants in the key conditions of Miller's first experiment did an initial task alone and then, by a coin flip, one of them was assigned to observe through a one-way mirror as the other performed a set of four tasks. For some participants, the four tasks were designed to evoke embarrassment—dance for 60 seconds to recorded rock music, laugh for 30 seconds as if just hearing a joke, sing the "Star Spangled Banner," and imitate a five-year-old throwing a temper tantrum (embarrassment condition). For others, the tasks were parallel but not embarrassing—listen to the rock music, copy the words of the "Star Spangled Banner," and so on (no-embarrassment condition). To manipulate empathy, half of the observers in the embarrassment condition were instructed to "picture how the actor feels, visualizing how it feels to him [or her] to be performing the task" (high-empathy/embarrassment cell); the other half were instructed to "watch the actor's behavior closely" (low-empathy/embarrassment cell). All observers in the no-embarrassment condition received the watch-behavior (low-empathy) instructions.

Confirming that the embarrassing tasks caused embarrassment, actors doing them reported feeling more embarrassed than did actors doing the not-embarrassing tasks. Observers, too, rated their actor's embarrassment higher when the actor performed the embarrassing tasks. And providing evidence of one or more of the states Miller called empathic embarrassment, observers in the embarrassment condition also reported feeling more embarrassed themselves. Moreover, among observers in the embarrassment condition, those given the high-empathy instructions reported feeling more embarrassed than those given low-empathy instructions.

The observers in the high-empathy/embarrassment cell also reported feeling sorrier for the actor and feeling more sympathetic toward him or her, indicating increased empathic concern. And they were more physiologically aroused while observing. Moreover, observers' reports of embarrassment and of feeling sympathetic toward the actor were positively correlated. But reports of embarrassment correlated positively with displayed physiological arousal, whereas reports of feeling sympathetic didn't. In sum, observers who pictured how the actor felt while performing the embarrassing tasks reported feeling both more embarrassment themselves and more empathic concern for the actor, but their embarrassment and their empathic concern seemed to be two distinct emotional responses, not other-oriented empathic embarrassment.

These results suggest, I think, that although observers in Miller's high-empathy/embarrassment cell felt more empathic concern for the actor, the embarrassment they reported wasn't a form of empathic concern. Instead, it was a product either of emotional contagion or of imagining themselves—not only the actor—in the embarrassing situations. My confidence in this interpretation is increased by the results of Miller's second experiment, which provided evidence that those observers who showed increased embarrassment

Varieties of Empathic Concern · 103

and physiological arousal also reported being, in general, more personally prone to feel embarrassed in awkward situations.

More Support for Doubt

Eric Stocks, David Lishner, Bethany Waits, and Eirah Downum reported two experiments that further supported the suggestion that empathic embarrassment isn't a form of empathic concern (Stocks, Lishner, Waits, & Downum, 2011). In their first experiment—ostensibly run to help the university's Office of Student Transition identify adjustment issues commonly faced by entering students—participants (freshman and sophomore undergraduates) were asked to evaluate the typicality of one or more experiences of a randomly selected incoming freshman. In fact, all participants were assigned (ostensibly randomly) to evaluate two experiences of a freshman named Zack. They learned about Zack's first experience by reading the transcript of an initial interview with him, then learned about his second experience by listening to an audiotape of a follow-up interview.

To manipulate valuing of Zack's welfare, two versions of the transcript of the initial interview were created—each adapted from the transcripts developed by Batson, Eklund, and colleagues (2007) in which Bryan Banks encountered a lost and confused old woman (described in Chapter 4). Participants in Stocks and colleagues' high-valuing condition read that when Zack encountered a lost and confused old woman, he was nice to her. Those assigned to the low-valuing condition read that he was rude. All participants then listened to the follow-up interview, in which Zack ruefully described an embarrassing incident on his first date with a girl he really wanted to impress. Toward the end of the evening, with the date going really well, Zack got laughing too hard and blew Coke out his nose—and then, laughing even harder, he let loose a loud and smelly fart.

After hearing about Zack's disastrous date, participants in the high-valuing condition reported feeling more empathic concern and also feeling more embarrassed than did participants in the low-valuing condition. Moreover, participants' reports of empathic concern and embarrassment were positively correlated ($r = .62$). These results, which parallel those of Miller's (1987) first experiment, were consistent with the possibility that the reported embarrassment was a form of empathic concern.

But results of Stocks and colleagues' second experiment suggested a different interpretation. All participants heard the audiotaped interview about Zack's disastrous date. However, this time there was no prior valuing manipulation—that is, participants didn't first read about his encounter with the old woman. Instead, participants were randomly assigned one of three listening perspectives prior to hearing about Zack's date: remain objective, imagine how the person in the interview feels, and imagine how you would think and feel if the events described happened to you. These listening-perspective instructions were modeled on the objective, imagine-other, and imagine-self instructions used by Batson, Early, and Salvarani (1997), described in Chapter 2.

Hearing about Zack's date, participants in the imagine-other condition reported feeling significantly more empathic concern than did participants in the remain-objective condition, whereas participants in the imagine-self condition didn't. In contrast, participants in the imagine-self condition reported feeling significantly more embarrassed than those in the objective condition, whereas participants in the imagine-other condition didn't. To find that empathic concern was high and embarrassment low in the imagine-other condition, but embarrassment high and empathic concern low in the imagine-self condition, suggests that the reported embarrassment in the latter condition wasn't a form of empathic concern; instead, it was personal embarrassment participants imagined feeling had they committed such a faux pas. Overall, reported embarrassment correlated .61 with reported distress and only .33 with reported empathic concern.

The results of Stocks and colleagues' second experiment suggest that the relatively high empathic concern reported in the imagine-other condition reflected feeling sorry for Zack, but not empathic embarrassment. And the relatively high embarrassment reported in the imagine-self condition reflected imagined personal embarrassment, not other-oriented concern for Zack. Further supporting this interpretation, reported empathic concern was positively correlated both with participants' reported desire to see Zack receive help with his transition to college ($r = .42$) and with their desire to receive updates on his welfare ($r = .53$). Reported embarrassment wasn't significantly correlated with either of these desires ($rs = .05$ and .08, respectively).

Overall, Stocks and colleagues' results support the idea that empathic concern and self-oriented personal embarrassment are two distinct emotional responses to learning of another's embarrassment. Imagining how the other feels heightens awareness of his or her distress and, if the other's welfare is valued, evokes empathic concern. Imagining oneself in another's embarrassing situation evokes imagined personal embarrassment, a form of personal distress.

Conclusion

The existing empirical evidence suggests that two distinct forms of empathic concern are measured by the Empathic Concern Index—and that each is evoked by a different type of need. Sympathy is evoked by a cared-for other's current need. Tenderness, by a cared-for other's vulnerability. Two additional forms of empathic concern, empathic distress and empathic sadness, are sometimes measured by the distress and sadness adjectives on the Emotional Response Questionnaire that aren't part of the Empathic Concern Index. When the other's need involves physical harm or pain, the distress and sadness adjectives seem to measure self-oriented personal distress and sadness. When the other's need is a coping/adjustment problem, these adjectives seem to measure empathic distress and sadness felt for the other.

Empathic anger is a form of empathic concern that differs importantly from the previous four forms. Although evoked by and motivating action designed to address the cared-for other's need, empathic anger is directed toward the person or persons seen as causing the other's need, not toward the cared-for other.

What has been called empathic embarrassment doesn't seem to be a form of empathic concern. Instead, it appears to be a product of one or both of two other psychological states that have been called empathy—(a) emotional contagion and (b) imagining yourself in the other's situation. Either of these can lead you to feel embarrassed, but your embarrassment seems to be a form of personal distress.

In sum, we currently have evidence for five different forms of empathic concern. And there's no reason to think that these five exhaust the possibilities. There may well be others produced by other types of need.

Why is it important to recognize the different forms of empathic concern? Once again, appraisal theories of emotion offer an answer: Our emotions evoked by different needs produce motivation and behavior to address those specific needs (Batson, Shaw, & Oleson, 1992; Frijda, 1988; Keltner & Haidt, 1999, 2001; Scherer, 1984). To illustrate with sympathy and tenderness, sympathy should produce motivation to address the current need. Often, but not always, this motivation will lead to helping behavior. Tenderness should produce motivation to address the target's vulnerability. More precisely, tenderness evoked by chronic vulnerability should produce a desire to protect and shield the other from harm. Rather than immediate helping, this motivation should promote vigilance and long-range forms of assistance that, if possible, help the target overcome vulnerability through growth and learning.

Part II of this book considers the motivational and behavioral consequences of feeling empathic concern in its various forms. Chapter 7 focuses on motivational consequences—specifically, on the suggestion that the motivation produced by empathic concern is altruistic not egoistic. This suggestion returns us to the fundamental question of whether, when we feel empathic concern, we're motivated to care for the target of our empathy for his or her sake, not for ours.

WHY EMPATHIC CONCERN IS IMPORTANT

7 MOTIVATIONAL CONSEQUENCES

THE EMPATHY-ALTRUISM HYPOTHESIS

It probably comes as no surprise that feeling empathic concern for a person in need can motivate you to help that person. This observation has been around at least since the Middle Ages, when Thomas Aquinas noted that "mercy is heartfelt sympathy for another's distress, impelling us to succor him if we can" (Aquinas, 1270/1917, II-II, 30,3). Moreover, empirical research supports the observation (see, for example, Coke et al., 1978; Dovidio, Allen, & Schroeder, 1990; and Krebs, 1975—see Batson, 1991, 2011, and Eisenberg & Miller, 1987, for reviews). But to observe that empathic concern motivates helping tells us nothing about the nature of this motivation. Is the goal to benefit the person for whom empathic concern is felt, or is it to benefit ourselves?

The dominant view in Western thought has long been that the real reason we benefit others—even others for whom we care dearly—is to benefit ourselves. In the words of the wise and witty Duke de la Rochefoucauld, "the most disinterested love is, after all, but a kind of bargain, in which the dear love of our own selves always proposes to be the gainer some way or other" (La Rochefoucauld, 1691, Maxim 82). The *empathy-altruism hypothesis* challenges this doctrine of universal egoism by proposing that empathic concern produces altruistic motivation. Although never a majority view, this alternative hypothesis has been around in one form or another for a long time, being espoused not only by Aquinas but also by, among others, David Hume, Adam Smith, and Charles Darwin.

The significance of an empathy-altruism hypothesis depends on what you think altruism is. If, like most behavioral and social scientists today, you think of altruism as personally costly

Empathic Concern. C. Daniel Batson, Oxford University Press. © Oxford University Press 2023.
DOI: 10.1093/oso/9780197610923.003.0008

helping—or as helping to gain internal rewards (e.g., a warm glow for doing a good deed) rather than external rewards (e.g., payment or praise)—then the existence of empathy-induced altruistic motivation can't be doubted. But to claim that such altruism exists tells us nothing we didn't already know. These conceptions of altruism don't challenge the doctrine of universal egoism; they trivialize the centuries-old egoism-altruism debate. If you instead adopt a conception of altruism that's true to that debate and not just a subtle form of egoism, an empathy-altruism hypothesis is profound.

In the egoism-altruism debate, *altruism* refers to a motivational state with the ultimate goal of increasing another's welfare. *Egoism* refers to a motivational state with the ultimate goal of increasing our own welfare. So defined, altruism and egoism have much in common. Each specifies the ultimate goal of a motivational state, and for each, the ultimate goal is to increase someone's welfare. These common features provide the context for specifying the crucial difference: Whose welfare is the ultimate goal? Is it that of the person in need, or our own? Accepting the terms as defined in the debate, the empathy-altruism hypothesis claims that *empathic concern*—defined as in Chapter 1—*produces altruistic motivation*—a motivational state with the ultimate goal of increasing another's welfare.

To clarify, "ultimate goal" in this hypothesis refers to what we're after in the psychological present, not to a metaphysical first or final cause and not to biological function. An *ultimate goal* is an end in itself. In contrast, an *instrumental goal* is a stepping-stone on the way to an ultimate goal. If barriers to reaching an instrumental goal arise, alternative routes to the ultimate goal will be sought. And if the ultimate goal is reached bypassing the instrumental goal, the motivational force will disappear. An ultimate goal can't be bypassed in this way. Ultimate goals should also be distinguished from their *unintended consequences*—results of goal-directed action that aren't goals.

Each of a person's ultimate goals defines a distinct goal-directed motive. So, because altruism and egoism as defined have different ultimate goals, they are distinct goal-directed motives—even though they can co-occur. Moreover, each is a motivational *state*, not a personal disposition or *trait*. The empathy-altruism hypothesis is about the motive produced by empathic concern in people like you and me, not about what motivates saints and martyrs. Finally, the hypothesis doesn't claim that when we feel empathic concern we experience only or even primarily altruistic motivation. We can experience other motives, including motives for helping, produced by thoughts and feelings other than empathic concern.

Testing the Empathy-Altruism Hypothesis Against Its Egoistic Alternatives

Is this empathy-altruism hypothesis true? That is, does empathic concern felt for a person in need produce motivation directed toward the ultimate goal of relieving that need? The evidence, mentioned earlier, that empathic concern produces motivation to help the person for whom it's felt is consistent with this hypothesis but doesn't provide clear support. As depicted in Table 7.1, removing the other's need could be (a) an ultimate goal, with any self-benefits being unintended consequences, or (b) an instrumental goal on the way to the ultimate goal of gaining one or another self-benefit. That is, the motivation could be either altruistic or egoistic. To know which it is, we need to do more than show evidence that empathic concern produces helping; we need to ascertain the ultimate goal.

Three types of egoistic ultimate goals have been proposed to account for empathy-induced helping. The most popular proposal—both in classical philosophy and in contemporary behavioral and social science—is that empathy-induced helping is directed toward the ultimate goal of *aversive-arousal reduction*. As discussed in Chapter 2, this egoistic explanation claims that feeling empathic concern for another in need is unpleasant, and we help because removing the other's need is a way to remove our own unpleasant arousal (e.g., Piliavin et al., 1981).

A second proposal is that empathic concern motivates us to *avoid empathy-specific punishment*. (The punishment must be empathy-specific if it's to account for empathy-induced helping.) There are two versions of this possibility. One, introduced by Archer, Diaz-Loving, Gollwitzer, Davis, and Foushee (1981), focuses on avoidance of social punishment. It claims that we've learned through socialization that others will judge us negatively if we fail to help a person for whom we feel empathic concern. So, we help in order to avoid this social censure. The second version, suggested by, among others, Dovidio (1984), Batson (1987), and Schaller and Cialdini (1988), focuses on self-punishment. It claims we've learned through socialization that feeling empathic concern introduces a special obligation to help and, as a result, an extra dose of self-administered shame and guilt if we don't. When we feel empathic concern, we think of this impending self-punishment and help in order to avoid it. (Both versions could, of course, be true.)

The third egoistic proposal is that empathic concern produces motivation to *gain empathy-specific reward*. Three different versions of this possibility have been suggested. Most common is the claim that we learn through

112 • EMPATHIC CONCERN

Table 7.1 Logical Structure of the Question About the Nature of the Motivation Produced by Empathic Concern

Nature of the motivation	Outcomes of helping	
	Remove the other's need	Receive self-benefits
Altruistic	Ultimate goal	Unintended consequence
Egoistic	Instrumental goal	Ultimate goal

socialization that special rewards follow helping someone for whom we feel empathy—rewards in the form of extra praise from others or extra feelings of pride in ourselves. Thinking of these rewards, we help in order to get them. This possibility was suggested by Thompson, Cowan, and Rosenhan (1980), Meindl and Lerner (1983), and Batson (1987).

The second version is that, rather than a desire for empathy-specific rewards, empathic concern creates additional need for the general mood-enhancing rewards associated with helping. Much as a hungry person desires food more than someone comfortably replete, the claim is that feeling empathic concern depresses our mood and creates a desire to feel better. This desire for mood enhancement, in turn, makes the positive feelings that come from helping more attractive—and helping more likely. Cialdini, Schaller, Houlihan, Arps, Fultz, and Beaman (1987) proposed this *negative-state-relief hypothesis*. They reasoned that individuals who experience empathic concern find themselves in a negative affective state of temporary sadness or sorrow, which leads them to help "because helping contains a rewarding component for most normally socialized adults . . . [and] can be used instrumentally to restore mood" (Cialdini et al., 1987, p. 750).

At first glance, the negative-state-relief hypothesis may look like the aversive-arousal-reduction explanation. In fact, it's quite different. Both explanations begin with the proposition that empathic concern is unpleasant, a negative affective state. But from this common starting point, they diverge. Negative-state-relief claims that the resulting motivation is directed toward the goal of adding mood-enhancing rewards that we've learned are associated with helping. Aversive-arousal-reduction claims that the motivation is directed toward the goal of eliminating the negative affect itself—and helping is one way to do so.

The third version of empathy-specific reward is the *empathic-joy hypothesis*, proposed by Smith, Keating, and Stotland (1989). They argued that when we feel empathic concern, we don't help to gain the empathy-specific rewards of being seen or seeing ourselves as helpful—nor do we help because of an added need for mood-enhancing rewards. Instead, we help to gain the pleasant, happy feeling of sharing vicariously in the joy that the needy individual experiences when his or her need is removed. In their words, "The prospect of empathic joy, conveyed by feedback from the help recipient, is essential to the special tendency of empathic witnesses to help . . . . The empathically concerned witness to the distress of others helps in order to be happy" (Smith et al., 1989, p. 641).

The empathy-altruism hypothesis doesn't deny that empathy-induced helping can bring self-benefits—including the ones just described. But it claims that insofar as our motivation for helping stems from empathic concern, any self-benefits that result are unintended consequences rather than ultimate goals (see Row 1 of Table 7.1). Each of the egoistic alternatives disagrees, specifying a self-benefit as the ultimate goal, with removal of the other's need as an instrumental means to reach this egoistic end (see Row 2).

Why the Ultimate Goal Matters

As long as empathic concern motivates helping, why worry about whether the motivation is altruistic or egoistic? The answer depends on your interest. If you're only interested in removal of the specific target's current need, the ultimate goal may not matter. But if you're interested in knowing when and where empathy-induced help is likely to occur and how effective it's likely to be—perhaps with an eye to creating a more caring society—then to understand the ultimate goal is essential. To give but one example, if empathic concern motivates me to help in order to avoid your censure or get your praise, then when you won't know I was the one who helped, the empathy-helping relationship will disappear.

Like any other goal-directed behavior, occurrence of empathy-induced helping depends not only on the strength of the empathy-induced motive but also on the strength of other motives present at the time—and on how helping relates to each of these motives. It also depends on whether helping in the specific situation can promote the ultimate goal of the empathy-induced motive. The more directly that helping promotes the ultimate goal(s), and the more uniquely it does so among the behavioral options available, the more likely it is to occur. If it instead promotes an instrumental goal, empathy-induced helping will vanish if (a) the causal association between the instrumental and ultimate goal(s) is broken (as in the example in the preceding paragraph) or (b) a better behavioral path to the ultimate goal(s) appears that bypasses the instrumental goal. Invariance—and predictive power—is found in ultimate goals and motives, not in behavior or consequences (Lewin, 1938, 1944/1951).

Turning to Experiments

But if, as noted in Table 7.1, empathy-induced helping typically benefits both the person in need and the helper, how are we to know whose benefit is its ultimate goal? This puzzle has led many scientists to give up on the question of whether the motivation produced by empathic concern is altruistic or egoistic, concluding that the question can't be addressed empirically. They often add that the motive doesn't really matter anyway; only behavior matters (e.g., de Waal, 2008).

I think such surrender is premature. I think that we can empirically discern people's ultimate goals, indeed, that we often do. We do it when we infer whether a student is really interested or only seeking a better grade (What happens to the interest after the grades are turned in?), why a friend chose one job over another (What features did the chosen job have that the unchosen one didn't?), and whether politicians mean what they say or are only after votes (What do they do once elected?). We also do it when someone does us a favor or is kind. How do we discern ultimate goals? The following four principles seem key:

1. We can't trust self-reports. People often don't know—or won't tell—what their ultimate goals are.
2. We don't observe goals directly; we infer them from behavior.
3. If we observe a behavior that has two (or more) possible ultimate goals, the true ultimate goal(s) can't be discerned. It's like having one equation with two (or more) unknowns.
4. However, if we change the situation so that this behavior is no longer the best route to one of the possible ultimate goals and we still observe the behavior, then that goal isn't an ultimate goal of the behavior. It can be crossed off the list of possibilities.

These principles suggest that experiments are the most appropriate research method to determine the nature of the motivation produced by empathic concern. No other method seems up to the task. To report dramatic examples of helping, even highly costly helping, isn't enough because examples don't reveal the nature of the underlying motivation (Principle 2). The ultimate goal could be to benefit the individual in need, or it could be to benefit oneself (Principle 3). Only by systematically varying the situation under which the behavior occurs, as is possible in an experiment, can we draw clear inferences about the ultimate goals (Principle 4). Experiments aren't the method of choice to address every research question, but they seem uniquely well suited to determine the nature of a person's motivation.

Competing Predictions

The number of proposed empathy-specific egoistic motives that can produce helping complicates the task of determining whether the motivation produced by empathic concern is altruistic or egoistic. Careful analysis, however, reveals that under at least one diagnostic situational change, competing behavioral predictions are made by the empathy-altruism hypothesis and each of the proposed egoistic motives. These predictions, which are summarized in Table 7.2, provide opportunities to test the empathy-altruism hypothesis against each of the six proposed egoistic alternatives. The diagnostic change in a given row of the table can be used to test the empathy-altruism hypothesis against any egoistic alternative that makes a different prediction from the prediction of the empathy-altruism hypothesis for that change.

Most of the behavioral predictions in Table 7.2 are, I hope, clear. However, the predictions for salient thoughts (the last row) may need some explanation. When a person is motivated to reach some goal, thoughts related to this goal will be salient. But how can we know a person's salient thoughts? To ask the person seems futile because, as said earlier, he or she may not know or be willing to say (Principle 1). Fortunately, almost a century ago John Stroop discovered a way to assess salient thoughts that doesn't require self-reports (Stroop, 1938). He found that (a) presenting people with a reminder of their thoughts (by, for example, seeing a word related to the thoughts), then (b) having the people make a response to the reminder *unrelated* to these thoughts (e.g., name as quickly as possible the color of the ink in which the word is printed), creates cognitive interference and increases the response latency (i.e., slows the speed) of the unrelated response.

Despite being an indirect measure, these latencies have the virtue that the reminders that should increase the response latency if the motivation is altruistic differ from those that should increase the latency if the motivation is any of four of the six egoistic alternatives. Consider: If the motive is altruistic, the ultimate goal is to remove the empathy-evoking need, so seeing a word related

Table 7.2 Behavioral Predictions from the Empathy-Altruism Hypothesis and Its Egoistic Alternatives

Diagnostic Situational Changes	Empathy-altruism hypothesis	Egoistic Alternatives		
		Aversive-arousal reduction	Avoid empathy-specific punishment	Gain empathy-specific reward
Viability of escape. Can the goal be reached by escape without helping?	Escape without helping not viable	Escape viable (from needy other's distress)	Escape viable (from social and self-censure)	Escape without helping not viable
Necessity of help being effective. Must the help be effective to reach goal?	Effectiveness necessary	Effectiveness necessary	Not necessary (if ineffectiveness justified)	Necessary for empathic-joy; not necessary (if ineffectiveness justified) for other two versions
Acceptable helpers. Whose help can attain goal?	One's own, others'	One's own, others'	One's own, others'	One's own, others' for empathic-joy; only one's own for other two versions
Receive or anticipate mood-enhancing rewards. Does this reduce motivation to help?	No; mood-enhancement doesn't reach goal	Possibly, if mood-enhancement Overrides aversive arousal	No; mood-enhancement doesn't reach goal	Reaches goal only of negative-state- relief version
Diagnostic Situational Changes	Empathy-induced altruistic motivation	Egoistic Alternatives		
		Aversive-arousal reduction	Avoid empathy-specific punishment	Gain empathy-specific reward
Probability that update on other's need will be positive (no chance to help). Does this affect desire to get update?	Update desired even if not likely to be positive	Update desired only if likely to be positive	Positivity of update not relevant to punishment avoidance	Update desired only if likely to be positive if goal is negative-state relief or empathic joy; not relevant to other Version
Salient thoughts. What thoughts are salient when deciding whether to help?	Needy other's welfare; costs of helping	Aversive arousal; costs of helping	Possible punishments; costs of helping	Possible rewards; costs of helping; needy other's welfare if goal is empathic joy

to the need should produce longer latency when reporting the color of the ink. The only egoistic alternative for which words related to the need should produce longer latency is the empathic-joy hypothesis. Removal of the other's need is necessary to experience empathic joy, so for a person seeking this joy, thoughts about the need should be salient.

The other two versions of empathy-specific reward predict longer latency to name the color of words related to rewards (e.g., praise, pride). Versions of empathy-specific punishment predict longer color-naming latency to words related to social or self-punishments (e.g., blame, guilt). Although aversive-arousal reduction predicts longer latency to words related to aversive arousal (e.g., distress, upset), I don't think this prediction can be effectively tested, at least not with our existing measures. As discussed in Chapters 2 and 6, distress felt on encountering another in need can reflect either direct personal distress, a form of aversive arousal, or distress for the person in need, a form of empathic concern. Thus, it wouldn't be clear which motive—aversive-arousal reduction or empathy-induced altruism—underlies increased latency due to reminders of thoughts about distress or upset. (If you wish to have more detail on this or any other of the predictions in Table 7.2, see Batson, 2011, Appendix A.)

The Evidence

From 1978 to 1996, thirty-one experiments were conducted to test the empathy-altruism hypothesis against the egoistic alternatives. In each of these experiments, a behavior from Table 7.2 that could differentiate an empathy-induced altruistic motive from one or more of the egoistic alternatives was measured. Participants in the experiments were confronted with what they believed were real need situations, allowing them to actually feel empathic concern and not simply imagine feeling it. Empathic concern for the person in need was either manipulated, measured, or both. In almost all the experiments, a cross-cutting factor based on one of the six diagnostic changes listed in Table 7.2 was manipulated (e.g., easy vs. difficult escape without helping), creating conditions that allowed clear competing predictions from the empathy-altruism hypothesis and one or more of the egoistic alternatives. The remaining few experiments used a single level of the cross-cutting factor, a level that produced competing predictions (e.g., easy escape).

None of the cross-cutting factors in Table 7.2 allowed a clear test of the empathy-altruism hypothesis against all six proposed egoistic alternatives. As a result, it was necessary either to conduct experiments in which several

118 • EMPATHIC CONCERN

different factors were varied at once—which seemed unwieldy and unwise— or to conduct a series of experiments in which the egoistic alternatives were tested one after another. The latter strategy seemed clearly preferable, but to follow it required care. To be maximally informative, experiments testing different egoistic explanations should use the same need situation and the same technique for inducing empathic concern, varying only the hypothesis-relevant cross-cutting factor. Also, insofar as possible, each egoistic alternative should be tested in multiple experiments using different need situations, different techniques for inducing empathy, and different cross-cutting factors. Both strategies—testing different hypotheses using similar procedures and testing the same hypothesis using different procedures—were employed across the 31 experiments.

Cumulatively, the experiments tested all the competing predictions in Table 7.2. To cite but one example of research testing each prediction, *viability of escape from the needy other's distress without helping*—Row 1, Cell 2—was tested by Batson, Duncan, Ackerman, Buckley, and Birch (1981). *Viability of escape from social punishment* —Row 1, Cell 3—was tested by Fultz, Batson, Fortenbach, McCarthy, and Varney (1986). *Viability of escape from self-punishment*—Row 1, Cell 3—was tested by Batson, Dyck, Brandt, Batson, Powell, McMaster, and Griffitt (1988, Studies 2–4). *Necessity of help being effective even if ineffectiveness is justified*—Row 2, Cells 3–4—was tested by Batson and Weeks (1996). *Acceptability of the need being removed without one's own help*—Row 3, Cell 4—was tested by Batson, Dyck, and colleagues (1988, Study 1). *Receipt or anticipation of mood-enhancing rewards unrelated to helping*—Row 4, Cell 4—was tested by Batson, Batson, Griffitt, Barrientos, Brandt, Sprengelmeyer, and Bayly (1989). *Effect of the likely positivity of an update on desire to receive the update*—Row 5, Cells 2–4—was tested by Batson, Batson, Slingsby, Harrell, Peekna, and Todd (1991). *Salience of need-relevant, punishment-relevant, and reward-relevant cognitions*—Row 6, Cells 3–4— was tested by Batson, Dyck, and colleagues (1988, Study 5).

With remarkable consistency, results of the 31 experiments provided clear support for the empathy-altruism hypothesis (i.e., support for the predictions in Cell 1 of each row). A few experiments were initially interpreted as supporting one of the egoistic alternatives—most notably, the experiments reported by Cialdini and colleagues (1987) and Smith and colleagues (1989)— but in each case, subsequent experiments designed to eliminate ambiguities or potential confounds supported the empathy-altruism hypothesis. (For a summary of the procedures and results of all 31 experiments, as well as references to the original journal article reporting each, see Batson, 2011, Chapter 5 and Appendixes B–G.)

An All-At-Once Combination

Not only did the experimental evidence fail to support any of the six proposed egoistic alternatives; it also failed to support any combination of the six. It even failed to support an all-at-once combination, which claimed that empathic concern simultaneously evokes all six proposed empathy-specific egoistic motives.

This all-at-once combination could account for many of the results that seemed to support the empathy-altruism hypothesis because one egoistic alternative could explain results that another couldn't. To illustrate, the finding by Batson, Duncan, and colleagues (1981) of an empathy-helping relationship even when escape without helping was easy, predicted by the empathy-altruism hypothesis but not by aversive-arousal reduction (see Row 1, Cells 1 and 2 of Table 7.2), could be accounted for by any of the three versions of empathy-specific reward because the three made the same prediction for easy escape as did the empathy-altruism hypothesis (Row 1, Cells 1 & 4).

There were, however, some results that an all-at-once combination couldn't explain. To cite but one example, Dovidio, Allen, and Schroeder (1990) gave some participants a chance to help with the need for which empathy was induced, while others had a chance to help the same person, but with a different need. Given that escape without helping was easy in this experiment, none of the six egoistic alternatives made the same prediction as the empathy-altruism hypothesis—more helping in the high-empathy condition than in the low among participants who could help with the need that originally induced empathy, but not among those who could help with the different need. Yet this is what was found. (For a summary of other results contrary to the all-at-once alternative, see Batson, 2011, pp. 131–134.)

Two New Challenges

Even with all the apparent support for the empathy-altruism hypothesis found by 1996, controversy over its truth remained. Two new challenges came to the fore:

Psychological escape. One new challenge was that the experiments purporting to test the aversive-arousal-reduction alternative didn't adequately do so because these experiments manipulated the ease of physical escape from the empathy-arousing need, whereas the form of escape necessary for aversive-arousal reduction is psychological escape. If research participants didn't anticipate that by getting the empathy-arousing need out of sight they could also get it out of mind, then manipulating ease of physical escape wouldn't provide a valid test. In one way or another, this challenge was raised by Hoffman (1991), Hornstein (1991), Sober (1991), Wallach and Wallach (1991), Sober and Wilson (1998), Nichols (2004), and Stich, Doris, and Roedder (2010).

But, casting doubt on this first new challenge, participants in the experiments that had manipulated ease of physical escape didn't know and had no direct contact with the person in need (e.g., Batson, Duncan et al., 1981). Under these conditions, it seemed likely that physical escape *could* provide an effective manipulation of psychological escape. Further, two experiments reported by Batson, Batson, and colleagues (1991) had varied psychological escape from the person's need (although they weren't designed for this purpose). Each experiment manipulated the probability that the young woman for whom empathy was or wasn't induced would no longer be in need by the time participants received an update on her condition. Some participants learned that the probability was high that the young woman would still be in need; others learned the probability was low. Then participants were allowed to choose whether or not to receive the update. High-empathy participants chose to receive the update more than low-empathy participants even when doing so carried a high probability of future exposure to the empathy-arousing need.

Finally, Stocks, Lishner, and Decker (2009) reported two experiments expressly designed to manipulate psychological escape (difficult vs. easy) by leading participants to believe they either would or wouldn't remember learning of the empathy-inducing need. High-empathy participants were more likely than low-empathy participants to help remove the need even when they believed they'd soon be free of it without helping. All this evidence made the first new challenge implausible. (Again, see Batson, 2011, pp. 135–145, for more detail.)

Self-other merging. The second new challenge claimed that when people feel empathic concern they experience a merging of their concepts of self and of the person for whom they feel empathy, creating a psychological "one." Self-interest then leads the empathically aroused individual to care about the welfare of this self-other unit.

A number of researchers have claimed that some version of self-other merging can account for the effects of empathic concern—most notably

Cialdini, Brown, Lewis, Luce, and Neuberg (1997). (See Batson, 2011, pp. 145–149, for an overview of various versions.) However, a careful look at the available research reveals no clear support for any of these claims. Instead, there's considerable contrary evidence, both from behavioral research and from neuroscience research. (See Batson, 2011, pp. 149–160, for a review and assessment of the evidence; also see Stocks & Lishner, 2010.) Either similarity or relationship closeness (e.g., kinship, friendship, shared group membership), which are often used to operationalize merging, can at times be more powerful instigators of helping than feelings of empathic concern—as, for example when helping involves providing the person in need a place to live or involves raising two orphaned children (see Cialdini et al., 1997). But evidence indicates that these merging effects are independent of the effect of empathic emotion on helping (see Batson, Sager et al., 1997, and Maner, Luce, Neuberg, Cialdini, Brown, & Sagrin, 2002). Based on this evidence, it seems that self-other merging can't account for the motivation to help produced by empathic concern.

Current Status of the Empathy-Altruism Hypothesis

In the words of Sherlock Holmes, "When you have eliminated the impossible, whatever remains, *however improbable*, must be the truth" (Doyle, 1890, p. 111, italics in original). It seems impossible for any of the proposed egoistic explanations to account for the motivation produced by empathic concern, so what remains? The empathy-altruism hypothesis. Pending a plausible new egoistic explanation of all the evidence supporting the empathy-altruism hypothesis—ideally accompanied by evidence that clearly supports the new egoistic explanation—it seems necessary to accept the empathy-altruism hypothesis, however, improbable, as true.

Limits on the Empathy-Altruism Relationship

That said, let me immediately add two important qualifiers—one about the scope of empathy and the other about competing concerns.

The Scope of Empathy

All the research testing the empathy-altruism hypothesis suggests that the human capacity for altruism may be limited to those for whom we feel empathic concern. In experiment after experiment, when empathy for the person in need was low, the pattern of helping pointed to underlying egoistic motivation. It's not that we never help people for whom we feel little empathy; we often do. But only, the research indicates, when it's in our own best interest.

Sources of altruistic motivation other than empathic concern have been proposed, including an "altruistic personality" (Oliner & Oliner, 1988; Rushton, 1980; Staub, 1974), principled moral reasoning (Kohlberg, 1976; Staub, 1974), and internalized prosocial values (Batson, 1989; Schwartz & Howard, 1984; Staub, 1989). Evidence exists that each of these potential sources is associated with increased helping, but there's no clear evidence that the underlying motivation is altruistic. Instead, relevant research suggests that the care for others associated with these sources is instrumental to gaining the self-benefit of seeing oneself or being seen by others as an altruistic, moral person (e.g., Batson, Bolen et al., 1986). At present, empathic concern is the only source of altruistic motivation for which we have good evidence. We need more research on these other possibilities.

To say that empathic concern is the only known source of altruistic motivation raises the question of how easy it is for us to become empathically concerned about the plight of others in need—especially others who aren't family or friends. There certainly seem to be strong perceptual and conceptual forces working against the arousal of such concern. These forces include anything and everything that makes it difficult to meet the two necessary conditions for feeling empathic concern discussed in Chapter 4—perceiving another as in need and valuing his or her welfare. As discussed in Chapters 8 through 11, there's self-preoccupation or absorption in an ongoing task; seeing the other as a statistic not as a person with feelings and desires; seeing the other as a person but as one of "them" not "us"—as black not white, male not female, Arab not Jew, Catholic not Protestant. Under the influence of such forces, we can find ourselves responding to those who have no bread by suggesting they eat cake instead.

Yet, despite the perceptual and conceptual inhibitors of empathic concern, we still seem to have a remarkable capacity to get invested in the welfare of others as long as we have no prior antipathy. Think of our capacity to feel for characters in novels, movies, or on television. We may have known these characters only for minutes, and we know they're fictitious. Still, we find ourselves churning when they're in danger, yearning when they're in need, weeping over their losses—and successes. Indeed, it often seems we must take steps to avoid feeling empathic concern for total strangers in need, be they in a homeless camp, starving in the South Sudan, or fleeing as refugees from Syria, Ukraine, or Central America. To avoid becoming empathically aroused, we turn the corner, switch channels, flip the page, think of something else. The necessity to defend ourselves against feeling empathic concern suggests that our potential for such feeling is strong.

Competing Concerns

The second qualifier is that, while being capable of care for others, we also care for ourselves. Batson, O'Quin, and colleagues (1983, Study 3) found that if the cost of helping was high (taking shocks that were "clearly painful but of course not harmful"), the motivation even of individuals who had previously reported feeling high empathic concern for a stranger reacting badly to the shocks appeared to be egoistic. This finding suggested that empathy can be "a fragile flower, easily crushed by self-concern" (Batson, O'Quin et al., 1983, p. 718). Even if we experience empathic concern for someone in need, that concern can be overridden by other, more pressing concerns.

Of course, this isn't all bad. Life would be quite awkward if we were only looking out for others' concerns and not also for our own. It would be, as one philosopher suggested, like a community in which everyone tries to do everyone else's washing. Nobody's washing would get done.

Nor does self-concern always triumph. The ease with which it can override empathic concern is a function of its strength relative to the strength of our empathic concern. In the study just mentioned, participants didn't know or even meet the person reacting badly to the shocks, whom they saw over closed-circuit TV. With stronger intrinsic valuing of the welfare of the person in need, empathic concern is likely to be less fragile. Think, for example, of a father's response to seeing his young daughter toddling into the path of an oncoming car. His concern is apt to remain riveted on her welfare, with little thought for his own.

Implications for Our View of Human Nature

Thinking more broadly, if the empathy-altruism hypothesis is true, we need to revise our views about human nature and the human capacity for caring. To find that we're capable of empathy-induced altruistic motivation means that ours is a more social species than dominant views of human nature have led us to believe. Accounts of human motivation in terms of universal egoism must give way to a pluralistic view that includes such altruism.

When we act to benefit others, it's often unclear what our motives are (hence, the need for experiments). In some cases, the motivation is almost certainly exclusively egoistic, but in many others, it might be at least in part altruistic. A teacher rushes across the playground to comfort a child who skinned a knee. A middle-aged man tearfully decides to acquiesce to the quiet pleas of his cancer-riddled mother and have her life-support removed. You and I do favors for family and friends—we contribute to charities, to civic causes, to help flood victims, to save whales. In each of these cases, the motivation could be at least partially altruistic. Yet in each case, and in any other that comes to mind, the motivation could be exclusively egoistic.

Prior to the support for the empathy-altruism hypothesis, parsimony adjudicated these cases in favor of universal egoism. All could be attributed to egoistic motivation but only some, even partially, to altruistic motivation. Under these circumstances, it made sense to favor universal egoism. The situation is different now. If both egoism and empathy-induced altruism are within the human repertoire, then the cases in which our motivation might be at least partially altruistic are open to dispute. Here's one example:

Challenging the Value Assumption of the Theory of Rational Choice

For almost a century now, the most influential view of economic decision-making has been the theory of rational choice (Von Neumann & Morgenstern, 1944). This theory rests on two assumptions, a rationality assumption and a value assumption. The rationality assumption is that we humans will choose whatever action is most likely to get us what we want. The value assumption is that what we want is to maximize self-interest. In the words of economist Mancur Olson, "rational, self-interested individuals will not act to achieve their common or group interest" (Olson, 1971, p. 2). I would add that, according to the theory, they also won't act to achieve another individual's interest—only their own.

A long line of research by Daniel Kahneman, Amos Tversky, and others has challenged the rationality assumption of the theory of rational choice, showing that our decisions are often illogical and suboptimal for getting us what we want (e.g., Kahneman, Slovic, & Tversky, 1982). But this research hasn't challenged the value assumption, the assumption that we only want to maximize self-interest. Research testing the empathy-altruism hypothesis has. It provides evidence that we can value more than ourselves.

Two Tests of the Value Assumption

To directly test the implications of the empathy-altruism hypothesis for the value assumption of rational choice, colleagues and I conducted two experiments in which we used an imagine-other perspective to introduce empathic concern into a situation designed to model economic decision making—the one-trial Prisoner's Dilemma (Rapoport & Chammah, 1965). In this dilemma, two people each make a decision whether to cooperate with the other person or to defect. The consequences of this decision are set so that, regardless what the other person decides, defection always maximizes self-benefit and cooperation always maximizes the other's benefit.

Our first experiment showed that leading one participant in a one-trial Prisoner's Dilemma to feel empathic concern for the other significantly increased the empathizer's cooperation (Batson & Moran, 1999). The second experiment showed that feeling empathic concern also significantly increased cooperation in a modified version of the dilemma where (a) participants' choices were made sequentially rather than simultaneously; (b) the empathizer was always "randomly" selected to choose last; and (c) before choosing, the empathizer learned that the other person had defected (Batson & Ahmad, 2001). Under these conditions, a choice to cooperate would greatly benefit the other but entirely at the empathizer's expense. In this extreme circumstance, only 5% of participants not induced to feel empathy cooperated. But 45% of those induced to empathize did. Although empathic concern didn't override economic self-interest for everyone in the high-empathy condition (recall the second limit noted earlier), it did for almost half. These two experiments provided evidence that empathic concern can lead people to care for another even in economic decision-making, challenging the value assumption of rational choice on the theory's home ground.

Outside the Lab

Lest we overinterpret these results, it's worth asking how often people feel empathic concern in a Prisoner's Dilemma or other economic exchanges? Only rarely, I suspect, in the typical dilemma experiment. There, participants are dealing with a stranger about whom they know nothing and whom they never meet. Without an explicit empathy induction, there should be little empathic concern in such a situation. In everyday life, however, the people with whom we find ourselves in conflict over things, money, opportunities, and privileges are often people we know and care about—coworkers, colleagues,

126 • EMPATHIC CONCERN

classmates, teammates, friends, and family. For them, empathic concern may be frequently felt. And if it is, the theory of rational choice is likely to provide a distorted view of our motives and behavior.

Recognizing this problem, economist Samuel Bowles advocated abandonment of the theory of rational choice. He argued that there's nothing to preclude "more realistic psychological assumptions" (Bowles, 2008, p. 1609). But is that true? After all, more realistic assumptions complicate matters. They force us to recognize that the human motivational repertoire is broader than material gain—indeed, broader than self-interest in all its forms. They force us to rethink human nature.

Conclusion

Across the past four decades, more than 30 experiments have been conducted to test the empathy-altruism hypothesis against a range of egoistic alternative explanations—explanations claiming that the motivation produced by empathic concern is directed toward the ultimate goal of obtaining one or another self-benefit. With remarkable consistency, results of these experiments failed to support any of the egoistic alternatives, supporting the empathy-altruism hypothesis instead. The few results that initially seemed to contradict the empathy-altruism hypothesis haven't stood up to further examination. To the best of my knowledge, we now have no plausible egoistic explanation for the cumulative results of these experiments, which has led me to conclude, tentatively, that the empathy-altruism hypothesis is true. Other-oriented feeling for a person in need (empathic concern) does indeed seem to produce motivation with the ultimate goal of removing the empathy-inducing need. The strength of the experimental results has also led me to believe that this motivation can be surprisingly powerful.

Yet, even if empathy-induced altruistic motivation exists and can be strong, it's no panacea. The range of people and problems that evoke our empathic concern is limited, and empathy-induced altruistic motivation can be overridden by self-concerns. These limits set bounds on the societal benefits of such motivation. So it would be wrong to bottle empathy-induced altruism as a tonic that's good for whatever ails you.

But it would also be wrong to think it's good for nothing. As we shall see in the remaining chapters, empathic concern and the altruistic motivation it produces are potentially important psychological resources that, if harnessed and put to work, could prove transformative.

8 BEHAVIORAL CONSEQUENCES

INTERPERSONAL BENEFITS

Behavioral consequences of feeling empathic concern are most obvious at the interpersonal level—in our relations with other individuals. As suggested in Chapter 5, there's good reason to think that the biological roots of empathic concern lie in parental care, and in the ability to generalize from there not only to non-progeny with whom we're close but also to strangers toward whom we harbor no antipathy—and even, as we shall see, to members of stigmatized groups. In this chapter, I'll focus on evidence of benefits for strangers in need. But first, let me add to the benefits for parental care and close relationships mentioned in Chapter 5 by citing some relevant behavioral research.

Parental Care

Lou Penner and colleagues examined the effect of empathic concern felt by parents for their child who was receiving a painful treatment for pediatric cancer (Penner, Cline, Albrecht, Harper, Peterson, Taub, & Ruckdeschel, 2008). They found a significant negative correlation between the parent's empathy reported just prior to their child's treatment and the level of pain and distress the child experienced during the treatment.

What produced this correlation? The parents couldn't remove their child's pain, which was unavoidable given the treatment. What they could do was help the child endure the pain as easily as possible. Penner and colleagues found that parents who felt high empathic concern differed from those who felt low empathy in both verbal and nonverbal behaviors as they interacted with their

Empathic Concern. C. Daniel Batson, Oxford University Press. © Oxford University Press 2023.
DOI: 10.1093/oso/9780197610923.003.0009

child. High-empathy parents were more likely to comfort, reassure, and engage the child in everyday activities such as reading and play. Low-empathy parents tried to minimize or deny the pain. The more sensitive care provided by high-empathy parents—presumably a result of empathy-induced altruistic motivation—seemed to enable their child to better handle his or her pain (as judged by the child, by nurses, and by trained observers).

Research also suggests that empathic concern may be an important antidote to child abuse and neglect. Milner, Halsey, and Fultz (1995) assessed the empathic responsiveness of mothers while they watched video clips of an infant (not their own) who was (a) smiling and laughing, (b) looking around, or (c) crying. The mothers were from two matched groups—those identified as being at high risk of physically abusing a child and those identified as being at low risk. Low-risk mothers showed a significant increase in empathic concern while watching the crying infant. High-risk mothers showed a similar trend, but the increase wasn't statistically reliable. Instead, high-risk mothers reported significant increases in personal distress and hostility while watching the crying infant, whereas low-risk mothers didn't (see Frodi & Lamb, 1980, for parallel results using physiological measures). The pattern of response by the high-risk mothers is congruent with clinical reports that child abusers experience less empathic concern and more hostility in response to a crying child (de Paúl, Pérez-Albéniz, Guibert, Asla, & Ormaechea, 2008).

Turning to neglect, de Paúl and Guibert (2008) provided a thoughtful analysis of the ways in which child neglect can result from breakdown of the causal sequence described in Chapters 4 and 7 from perception of need and valuing the other's welfare to empathic concern and, thereby, to altruistic motivation and care. Their analysis seems plausible, but insofar as I know, it hasn't been directly tested.

Close Relationships

As one would expect, there's much evidence that greater intrinsic valuing of a relationship partner's welfare—greater love—predicts satisfaction in and duration of close relationships (Berscheid & Reis, 1998). Unfortunately, research is sparse on the role that empathic concern and empathy-induced altruistic motivation play in this association. Far more research has focused on how each partner gets his or her personal needs met in a close relationship (see Berscheid, 1983; Kelley, 1979; Rusbult, 1980). Still, the limited research that exists suggests that empathy can be an important contributor.

Romantic Relationships

The role of empathic concern in romantic relationships has most often been looked at from the perspective of attachment theory (Bowlby, 1969; Mikulincer & Shaver, 2003). For example, Feeney and Collins (2001, 2003) found that people who say that the help and support they provide to their romantic partner is altruistically rather than egoistically motivated also say that their care is more sensitive and responsive. Their partners, too, say the care is more sensitive and supportive, but to a lesser degree. Feeney and Collins found further that the partner's assessment of the care received was associated with his or her satisfaction with the relationship both in the present and (again, to a lesser degree) two to three months later. Similarly, using daily reports, Maisel and Gable (2009) found need-responsive social support by one partner was associated with less sadness and anxiety in the second partner, and with more positive ratings of relationship quality.

Focusing explicitly on empathic concern, Feeney and Collins (2001) used a procedure developed by Simpson, Rholes, and Nelligan (1992) that involved bringing couples into the lab and having one partner prepare to give a videotaped speech that was to be evaluated by peers. The other partner (the potential caregiver) was told how nervous the speechmaker reported feeling about giving the speech, either very nervous (high need) or not nervous (low need), which provided a manipulation of the potential caregiver's perception of the speechmaker's need. The potential caregiver then had an opportunity to write a private note to the speechmaker. Several days earlier, potential caregivers had reported their general empathic tendencies and altruistic motivation. These self-reports were positively correlated with writing a note that was rated by both the speechmaker and the researchers as showing greater sensitivity to the speechmaker's level of need.

Caution is, of course, needed when interpreting the results of studies that rely on self-reported empathic tendencies and altruistic motives in close relationships. As Hal Kelley aptly put it:

> The rules for showing altruism [in a romantic relationship] . . . . are well known to ordinary people and therefore afford the basis for favorable self-presentations that may misrepresent a person's true motives. There is much to be gained from convincing our partners that we are attuned to their interests and willing to put them before our own. And there is even more to be gained, for many persons, from convincing themselves of their beneficent motives. (Kelley, 1983, p. 285)

130 • EMPATHIC CONCERN

Fortunately, Collins, Ford, Guichard, Kane, and Feeney (2010) ran a follow-up experiment to the Feeney and Collins research just described. In the follow-up, they used the same stressor (giving a videotaped speech) and the same manipulation of level of need, but they moved beyond general self-reports and instead assessed empathic concern felt by the caregiving partner as the speechmaker prepared to give the speech. Moreover, they took two objective, behavioral measures of care: (a) how often the caregiver checked for a message from the speechmaker requesting help with the speech, and (b) the caregiver's willingness to forego working on enjoyable puzzles in order to make the speech in the partner's place.

Results revealed that secure caregivers—those low in relationship anxiety and avoidance—not only expressed more empathic concern but also more often checked the computer monitor for a message from their partner and more often volunteered to make the speech in the partner's place. Collins and colleagues concluded that relationship security enables individuals to shift from self-focus and self-concern to partner-focused empathic concern and altruistic care.

Finally, another line of research has shown that empathic concern for one's relationship partner after the partner transgresses is a strong predictor of forgiveness. Forgiveness, in turn, makes for more positive—and enduring—relationships. (See Fincham, Paleari, & Regalia, 2002: McCullough, Rachal, Sandage, Worthington, Brown, & Hight, 1998; McCullough, Worthington, & Rachal, 1997; Worthington, 1998.)

Friendships

While not explicitly assessing the effects of empathic concern, Schlenker and Britt (1997) showed that people will selectively present information about a friend to a third person in order to benefit the friend. Participants in Schlenker and Britt's experiment were asked to describe a same-sex friend to a person of the opposite sex whom they thought the friend either regarded as extremely attractive or regarded as unattractive. The participants tended to present the friend as having attributes they had been led to believe the attractive person liked, but as not having attributes the unattractive person liked. So doing, they promoted their friend's chances with the attractive person but communicated to the unattractive person that the friend was "not your type." This need-sensitive strategy may have been due to empathy-induced altruism, but we can't be sure because empathic concern wasn't measured.

Providing self-report evidence for the role of empathy-induced altruism in friendship development, Crocker and Canevello (2008) found that first-semester university students who reported other-oriented, compassionate goals for developing relationships with friends and roommates (rather than self-image-enhancing goals) also reported more closeness, support, and trust in their relationships. Once again, these findings are suggestive but, clearly, much more research is needed on the role of empathy and altruism in friendships. To date, there has been remarkably little.

Benefit to Strangers in Need

Research testing the empathy-altruism hypothesis reviewed in Chapter 7 revealed a number of circumstances in which feeling empathic concern for a stranger in need increases the likelihood of helping him or her—when escape from the need situation is easy; when helping is anonymous; when failure to help is justified; when anticipating a mood-enhancing experience if one doesn't help; and when there will be no feedback about the effectiveness of one's helping effort. In each of these circumstances, greater empathic concern produced more help for a stranger in need.

More Sensitive Help

Not only can empathic concern produce more help, it can also produce more sensitive help. Empathy-induced altruistic motivation is directed toward enhancing the welfare of the person in need, so the behavior it evokes is likely to be responsive to the nature of the need. Egoistic goals such as gaining rewards and avoiding punishments can often be reached even if our help doesn't effectively remove the need. To satisfy these motives, the thought counts. But good intentions aren't enough for empathy-induced altruism. It's directed toward what's good for the target(s) of empathy, not toward a display of our own goodness.

Again, research reviewed in Chapter 7 supports this reasoning. Unlike those feeling little empathic concern for a person in need, people who are empathically aroused feel bad if their own or another person's efforts to remove the need don't succeed, even when they can in no way be blamed for the ineffectiveness (Batson, Dyck et al., 1988; Batson & Weeks, 1996). Capitalizing on this distinction, economists have used concern for the effectiveness of one's help to differentiate altruistic from egoistic motives for contributing to charities (e.g., Ribar & Wilhelm, 2002).

132 • EMPATHIC CONCERN

An experiment by Sibicky, Schroeder, and Dovidio (1995) nicely demonstrates the sensitivity that characterizes help evoked by empathic concern. Participants either were or weren't induced to feel empathy for a stranger in need, then were given a chance to help this person. In addition to the typical condition in which helping would address the need, there was a condition in which even though helping beyond a minimal level would better meet the immediate need, it would result in greater need in the future. Based on the empathy-altruism hypothesis, Sibicky and colleagues predicted that participants induced to feel empathic concern would help less in the new condition. Results supported this prediction. In contrast, participants feeling low empathy didn't help less in the new condition. Their focus seemed to be on the self-benefits of being seen as helpful. Sibicky and colleagues concluded that empathic concern enhances sensitivity to what the target really needs.

Empathy-induced helping is also likely to be less fickle. As discussed in Chapter 7, individuals experiencing relatively low empathic concern, and so, a relative predominance of egoistic over altruistic motivation, are far less likely to help when they either can easily escape exposure to the need situation without helping or can easily justify to themselves and others a failure to help (Batson, Duncan et al., 1981; Batson, Dyck et al., 1988; Toi & Batson, 1982). In contrast, individuals experiencing relatively high empathic concern show no noticeable decrease in readiness to help under these conditions.

The practical implications of the low-empathy findings are troubling. Easy escape and high justification for not helping are common features of many need situations. Amidst the blooming, buzzing confusion of life, we can almost always find a way to direct attention elsewhere—or to convince ourselves that inaction is justified. If empathy-induced altruism isn't vulnerable to these outs, its practical potential looks promising indeed.

Less Aggression

Not only does empathic concern produce more and more sensitive care for strangers in need, it can also inhibit any inclination to aggress against or harm the person for whom empathy is felt, even in the face of provocation. Of course, empathic concern shouldn't inhibit all aggressive impulses, only those directed toward the target of empathy. As discussed in Chapter 6, it's easy to imagine *altruistic aggression*, in which empathic concern felt for Person A leads to empathic anger and, thereby, to increased aggression toward Person B if B is perceived to be a threat to A's welfare (for supporting evidence, see Hoffman, 2000; Pfallheicher et al., 2019; Vitaglione & Barnett, 2003).

Miller and Eisenberg's meta-analysis. In an early meta-analysis of approximately 50 studies, Miller and Eisenberg (1988) concluded that "empathy is negatively related to aggression, externalizing [i.e., threatening, attacking, and fighting], and antisocial behaviors" (p. 338). However, a close look at the studies reviewed by Miller and Eisenberg suggests the need for a more guarded conclusion.

In many of the reviewed studies, the negative relation between empathy and aggression was weak. Overall, there was "modest but not entirely consistent support for the notion that empathic responsiveness may be an inhibitor of aggression" (Miller & Eisenberg, 1988, p. 339). Moreover, the clearest evidence for inhibition was found in studies that assessed empathy using self-report questionnaire measures of a general disposition to experience empathic concern. As explained in Chapter 3, responses on self-report measures of dispositional empathy may reflect a desire to present oneself as a nice, sensitive, caring person rather than a readiness to feel empathy (for empirical support of this possibility, see Batson, Bolen et al., 1986). Thus, reduced aggression associated with these dispositional measures may not be the result of empathic concern but of a desire to be nice—or to appear so.

Additionally, in virtually all the studies reviewed by Miller and Eisenberg that assessed empathy felt for a specific person, that person wasn't the one who provoked potential aggression. To find that feeling empathic concern for one person is associated with displaying less aggression toward another could indicate a general disposition toward empathic concern that produces a general inhibition of aggression. But, again, this association could indicate a desire to be or appear nice.

In the one study reported by Miller and Eisenberg in which self-reported empathic concern for the provocateur was assessed and found to be present after provocation (Gaines, Kirwin, & Gentry, 1977), the association between inhibition of aggression and reported empathy was highly significant. But in this study the causal relationship between empathy and aggression was unclear because assessment of empathy occurred after the opportunity to harm the provocateur. Those who aggressed less may have inferred that they felt more empathic concern, rather than empathic concern inhibiting their impulse to aggress.

Miller and Eisenberg reported only four studies in which attempts were made to induce (as opposed to simply measure) empathic concern for the person who provoked the potential aggression, and the evidence from these four studies was inconclusive. Eliasz (1980) failed to find a negative relation between empathy and aggression. However, prior to the empathy manipulation in his experiment, participants received a harsh evaluation designed to provoke anger and possible retaliatory aggression. This ordering of events may have prevented empathic concern from ever developing. In each of the other three experiments, the induction of empathy significantly inhibited harming the person for whom empathy was felt. But these three studies were all reported in unpublished dissertations.

Subsequent to the Miller and Eisenberg review, Richardson, Hammock, Smith, Gardner, and Signo (1994, Study 2) attempted to induce male undergraduates to feel empathic concern for a target before the target harmed them. These undergraduates aggressed no less in return than did male undergraduates not induced to feel empathy. But no measure of empathic feeling for the target was taken in this study, so we can't be sure that empathy existed at the time of the opportunity to retaliate. There would be no reason to expect empathy to inhibit aggression unless it was present when participants had the chance to aggress. Overall, then, results of empathy-aggression research prior to 1995 were far from clear.

More recent research on the empathy-aggression relationship. Two newer lines of research provide clearer evidence that empathic concern felt for a provocateur can inhibit aggression toward that person. First, research on forgiveness after being harmed has found that an important step in the forgiveness process is to replace feelings of anger toward a harm-doer with empathic feelings (Witvliet, Ludwig, & Vander Laan, 2001). Of course, replacing feelings of anger with empathic feelings is often easier said than done.

Second, in an intriguing and ambitious experiment, Harmon-Jones, Vaughn-Scott, Mohr, Sigelman, and Harmon-Jones (2004) sought to assess the effect of empathic concern on anger-related left-frontal cortical electroencephalographic (EEG) activity. In the initial phase of the experiment, a perspective-taking manipulation (imagine the other's feelings; remain objective) was used to induce undergraduate men and women to experience either high or low empathic concern for another student who was suffering from multiple sclerosis. In the next phase, this other student provided either (a) a harsh and insulting (potentially aggression provoking) evaluation of an essay the participant had written or (b) a neutral evaluation. EEG activity was recorded immediately after participants received the evaluation, then attitudes toward the other student were measured. As predicted based on the empathy-altruism hypothesis, relative left-frontal cortical EEG activity—which typically increases after insult and is associated with aggressive behavior, and which increased in the low-empathy condition—was inhibited in the high-empathy condition. Hostile attitudes toward the other student were also inhibited. This experiment provides the clearest evidence to date that empathic concern in place before provocation can directly inhibit the desire to aggress.

Reduced derogation and blaming of victims of injustice. There is also evidence that empathic concern can inhibit a particularly subtle and insidious form of aggression: blaming the victims of injustice. In his classic experiments on the just-world hypothesis, Mel Lerner (1980) found that research participants were likely to derogate an innocent victim of suffering. Lerner argued that this derogation was motivated by our desire to maintain belief in a just world—belief that people get what they deserve and deserve what they get. To maintain this belief, we assume that if victims of injustice have less, they must be less deserving.

Protecting our belief in a just world in this way can lead to what William Ryan called "blaming the victim" (Ryan, 1971)—that is, responding to targets of unjust discrimination and oppression by unconsciously blaming them for their fate. Ryan thought the prototypical victim-blamer is someone fairly well-off financially but not entirely secure. By blaming the poor and oppressed, such people can reassure themselves that they really do deserve their relative advantage.

Derogation and blaming the victim are all too common alternatives to caring about poverty and social injustice. These alternatives can lead to smug acceptance of the suffering of the disadvantaged as just and right. But empathic concern may counteract this tendency. In an important follow-up to Lerner's classic experiments, Aderman, Brehm, and Katz (1974) found that perspective-taking instructions designed to induce empathic concern eliminated the tendency for participants to derogate an innocent victim.

Feeling for Members of Stigmatized Groups

What constitutes a stigmatized group is in the eye of the beholder. To suggest that empathic concern and the altruistic motivation it produces can be felt for members of a group the empathizer sees as stigmatized—including religious, racial, or ethnic out-groups, as well as people with some disability or disease—may seem hopelessly naive. Relations with such groups often have a history of disdain and mistrust if not outright hostility. In the face of such history, isn't empathic concern too much to ask? After all, to feel empathic

136 • EMPATHIC CONCERN

concern requires that one be other-oriented, valuing the other's welfare and attending with sensitivity to his or her plight.

Personalizing Contact and Superordinate Goals

A strategy designed to address this problem is to provide *personalizing contact* with the stigmatized group member, contact that (a) involves interaction with the other as an individual, not simply as one of *them*, and (b) occurs in a nonadversarial, low-threat situation in which mistrust and conflict are either not evoked or, even better, are counterproductive. (As I am using the term, "personalizing" refers to the nature of one's interaction with the group member, not to perception of him or her in terms of personality traits instead of group membership; see Brewer, 1988, and Miller, 2002, for discussions of "personalization" in this second, perceptual sense.)

Personalizing contact should encourage empathic concern for the stigmatized group member in two ways. First, it increases the likelihood of accurately perceiving the group member's needs, hopes, and fears. In addition, it increases the likelihood of valuing his or her welfare. As discussed in Chapter 4, these are the necessary conditions to experience empathic concern.

But how can personalizing contact with individuals in a stigmatized group be achieved? Obviously, it's not easy. More is required than providing face-to-face contact. Such contact is likely to heighten suspicion, hostility, discomfort, and dislike (Pettigrew, 1998). One structural technique that has proved effective in creating nonadversarial personalizing contact, and thereby reducing intergroup conflict and hostility, is to introduce a *superordinate goal* (Sherif, Harvey, White, Hood, & Sherif, 1961). A superordinate goal is something that those on both sides of an intergroup conflict want but can attain only if they join forces and work together. Potential antagonists find themselves united in the effort to reach a common goal—strange bedfellows, perhaps, but bedfellows nonetheless.

Think of the psychological consequences. When working together toward a common goal, hostility and aggression are counterproductive. Instead, members of each group must attend to and understand what members of the other group value; that is, what they want and need. And, to coordinate efforts in pursuit of the goal, members of each group must attend to the perspective of those in the other group. In combination, these two consequences should increase feelings of empathic concern for members of the out-group. Importantly, these effects on empathy don't require that group members give up their own group identity in order to pursue the superordinate goal (Dovidio, Gaertner, & Saguy, 2009).

Using an Imagine-Other Perspective to Induce Empathic Concern for a Member of a Stigmatized Group

An imagine-other perspective like that used in many of the experiments described in earlier chapters is another way to induce empathic concern for a member of a stigmatized group—and to do so without the complications and challenges of face-to-face contact. In a series of three experiments, Batson, Polycarpou, and colleagues (1997) employed this strategy to increase empathic concern for a member of three different groups likely to be stigmatized in the United States in the 1990s—people with AIDS (Experiment 1), the homeless (Experiment 2), and convicted murderers (Experiment 3).

As in other experiments using an imagine-other perspective to induce empathic concern (see Chapters 1, 2, and 7), considerable information was presented about the stigmatized group member whose thoughts and feelings participants were asked to imagine (unlike research using an imagine-self perspective—e.g., Galinsky & Moskowitz, 2000). Moreover, the information had three features. First, it clearly presented the target's thoughts and feelings. Second, it presented the target in a sympathetic light—as human and fallible rather than accusing and aggressive. Third, it made salient the target's membership in the stigmatized group. In addition to these features, the information was presented in a nonthreatening situation; participants listened to a tape-recorded interview with the out-group member. Together, the features provided personalizing contact without a face-to-face meeting.

In the first experiment, which was run when AIDS was a major societal concern, female undergraduates listened to an interview with another undergraduate, Julie, who talked about her life since unexpectedly learning three months ago that she was HIV positive. Prior to listening, some participants received instructions to "imagine how the woman who is interviewed feels about what has happened and how it has affected her life," whereas others were instructed to remain objective and detached. A cross-cutting manipulation varied information about Julie's responsibility for contracting AIDS. In a not-responsible condition, she explained that she got the virus while being treated in hospital after the car in which she was riding was hit by a drunk driver. In the responsible condition, Julie got AIDS after a wild summer in which she "slept around quite a bit and didn't really protect myself." The responsibility manipulation allowed us to assess whether empathy could be induced even when Julie was responsible for her plight.

Participants in the imagine-other condition of this experiment reported feeling significantly more empathic concern for Julie than did participants in the remain-objective condition—and did so both when she wasn't responsible and when she was. Although the perspective effect was greater in the not-responsible condition, this wasn't because little empathy occurred in the responsible condition. Rather, some participants in the responsible condition who had been instructed to adopt an objective perspective reported relatively high empathy. Perhaps they or someone they knew had also engaged in unsafe sex, making it difficult to remain objective about Julie's plight.

In Experiment 2, male and female undergraduates randomly assigned to the same two perspective conditions listened to an interview with Harold Mitchell, a 56-year-old homeless man. Responsibility was again manipulated. Half of the participants in each perspective condition learned that Harold became homeless "after losing his job because of an illness"; the other half, "after he was tired of working and quit his job." Once again, participants in the imagine-feelings perspective condition reported feeling significantly more empathic concern for Harold than did participants in the remain-objective condition—and, this time, the difference was as great when Harold was responsible for being homeless as when he wasn't.

Experiment 3 provided a more extreme test of the ability of an imagine-other perspective to induce empathic concern for a stigmatized out-group member. Undergraduate men and women who were randomly assigned to adopt either an imagine-other or objective perspective listened to an interview with James Stevens, a convicted murderer serving a sentence of life without parole. In the interview, ostensibly conducted at a federal penitentiary, James described a longstanding feud with his next-door neighbor, Paul, then told how he shot and killed Paul, was arrested, and was now serving a life sentence—and how he felt about it all. (Responsibility wasn't manipulated in this experiment because James was clearly responsible for killing Paul.) Again, the imagine-other perspective produced significantly more empathic concern than the objective, providing evidence that it's possible to induce at least some empathic concern for a member of a highly negatively stigmatized out-group. However, the reported empathy in each perspective condition of this experiment was considerably lower than in the first two experiments, presumably due to the highly negative stigma of being a murderer.

Finally, in a conceptually similar experiment, Batson, Chang, Orr, and Rowland (2002) found that an imagine-other perspective produced significantly more empathic concern for a jailed heroin dealer, Jared Briggs. And again, participants in each perspective condition reported considerably less empathic concern for Jared than participants in the first two experiments reported for Julie and Harold, presumably due to the highly negative stigma associated with dealing hard drugs.

In Chapter 4, I presented evidence that, often, people given no perspective instructions spontaneously imagine how the person in need feels rather than remain objective. The James and Jared experiments lead me to add an important qualifier: When the person in need is a member of a highly negatively stigmatized group, I suspect that many people find it more natural to remain objective rather than to imagine feelings. Unfortunately, neither of these experiments included a no-perspective condition, so this suspicion was untested.

A Likely Limit: When You Are about to Interact with the Stigmatized Other

Also important, Jacquie Vorauer provided evidence of a limit on use of imagine-other instructions to induce empathic concern for a member of a stigmatized group (Vorauer, 2013). She suggested that if you are about to interact face to face with such a person, then adopting an imagine-other perspective can lead you to focus on how this person thinks and feels about you—including about how you think and feel about him or her. In the words of Vorauer and Sasaki (2012),

> Because of the potential for evaluation that arises in such situations, individuals who try to take the out-group member's perspective may quickly become preoccupied with imagining how they themselves are viewed: The first thing that they are apt to see when they try to look at the world through an out-group interaction partner's eyes is themselves. (p. 520)

Such self-focus could undermine the ability of the perspective to induce empathic concern. But, given the results of an experiment by Vorauer and Sasaki (2009), a second possibility seems more likely. Although not inhibiting empathic concern, the self-focus may heighten egoistic motivation to avoid negative evaluation by the group member should you appear prejudiced against the group. This egoistic motive could, in turn, overpower empathy-induced altruistic motivation—much as did the desire to avoid painful electric shocks in Batson, O'Quin, and colleagues' (1983) Experiment 3 described in Chapter 7.

140 • EMPATHIC CONCERN

To test for this possibility, Vorauer and Sasaki (2009) had male and female White Canadian undergraduates anticipate a face-to-face discussion with a same-sex Aboriginal Canadian undergraduate about a segment from a recent documentary that featured an Aboriginal woman enduring great hardship. As expected, Vorauer and Sasaki found that their White participants instructed to imagine the woman's feelings reported significantly more empathic concern for her than did those instructed to remain objective. But, consistent with the possibility of overpowering, they also found that, whereas imagine-other participants who anticipated interacting with a same-sex White undergraduate showed increases in support for policies designed to help ethnic minorities and increases in recognition of discrimination as a problem, imagine-other participants expecting to interact with the Aboriginal undergraduate showed no significant increases.

A second experiment by Vorauer and Sasaki (2012) suggested a limit on this limit. The negative effects of adopting a stigmatized out-group member's perspective seemed to be limited to situations in which the out-group member (again, a same-sex Aboriginal Canadian undergraduate) expressed no need. When the out-group member expressed clear stigma-related need, an imagine-other perspective seemed to produce positive effects on participants' behavior in the interaction—at least among low-prejudice White participants. Vorauer and Sasaki (2012) interpreted these results as being due to participants' increased concern over the potential for negative evaluation by the out-group member leading them to try harder to look unprejudiced. I suggest a different interpretation. Although Vorauer and Sasaki didn't explicitly measure empathic concern, they did assess "warmth" and sensitivity directed toward the out-group member during the conversation. Participants in the imagine-other condition were found to display more warmth than participants in the objective condition, but only when the out-group member had disclosed hardships. This pattern is quite consistent with greater empathic concern being the source of the other-oriented sensitivity expressed by low-prejudice White participants who imagined the Aboriginal student's thoughts and feelings. After all, perception of need is a necessary condition for experiencing such concern (Chapter 4).

Is Religion Another Way to Expand Our Circle of Concern and Care?

Religions often seek to expand the range of those whose welfare we value. In the West, the faithful are admonished to "love your neighbor as yourself"

(Leviticus 19:18)—and are told that "the stranger who sojourns with you shall be to you as the native among you, and you shall love him as yourself" (Leviticus 19:34). The faithful are even instructed to "love your enemies, and do good to those who hate you" (Luke 6:27). Unfortunately, whether such admonitions lead the religiously devout to show more care for strangers and members of stigmatized groups than do the less religious—and, if so, whether these effects are mediated by empathic concern—is questionable (for relevant research see Batson, Denton, & Vollmecke, 2008; Batson, Floyd, Meyer, & Winner, 1999; and Batson, Schoenrade, & Ventis, 1993).

Looking to the East, compassion training based on the meditation practices of Tibetan Buddhism is thought to expand the meditator's circle of care. Consider two practices: First, *loving-kindness meditation* is designed to extend the range of others to whom the meditator wishes health, happiness, and well-being—that is, the range of others whose welfare is intrinsically valued. The strategy is to start with love felt for a clearly cared-for other (e.g., your mother), then gradually expand this loving care to include acquaintances, strangers, all humans (even enemies), and, eventually, all sentient beings. If, as claimed in Chapter 4, perception of need and intrinsic valuing of the other's welfare are the two necessary antecedents of empathic concern, loving-kindness meditation should increase the circle of people in need whose welfare the meditator intrinsically values and so feels empathic concern for, which should, in turn, produce empathy-induced altruistic motivation to have the need removed.

Second, *compassion meditation* is designed to extend the meditator's sensitivity to the needs of a wider range of others by increasing his or her readiness to recognize, understand, and feel for their suffering. Once again, the strategy is to start by focusing on the compassion we naturally feel for close others, then work to extend this response to a widening circle of others that eventually includes all sentient beings. If successful, compassion meditation should increase the range of targets whose needs we perceive, as well as the accuracy of our perception, thereby increasing the scope of our empathic concern and empathy-induced altruistic motivation. If these two closely related meditation practices have their intended effects, combining them should expand the meditator's empathic concern and empathy-induced altruistic motivation well beyond its normal bounds (see Ricard, 2006, 2015, for elaboration of this possibility).

Does practice of these forms of meditation in fact produce such expansion? Many anecdotes, legends, and testimonials tout meditation's effectiveness. And in recent years, researchers have gone beyond the anecdotes and testimonials to collect some relevant empirical evidence—the beginnings of a behavioral science of compassion. For example, there's evidence that loving-kindness meditation can (a) increase positive feelings toward a same-sex stranger (Hutcherson, Seppala, & Gross, 2008) and (b) decrease implicit intergroup bias against Blacks and the homeless (Kang, Gray, & Dovidio, 2014). There's also evidence that compassion meditation can (a) increase willingness to incur monetary cost to compel an unfair Decider in a Dictator Game to compensate the unfairly treated Recipient (Weng, Fox, Shackman, Stodola, Caldwell, Olson, Rogers, & Davidson, 2013), and (b) increase willingness to, without being asked, give one's seat in the research-lab waiting room to a woman on crutches (although this last effect wasn't statistically reliable, only a nonsignificant trend—Condon, Desbrodes, Miller, & DeSteno, 2013).

These results are encouraging, but systematic reviews of the empirical research to date fail to provide a clear answer to the question of whether meditation practices extend empathic concern and empathy-induced altruistic motivation in the ways predicted (see Berry, Cairo, Goodman, Quaglia, Green, & Brown, 2018; Berry, Hoerr, Cesko, Alayoubi, Carpio, Zirzow, Walters, Scram, Rodriguez, & Beaver, 2020; Kreplin, Farias, & Brazil, 2018). To bring clarity, better empirical tests are needed—ones that go beyond testing whether meditation training increases helping behavior to testing whether this effect is in fact due to extension of empathic concern (compassion) and altruistic motivation beyond the normal range, and not due to normative pressure and/or positive self-presentation.

Conclusion

More, more sensitive, and less fickle help for family, friends, and strangers in need. Less child abuse and neglect. Less aggression. Less derogation and blaming of victims of injustice. Increased concern for and openness to members of stigmatized groups. The list of potential interpersonal benefits for which there is at least preliminary empirical evidence is impressive. Empathic concern and the altruistic motivation it produces can, it seems, be powerful forces for good.

But as I said at the end of the previous chapter, empathic concern is no panacea. In this chapter, I've noted its several limits. In addition to these limits, empathic concern also has liabilities that can create problems rather than cure them. To fully understand its role in interpersonal relations, we need to recognize and appreciate the liabilities. Only then can we tap empathic concern's power responsibly.

9 BEHAVIORAL CONSEQUENCES

INTERPERSONAL LIABILITIES

Interpersonal liabilities of feeling empathic concern will be considered following roughly the same sequence as in Chapter 8. First, I'll note several liabilities for those near and dear, then focus on liabilities for strangers. In addition, I'll consider liabilities for the empathizer.

Liabilities for Close Others

At times, empathic concern felt for a close other can harm him or her. Loving one's child isn't all that's required of parents. Effective parenting also requires sensitivity about when to intervene and when to stand back in order to foster coping, confidence, and independence. Without such sensitivity, a parent's care can hurt rather than help. Honoré de Balzac, one of our most astute observers of human foibles, graphically portrayed this irony in his classic novel, *Pere Goriot* (1834/1962). Goriot's selfless love for his daughters spoiled them, drove them from him, and eventually doomed both them and him. Balzac's message: Empathic concern and the altruistic motivation it produces may be within the human repertoire, but if not held carefully in check, they can become destructive (also see Oakley, Knafo, Madhavan, & Wilson, 2012).

Paternalism, Maternalism, and Empathy-Induced Altruism

Just as effective parenting requires sensitivity, caring for close others who aren't our children requires the same. Again, empathy-induced

---

Empathic Concern. C. Daniel Batson, Oxford University Press. © Oxford University Press 2023.
DOI: 10.1093/oso/9780197610923.003.0010

altruism isn't all that's required for effective help (Fisher, Nadler, & DePaulo, 1983). Recall the adage about teaching the hungry to fish, not simply giving them fish.

If, as suggested in Chapter 5, empathic concern is based on cognitive generalization of human parental nurturance and tenderness, then it involves seeing those for whom we feel empathy, whether children or adults, as metaphorically childlike—as vulnerable, dependent, and in need of care. It also implies a status difference, at least as far as ability to address the need in question. Sometimes this difference poses no problem. Most of us happily defer to the expertise of firefighters, police officers, physicians, and plumbers when we need their help. At other times, it breeds harmful paternalism. Out of genuine concern, teachers and tutors can fail to help their students develop the ability and confidence to solve problems themselves, producing unnecessary dependence, low self-esteem, and a reduced sense of efficacy (Nadler, Fisher, & DePaulo, 1983; Vorauer, Quesnel, & St. Germain, 2016). Physicians, nurses, social workers, and physical therapists can do the same for patients with physical or mental disabilities (Nadler & Halabi, 2006).

The dangers of paternalism and dependence are real, but there's danger in the alternative as well. Paul Farmer of Partners in Health reserved some of his most biting criticism for White liberals who are so concerned not to offend or patronize that they fail to respond to immediate, crying needs. As Farmer put it, "There's a lot to be said for sacrifice, remorse, even pity" (Kidder, 2003, p. 40). How much help is too much, or too little, is often hard to ascertain. Again, wisdom is needed.

Imagining how the other feels about his or her situation—that is, adopting an imagine-other perspective—is particularly important to make empathic concern sensitive to what another person really needs. Drawing on her own practice as a physician and psychiatrist, Jodi Halpern (2001) presented the case of "Mr. Smith," a successful executive and family patriarch. Mr. Smith had experienced sudden paralysis from the neck down and was now ventilator dependent. Seeing his helpless condition, Halpern tried to provide comfort by communicating her deep sympathy and sorrow for him. He reacted with anger and frustration. Only after she made an active effort to imagine "what it would be like to be a powerful older man, suddenly enfeebled, handled by one young doctor after the next" (2001, p. 87) was Halpern able to appreciate and address his anger and frustration, enabling her to work *with* him rather than *on* him:

My initial sympathy was an unimaginative response to Mr. Smith's obvious vulnerability, which led me to treat him gently . . . . [His case] highlights the practical importance of imagining how a particular upsetting situation feels versus simply recognizing that a patient is upset. I imagined being unable to move and feeling rage at being an object of pity before "my" family. Imagining these specific experiences guided my interactions with Mr. Smith, shaping the timing of my remarks and my body language to communicate my respect for him and my capacity to withstand his anger. (Halpern, 2001, pp. 87–88)

A Warm Heart When You Need a Cool Head

Empathic concern can hurt close others in another way. Even when we know what help is needed, empathy-induced altruism can at times make matters worse, especially in situations that require a calm body and cool head. Think, for example, of the work of a surgeon. It's no accident, argued neurophysiologist Paul MacLean, that surgeons avoid operating on close kin or friends (MacLean, 1967). The problem isn't that surgeons feel no empathic concern for those they love—quite the opposite. When operating on your sister rather than a stranger, deep feelings of concern and a desperate desire to relieve her suffering may make a normally steady hand shake. Empathy-induced altruistic motivation could cost her life.

Testimony to another circumstance in which a warm heart made it difficult to do what was needed comes from survivors of the death camps in Nazi Europe. In the camps, members of the underground worked to save lives, but couldn't save everyone. At times they had to decide who would live and who would not. Survivors reported that empathic concern felt for those who would die made it difficult if not impossible to do what was necessary. In the words of Terrence Des Pres,

Compassion was seldom possible, self-pity never. Emotion not only blurred judgment and undermined decisiveness, it jeopardized the life of everyone in the underground. . . . Hard choices had to be made and not everyone was equal to the task, no one less than the kind of person whose goodness was most evident, most admired, but least available for action. (Des Pres, 1976, p. 131)

Liabilities for Strangers in Need

Turning from close others to strangers in need, one liability occurs even before empathic concern is experienced: To the degree that we believe empathic concern produces altruistic motivation, we may at times try to avoid feeling empathy in order to avoid the costs associated with the altruistic motivation it produces. And, in the absence of empathy, the stranger's need is less likely to be met.

Empathy Avoidance

What conditions produce motivation to avoid empathic concern? Shaw, Batson, and Todd (1994) suggested that empathy avoidance is likely when, before coming into contact with a stranger in need, we're aware that (a) we'll be asked to help this person and (b) helping will be costly. Shaw and colleagues tested this suggestion by having undergraduate men and women choose which of two audiotaped versions of a homeless man's appeal for help they wished to hear—a high-impact version, which was described as likely to evoke empathic emotion, or a low-impact version, described as objective and not emotional. Prior to making their choice, some participants learned that after they heard the appeal, they'd be given a chance to volunteer to help the homeless man. And of these participants, half were told that volunteering involved spending one hour preparing letters to send to potential contributors (aware/low-cost condition), whereas the other half were told that volunteering involved three one-and-a-half-hour meetings face-to-face with the homeless man, plus the possibility of further contact (aware/high-cost condition).

As suggested by the conditions specified for empathy avoidance, participants who were told both that they'd be asked to help and that helping involved high cost were significantly less likely to choose to hear the high-impact version of the homeless man's appeal than were participants either not told about the chance to help (unaware condition) or told that helping involved low cost. Apparently empathy avoidance—an egoistic motive to avoid an altruistic one—does exist. Awareness of our potential to experience empathy-induced altruism can at times lead us to turn away from those in need. (Cameron & Payne, 2011, provide further evidence of such a motive.)

Empathy avoidance can also occur in the helping professions, but the conditions for it occurring there probably aren't the same as those specified by Shaw and colleagues (1994). Professionals are more likely to avoid due to the perceived impossibility of providing effective help, not to the perceived cost of

Interpersonal Liabilities · 147

helping. Doctors and nurses caring for terminal patients, welfare case workers, therapists and counselors, may try to avoid feeling empathic concern in order to escape the frustration of not being able to satisfy the resulting altruistic motive (López-Peréz, Ambrona, Gregory, Stocks, & Oceja, 2013: Stotland, Mathews, Sherman, Hansson, & Richardson, 1978). Rather than feeling empathy, these professionals may distance themselves by turning their patients or clients into problems to be solved and treating them as such—a form of burnout (Maslach, 1982).

In Chapter 8, I noted that empathy-induced altruism can inhibit aggression—at least when empathy precedes the provocation to aggress. Empathy avoidance may help explain this qualifier. When an insult or other provocation to aggress precedes the induction of empathy, the desire to retaliate may make us want to avoid empathy because it might dampen this desire.

Consistent with this possibility, Worchel and Andreoli (1978) reported an experiment in which undergraduate men who were insulted by another research participant knew that they would soon have an opportunity to shock this other participant. While awaiting the chance to deliver shocks, the insulted men selectively attended to deindividuating, depersonalizing information about the other—information likely to inhibit empathic concern. Similarly, Zimbardo, Banks, Haney, and Jaffe (1973) reported that the "guards" in their famous prison simulation employed various deindividuating strategies that allowed them to avoid feeling sorry for the "prisoners," making it easier to treat them harshly.

In a far more extreme example of the same process, Rudolf Hoess, commandant of Auschwitz, reported that he "stifled all softer emotions" in order to carry out his assignment—the systematic extermination of 2.9 million people (Hoess, 1959). Empathy avoidance can, it seems, have devastating consequences both in what it prevents and in what it permits.

Empathic Concern Is Less Likely to be Evoked by Some Needs

In addition to sometimes being avoided, empathic concern is less likely to arise in response to certain needs—specifically, in response to needs of nonpersonalized others, needs that are abstract, and needs that are chronic. Our lack of empathy reduces the chance that those experiencing these types of needs will receive help.

Needs of nonpersonalized others. As discussed in Chapter 8, empathic concern is likely to be evoked by the needs of personalized others. This positive statement implies a negative: Empathic concern isn't likely to be evoked

148 • EMPATHIC CONCERN

by the needs of nonpersonalized others. Who are the nonpersonalized? A half-dozen answers to this question have been offered: (a) those who live far away, (b) those with whom we don't share group membership, (c) those not similar to us, (d) those who have needs we haven't experienced, (e) those we dislike, and (f) those we encounter as one among many individuals with similar needs.

Each of these characteristics has been proposed as a source of depersonalization, but existing research clearly supports only the last two. Before considering these two, let me briefly address the first four:

(a) As long as awareness of need and valuing of the other's welfare are held constant, distance doesn't seem to depersonalize. We can feel concern for a victim of some natural disaster or human atrocity on the other side of the globe. Distance may reduce felt responsibility to act, and reduce action, but these effects shouldn't be confused with either empathic concern or the altruistic motivation it produces.

(b) Although some have claimed that shared group membership is a necessary condition for personalization and for empathy-induced altruism (e.g., Stürmer, Snyder, Kropp, & Siem, 2006), research clearly shows that it isn't (e.g., Batson, Polycarpou et al., 1997; Batson, Sager et al., 1997).

(c) The same is true for similarity. In Chapter 4, I discussed the use of similarity to induce empathy, noting that perceived similarity can lead us to value another's welfare, which involves personalizing him or her. But I also noted that as long as perceived dissimilarity doesn't evoke antipathy, we can feel empathic concern for a wide range of targets, including people quite unlike ourselves, even members of other species (Batson, Lishner et al., 2005; Kahneman & Ritov, 1994; Shelton & Rogers, 1981—see Chapter 5).

(d) Nor is it necessary to have experienced the same need, despite claims by some that it is (e.g., Allport, 1924; Bandura, 1969; Hoffman, 1981a). As long as we can understand and appreciate another person's need, prior experience with that need isn't required (see Batson, Sympson, Hindman, Decruz, Todd, Weeks, Jennings, & Burris, 1996; Hodges, 2005; Hygge, 1976). Prior experience may heighten understanding of the other's need, and thereby empathic concern, but understanding can come from other sources as well. When it does, those who have never experienced a particular need can feel considerable empathy for a person suffering it. As Adam Smith pointed out long ago, "A man may sympathize with a woman in child-bed; though it is impossible that he should conceive himself as suffering her pains in his own proper person and character" (Smith, 1759/1853, p. 317).

Not only is prior experience not necessary, sometimes it can inhibit empathy. Sara Hodges and her colleagues found that among women presented with a woman who suffered a difficult childbirth, some of those who had given birth themselves compared the woman's reaction to their own and felt less, not more, empathic concern for her (Hodges, 2005; Hodges, Kiel, Kramer, Veach, & Villanueva, 2010; also see Israelashoeli et al., 2020).

The final two proposed depersonalizing conditions *do* inhibit empathic concern:

(e) As discussed in Chapter 4, dislike or antipathy toward another person can undermine one of the necessary antecedent conditions for feeling empathy—placing positive value on the other's welfare. Batson, Eklund, and colleagues (2007) provided clear evidence of the inhibiting effect of dislike on empathic concern and empathy-induced helping.

(f) There's also clear evidence of an inhibiting effect on personalization and empathy when an individual in need is one among a number of individuals with similar needs (Kogut & Ritov, 2005a, Experiments 1 & 2; Kogut & Ritov, 2005b, Experiment 3; Small, Lowenstein, & Slovic, 2007). To paraphrase Stalin, a person in need is a tragedy; a million in need is a statistic. Many of the pressing social problems we face today—mass starvation, refugees, genocide, pandemic—come at us in the form of statistics rather than individual persons in need. The consequence, argued Paul Slovic (2007), is "psychic numbing" and "the collapse of compassion," especially when the parade of problems never ends:

Confronted with the knowledge of dozens of apparently random disasters each day, what can a human heart do but slam its doors? No mortal can grieve that much. We didn't evolve to cope with tragedy on a global scale. Our defense is to pretend there's no thread of event that connects us, and that those lives are somehow not precious and real like our own. It's a practical strategy, to some ends, but the loss of empathy is also a loss of humanity, and that's no small tradeoff. (Slovic, 2007, p. 87; also see Slovic, Västfjäll, Erlandsson, & Gregory, 2017)

Daryl Cameron and Keith Payne demonstrated that such collapse of compassion can result from proactive regulation of compassionate feelings (i.e., empathy avoidance), which prevents overwhelming levels of emotion that might be produced by the number in need (Cameron & Payne, 2011; also see Ministero, Poulin, Buffone, & DeLury, 2018).

Abstract needs. Many social problems we face today don't involve individuals in immediate need. The problems are more abstract—climate change, nuclear proliferation, overpopulation. It's hard to feel empathic concern for these abstract needs, although personalizing metaphors such as "rape of the planet" may move us in that direction.

Not only is it difficult to feel empathy for these needs, such needs also can't be effectively addressed with a personal helping response. They require political action by governments. The process is long and slow, not the sort for which empathy-induced altruism is likely to be effective. Ecologist and philosopher Garrett Hardin (1977) concluded that in such cases you must appeal to self-interest:

> Is pure altruism possible? Yes, of course it is—on a small scale, over the short term, in certain circumstances, and within small, intimate groups. In family-like groups one should be able to give with little thought "of nicely calculated less or more." But only the most naive hope to adhere to a non-calculating policy in a group that numbers in the thousands (or millions!), and in which many preexisting antagonisms are known and many more suspected. . . .
>
> When those who have not appreciated the nature of large groups innocently call for "social policy institutions [to act] as agents of altruistic opportunities" they call for the impossible. In large groups, social policy institutions necessarily must be guided by what I have called the Cardinal Rule of Policy: *Never ask a person to act against his own self-interest.* (Hardin, 1977, pp. 26–27, italics in original)

Chronic needs. Even when addressing the needs of specific individuals, empathy-induced altruism may not suffice if the needs persist. Like other emotions, our feelings of empathy diminish over time. As a result, empathic concern may not sustain the kind of enduring help required of, for example, community-action volunteers (Omoto & Snyder, 2002). It may lead someone to volunteer to help people with AIDS or the homeless, but other motives may need to take over if a volunteer is to continue for the long haul.

Similarly, empathic concern and the altruistic motivation it produces may not suffice to sustain professional helpers who encounter people in need one after another, day after day. Empathic concern may lead a person to enter a helping profession but, by itself, may not be sufficient to sustain effectiveness. Over time, these helpers may find they no longer feel for their patients and clients, experiencing what has been called *compassion fatigue* (Figley, 2002; Rainer, 2000).

Empathic Concern Can Cause Us to Treat Others Unfairly

Empathic concern felt for a person in need can lead us to put his or her needs ahead of the needs of equally deserving others, thereby treating these others unfairly. To test for this kind of empathy-induced partiality, several colleagues and I conducted two experiments (Batson, Klein, Highberger, & Shaw, 1995).

When assigning workers to tasks. The first was presented to participants as a study of workplace interactions. Female Introductory Psychology students were, ostensibly randomly, placed in the role of a Supervisor. As Supervisor, they were to assign two other female Introductory Psychology students, the Workers, to tasks. One task had positive consequences; for each correct response the Worker would get a raffle ticket for a $30 gift certificate. The other task had negative consequences; for each incorrect response the Worker would get an uncomfortable electric shock (two to three times the strength of static electricity).

To make the issue of fairness salient, Supervisor instructions stated: "Most Supervisors feel that flipping a coin is the fairest way to assign the tasks, but the decision is entirely up to you. You can assign the Workers however you wish." Participants were provided with a coin to flip if they chose. The instructions also explained that neither of the Workers would learn how the tasks were assigned, only which task was hers. Finally, the instructions stated that among other variables, we were studying the effect of prior knowledge of one or both Workers. So, as Supervisor, they might receive a brief communication (a handwritten note) from one or both. The possibility of receiving a note set up our empathy manipulation.

Participants in a no-communication condition learned that they would receive no note. Those in two communication conditions received a note from one of the Workers ("Participant C") in which she was supposed to describe something interesting that happened to her recently. Of the participants who read C's note, half were instructed to imagine how the student writing the note felt about what was described (high-empathy condition), and half, to remain objective and detached (low-empathy condition). In the note, Participant C said the only thing she could think of was that two days ago she had been dumped by her boyfriend and was really upset. She added that her friends all said she just needed something good to happen to cheer her up, but so far that hadn't happened. (It was assumed that participants would think that giving C the positive-consequences task—raffle tickets—might cheer her up, whereas assigning her to the negative-consequences—electric shocks—wouldn't.)

How did participants in the three experimental conditions assign the Workers to tasks? Participants in the no-communication condition, who knew nothing about C's need for cheering up, all reported using a random method (flipping the coin) to assign the Workers. Consistent with this report—and with what would be expected if these participants used the coin—half (50%) assigned Participant C to the positive-consequences task. In the communication/low-empathy condition, 85% reported using a random method. The remaining 15% said they assigned C to the positive consequences without flipping the coin. Still, the overall result in this condition was the same as in the no-communication condition—half (50%) assigned C to the positive-consequences task.

Results were quite different in the communication/high-empathy condition, in which participants focused on C's feelings. Only half of the participants in that condition reported using a random method. The other half all assigned C to the positive consequences without flipping the coin. Thus, half of the participants in the communication/high-empathy condition unfairly favored the Worker for whom they had been led to feel empathy.

When later asked an open-ended question about the fairest way to assign the tasks, 95% in the communication/high-empathy condition said that using a random method was most fair. Yet, despite saying this, only half had acted accordingly. The other half assigned C the positive consequences without flipping the coin.

When deciding who gets help. In the second experiment, participants were given the chance to unfairly move a person for whom they felt empathic concern to the head of the line for help. Ostensibly to provide reactions to public-awareness materials produced by the Quality Life Foundation—a national organization devoted to improving the quality of life for children with terminal illnesses—participants (male and female) heard an interview with Sheri Summers, a 10-year-old girl with a slow-progressing terminal illness, myasthenia gravis. After listening, each participant was given an unexpected chance to help Sheri by moving her off a waiting list and into an immediate-treatment group ahead of other children who either had more severe illnesses or had been waiting longer for treatment. Once again, those in a low-empathy condition were instructed to remain objective; those in a high-empathy condition, to imagine Sheri's feelings.

Most participants in the low-empathy condition acted fairly, declining the opportunity to move Sheri into the immediate-treatment group ahead of more deserving children. Only 33% chose to move her. Participants in the high-empathy condition were far less likely to act fairly—73% chose to move Sheri into the immediate-treatment group.

Results of these two experiments support the claim that empathy-induced altruism can cause us to treat others unfairly. In each experiment, participants not induced to feel empathic concern for one of the individuals in need were likely to act fairly, but participants induced to feel empathy were likely to show partiality toward the target of their concern. It wasn't that the high-empathy participants abandoned fairness as a principle. When asked, almost all said that partiality was less fair than impartiality. Yet most were willing to act unfairly to benefit the person for whom they had been led to care.

In everyday life. Does empathy-induced unfairness occur in everyday life? It seems so. Empathic concern can introduce partiality into our decisions, both individually and as a nation, about which people among the many in need will get our assistance. To cite but one example, essayist Walter Isaacson suggested that the decision in 1992 by the U.S. to intervene in Somalia but not the Sudan occurred because photos of those suffering in Somalia evoked empathic concern in a way that photos of those in the Sudan didn't:

> In a democracy, policy (unless pursued in secret) must reflect public sentiment. But sentiment can ooze sentimentality, especially in the age of global information, when networks and newsmagazines can sear the vision of a suffering Somalian child or Bosnian orphan into the soft hearts of millions. Random bursts of compassion provoked by compelling pictures may be a suitable basis for Christmas charity drives, but are they the proper foundation for a foreign policy? Will the world end up rescuing Somalia while ignoring the Sudan mainly because the former proves more photogenic? (Isaacson, 1992)

In his book *Against Empathy*, Paul Bloom expressed similar concerns about the power of empathic concern to skew our moral judgment (Bloom, 2016). Although by empathy he meant feeling as another person feels rather than feeling for the other (see Chapter 1), most of Bloom's examples of the immoral effects of empathy—including the example from Isaacson just cited—involved feeling for individuals in need, not feeling as they feel.

It seems that empathy-induced altruism can produce moral myopia in much the same way as self-interested egoism. Each is focused on the welfare of a specific person or persons, so each is potentially at odds with appeals to impartial fairness.

Empathic Concern Can Hurt the Common Good

In addition to acting unfairly, empathic concern can lead a person to act against the common good if that good is at odds with the welfare of the cared-for other. Conflicts between an individual's welfare and the common good come to the fore in *social dilemmas*.

A social dilemma, of which the one-trial Prisoner's Dilemma described in Chapter 7 is a simple form, arises when four conditions exist: (a) a person has a choice about how to allocate scarce resources (e.g., time, money, energy) and, regardless of what others do, (b) allocation to the group is best for the group as a whole, but (c) allocation to a single individual (the allocator or another group member) is best for that individual, yet (d) if all allocations are to separate individuals (for example, if all individuals allocate to them-selves), each individual is worse off than if all allocations are to the group. Social dilemmas abound in modern society. To name but a few, we face one each time we decide whether to recycle, carpool, vote, or contribute to public television.

Empathy is a threat to the common good in a social dilemma. When listing the conditions for a social dilemma, I mentioned the possibility that the person could allocate resources to an individual other than self. Interestingly, insofar as I know, this possibility hadn't been considered in the extensive research on and discussion of social dilemmas prior to the 1990s. Guided by the assumption of universal egoism that underlies game theory and the theory of rational choice, it had been taken for granted that the only individual to whom people will allocate scarce resources is themselves. In contrast, the empathy-altruism hypothesis predicts that if we feel empathic concern for another member of a group, we'll be altruistically motivated to benefit that person. So, in addition to the two motives traditionally assumed to conflict in a social dilemma—self-interested egoism and interest in the common good— a third motive is in play.

The empathy-altruism hypothesis predicts, specifically, that empathic concern and the altruistic motivation it produces will conflict with the common good whenever three additional conditions exist: An allocator values the welfare of some but not all other individuals in the collective; the allocator perceives the cared-for other(s) to be in need of resources; and the allocator can give resources to others in the collective as individuals. How often do these additional conditions exist? It's hard to think of a real-world social dilemma in which they don't. They exist every time we try to decide whether to spend our time or money to benefit ourselves, the community, or another individual about whom we especially care. For example, a father may resist contributing to the United Way not to buy himself a new shirt but because he feels for his daughter who wants new shoes. Whalers may kill to extinction not out of personal greed but to provide for their families. An executive may retain an aging and ineffective employee for whom he or she feels compassion, thereby hurting the company.

To test this reasoning, Batson, Batson, Todd, Brummett, Shaw, and Aldeguer (1995) conducted two studies. In each, undergraduate participants faced a dilemma in which they could choose to benefit themselves, the group, or one or more other group members as individuals (all strangers). In each study, those led to experience high empathy for one of the other group members allocated more resources to that person as an individual, reducing the overall collective good. These results suggest the importance of considering self-interest, group-interest, and other-interest (i.e., empathy-induced altruism) as three distinct motives, each of which can operate in a social dilemma.

But is empathic concern a serious threat? How serious a threat to the common good is empathy-induced altruism? Most people would say that it's minor compared to self-interested egoism. After all, we experience our own needs directly; a cared-for stranger's needs are more remote.

True, yet empathy-induced altruism can still be a serious threat. Indeed, when our action is public, there's evidence that it can be a more serious threat to the common good than is self-interest. Clear social norms and sanctions exist to inhibit pursuit of our own interests at the expense of what's fair and best for all (Kerr, 1995). *Selfish* and *greedy* are stinging epithets. In contrast, norms and sanctions against showing concern for another's interests—even if doing so diminishes the common good—are less apparent. Favoritism toward another, especially another in need, isn't likely to be called selfish or greedy. We may be accused of being *naive, soft, a pushover,* or *a bleeding heart,* but these terms carry an implicit charge of gullibility, not greed.

To test the possibility that when our behavior is public, empathy-induced altruism can be a more serious threat to the common good than egoism, another set of colleagues and I conducted two more experiments (Batson, Ahmad, Yin, Bedell, Johnson, Templin, & Whiteside, 1999). In each, there were three experimental conditions: Some participants chose between allocation of resources to the group as a whole or to themselves alone (egoism condition). Some chose between allocation to a group of which they were not a member or to a member of that group for whom they were induced to feel empathy (altruism condition). Some chose between allocation to the group of which they were not a member or to the same member of that group but without empathy being induced (baseline condition). In the first experiment, all participants' allocations were kept private. In the second, half of the participants thought their decisions would be private. The other half thought that after deciding, the group would come together, and all allocation decisions would be made public.

When the decision was private, allocation to the group was significantly lower in both the egoism and altruism conditions compared to the baseline (both experiments). However, when the decision was public, allocation to the group was significantly lower only in the altruism condition. These results indicate, first, that both egoism and altruism can be potent threats to the common good. And second, that anticipated social evaluation is a powerful inhibitor of the egoistic but not the altruistic threat.

If altruism is a potent threat, why aren't there sanctions against it like there are against egoism? I suspect there aren't because society makes one or both of two assumptions: Altruism is always good. Altruism is weak. But we've seen that each of these assumptions is false. And if each is false, consider the implications. How do whalers and loggers stand up to the public outcry about overdepletion of natural resources? Easily. They're using these resources to care for their families, not themselves.

Empathic Concern Can Be Harmful to Your Health

Viewed from the perspective of personal survival and narrow self-interest, empathy-induced altruistic motivation is potentially dangerous. It can lead us to take risks that cost us dearly. When 28-year old Lenny Skutnik was asked why he dove into the ice-strewn Potomac River to rescue a drowning plane-crash victim, he said, "I just did what I had to do." I don't know the extent to which the motivation that impelled Skutnik's action was empathy-induced, but whatever motivated him to leave the safety of his car very nearly cost him his life. I also don't know the motivation of soldiers who save comrades by diving on live hand grenades or other explosive devices (Blake, 1978).

However, I suspect that empathy-induced altruism often plays a role. And I suspect it often plays a role in patients' willingness to take part in painful and risky medical research (Jansen, 2009). In such situations, empathic concern can indeed be life-threatening.

Empathic concern and the altruistic motivation it produces can be harmful to your health in less extreme situations as well. As noted earlier, both volunteer and professional helpers—AIDS buddies, hospice workers, doctors, social workers, therapists—who take on too heavy a load of other people's burdens may find themselves overwhelmed, with nothing more to give (Maslach, 1982; Omoto & Snyder, 2002; Schultz, Williamson, Morycz, & Biegel, 1991). Apparently, our capacity to experience empathic concern isn't a bottomless well. We can feel only so much compassion before we go numb. This compassion fatigue (Figley, 2002; Ranier, 2000) can not only harm others; it can also harm us. Caring for a loved one who is permanently physical disabled, or who requires extensive medical care, or who is terminally ill, can take a serious toll on the physical and mental health of the caregiver (Schultz & Beach, 1999; Schultz et al., 1991).

Although not a direct health risk, what might be called *compassion abuse* can clamp a tourniquet on the free flow of empathic concern. Professional panhandlers, "physically disabled" telemarketers who sell us lightbulbs, scam callers who pose as a friend or relative in need, all seek to take advantage of the empathic concern we feel. And when we realize—even suspect—that our compassion chain has been pulled once more, we're likely to vow: Never again. As described by Dan Gilbert (2007), a wedge of cynicism is driven between us and those in need. That wedge pinches us as well as them.

Empathic Concern Can Hurt Your Chances in Conflict Situations

Finally, empathic concern can hurt your chances in competitive sports, in business, and in political negotiations. Feeling for your opponent in situations like these can cause you to give ground. We've already seen one example: Empathic concern felt for the other participant in the Prisoner's Dilemma experiments described in Chapter 7 benefited the other at the empathizer's expense.

Research by Adam Galinsky and his colleagues suggests that empathy can have similar effects in negotiations. In one experiment, Galinsky, Maddux, Gilin, and White (2008) had M.B.A. students in a negotiation class pair up and engage in a 30-minute two-party bargaining exercise. One student

158 • EMPATHIC CONCERN

in each pair played the role of a Job Candidate, and the other, a Recruiter. The Candidate and Recruiter negotiated eight issues—salary, work location, bonus, vacation time, and so on. Both knew which issues mattered more to the Candidate, and which to the Recruiter. Joint gain could be maximized by being sensitive to which issues mattered most to whom and using this information to make trade-offs (a strategy called logrolling). As a perspective manipulation, each student in the Recruiter role was given one of three sets of instructions: (a) consider your own role carefully, (b) try to understand what the Candidate is thinking, or (c) try to imagine what the Candidate is feeling. The imagine-feelings instructions were like those often used to induce empathic concern.

Dyads with Recruiters assigned to either of the last two perspectives produced greater joint gain than dyads with Recruiters assigned to consider their own role. For Recruiters focused on the Candidate's thoughts, the difference was highly significant. For those focused on feelings, it was marginal. Of particular interest was how the greater joint gains were achieved in each condition. Recruiters who focused on the Candidate's thoughts got more of what they wanted than did Recruiters who focused on the Candidate's feelings. But Candidates who negotiated with a Recruiter focused on their feelings got more of what *they* wanted than did Candidates negotiating with a Recruiter focused either on the Recruiter's role or (non-significantly) on the Candidate's thoughts.

These results led Galinsky and his colleagues to conclude that when negotiating, it's more effective "to 'think for' than to 'feel for' one's adversaries" (Galinsky et al., 2008, p. 383). Recruiters who imagined the Candidate's feelings—which presumably induced empathic concern (we can't be sure because no measures of emotion were taken)—gave ground. They benefited the Candidate at cost to themselves. Recruiters who were able to get inside the Candidate's head, the way a skilled chess player might, got more of what they wanted. (For similar results, see Trötschel, Hüffmeier, Loschelder, Schwartz, & Gollwitzer, 2011.)

But note that these results were in a single negotiation. What about when there are multiple negotiations over time between the same people—as, for example, when a business person negotiates contracts with repeat customers? In future negotiations, the goodwill produced by giving ground in the present may tip the scales in favor of negotiators who imagine feelings rather than thoughts.

Consistent with this possibility, in a different bargaining exercise, Galinsky and colleagues (2008) found that Sellers who negotiated with an empathic

Buyer (one focused on the Seller's feelings) were significantly more satisfied with the way they were treated during the negotiation than were Sellers who negotiated with a Buyer focused on their thoughts. This was true even though agreement on a sale was (nonsignificantly) more likely in the latter case. Would the feelings of satisfaction engendered by being empathic lead to more productive subsequent negotiations? I don't know because that wasn't tested, but it's a possibility worth exploring in future research.

Conclusion

At the interpersonal level, empathic concern and the altruistic motivation it produces aren't unalloyed goods. Although Chapter 8 provided evidence that they can offer important benefits, this chapter provides evidence that there can also be important liabilities. Empathic concern can harm those in need when acted on unwisely, or when a cool head is required. It can be limited by empathy avoidance, and it's less likely to be evoked by nonpersonal, abstract, or chronic needs. It can lead you to show partiality toward those for whom you feel empathy, thereby acting unfairly or against the common good. It can, at times, jeopardize your mental and physical health, even your life. In conflict situations, it can cause you to give ground.

Identifying the conditions under which empathic concern is likely to be a benefit and when it's likely to be a liability is essential if we're to realize its potential to enhance and enrich our lives. The available research has made a start toward that goal, but only a start.

10 BEHAVIORAL CONSEQUENCES

INTERGROUP BENEFITS

The most frequently mentioned intergroup benefit of empathic concern is that it can produce more positive attitudes and action toward stigmatized out-groups.

Attitudes and Action Toward Stigmatized Groups

Chapter 8 provided evidence that we can be induced to feel empathy for a member of a stigmatized group as long as the induction process personalizes the member as an individual, not simply one of "them." Personalization can be produced by, for example, focusing on the member's thoughts and feelings (an imagine-other perspective) while listening to the member talk about his or her life. But note that the resulting empathic concern is an interpersonal not an intergroup emotion. It's felt for the individual member, not for the group. How can concern felt for an individual member of a stigmatized group improve attitudes and action toward the group as a whole?

Think of books such as *Uncle Tom's Cabin* (Stowe, 1852/2005), *Manchild in the Promised Land* (Brown, 1965), *House Made of Dawn* (Momaday, 1968), *One Flew Over the Cuckoo's Nest* (Kesey, 1962), *The Color Purple* (Walker, 1982), and *Borrowed Time* (Monette, 1988). Think of movies like *A Raisin in the Sun*, *The Elephant Man*, *Rain Man*, and *Longtime Companion*. Think of the television documentaries *Eyes on the Prize* and *Promises*. Each of these works, and many similar ones, appears designed to improve

Empathic Concern. C. Daniel Batson, Oxford University Press. © Oxford University Press 2023.
DOI: 10.1093/oso/9780197610923.003.0011

attitudes toward a stigmatized group—a racial or ethnic minority, people with some social stigma, disability, or disease. Creators of works like these seem to share two beliefs: First, that by inducing us to imagine the thoughts and feelings of a member of a stigmatized group as he or she attempts to cope, we can be led to value this person's welfare and feel empathic concern. Second, that these empathic feelings will generalize, leading us to feel more positively toward the group as a whole. Are these beliefs correct?

Improving Attitudes

To make the attitude-change process employed in these books, movies, and documentaries explicit, let me outline a three-step process originally proposed by Batson, Polycarpou, and colleagues (1997). The process moves from empathic concern at the interpersonal level to improved attitudes toward a stigmatized group at the intergroup level:

Step 1. Adoption of the perspective of a member of a stigmatized group as he or she describes stigma-related needs. This imagine-other perspective should increase empathic concern for the member.

Step 2. The empathic concern should in turn lead to increased valuing of the group-member's welfare (through the backward inference described in Chapter 4).

Step 3. As long as group membership is a salient aspect of the need for which empathy is induced, valuing the group-member's welfare should generalize to valuing the welfare of the stigmatized group as a whole, producing more positive beliefs about and feelings toward the group.

Research reviewed in Chapters 4 and 7 suggests that if empathic concern can be aroused for a member of a stigmatized group, positive feelings and actions are likely toward that specific member. But how does one get this effect to generalize to the group as a whole? Subtyping a known and cared-for out-group member as a special case—"the exception that proves the rule" of the stigmatizing stereotype—is a concern. That's why it's important to make the member's typicality as a group member salient in order for the enhanced valuing associated with empathy to generalize to other group members. Fortunately, subtyping should be less of a problem for empathy-based attitude change than it is when using cognitive strategies such as presenting stereotype-inconsistent information about an out-group member; such information highlights his or her atypicality (see Stephan & Finlay, 1999).

Intergroup Benefits · 163

Let me briefly review the evidence for each step of the three-step process:

Evidence for Steps 1 and 2. In Chapter 8, I reported four experiments that provided tests of the first step. In all four, adopting an imagine-other perspective significantly increased empathic concern felt for a member of a stigmatized group. What I didn't report in Chapter 8 is that the last three of these experiments included a measure of valuing the group-member's welfare and a measure of attitudes toward the stigmatized group. Thus, they also provided tests of Steps 2 and 3. (The first experiment, in which participants heard an interview with Julie who had AIDS, included an attitude measure that showed an effect of empathy on attitudes, but it didn't include a valuing measure.)

To test Step 2—that greater empathic concern leads to greater valuing of the out-group member's welfare—participants in the last three experiments were asked how much they valued the welfare of Harold Mitchell, a homeless man (Batson, Polycarpou et al., 1997, Experiment 2), James Stevens, a convicted murderer imprisoned for life without parole (Batson, Polycarpou et al., 1997, Experiment 3), or Jared Briggs, an imprisoned heroin addict and dealer (Batson, Chang et al., 2002). In the remain-objective (low-empathy) condition, valuing of Harold was a little above the midpoint of the rating scale of positivity of feeling toward him, whereas valuing of James and Jared, the two criminals, was well below the midpoint. In the imagine-other (high empathy) condition, valuing of each of these stigmatized-group members was significantly more positive—well above the midpoint for Harold and around the midpoint for James and Jared. Further supporting Step 2, a simple path analysis revealed that participants' self-reported empathic concern (measured with the six-item index—see Chapter 1) mediated the effect of the imagine-other perspective on increased valuing in each experiment.

Evidence for Step 3. Turning to Step 3, attitudes toward the stigmatized group were measured in each of the three experiments by group-specific attitude questionnaires modeled on McConahay's (1986) Modern Racism Scale. As predicted, imagining the feelings of Harold and Jared made attitudes significantly more positive toward homeless people and toward people addicted to hard drugs, respectively. Imagining James's feelings made attitudes toward convicted murderers somewhat more positive, but the effect wasn't statistically significant.

Additional light was shed on the effect of empathic concern felt for James on attitudes toward murderers by telephone interviews with the research participants conducted one to two weeks after they heard the interview with James and completed the empathy, valuing, and attitude measures in the

164 • EMPATHIC CONCERN

laboratory. For the interviews, an undergraduate woman with prior experience in telemarketing (but no knowledge of the lab session or the hypotheses being tested) called each participant and explained that she was "conducting a small survey for a class on current political issues":

> It's for a term paper on prison reform, and my task is to do a small survey to find out what KU [University of Kansas, where the experiment was conducted] students think about the issue . . . . There's a proposal for allowing more freedom inside prisons—and increasing education and rehabilitation efforts to give prisoners an opportunity to make a useful contribution to society. So, I would like to read you a few statements about this. Then you can give me your opinion about each.

The interviewer then read five statements designed to assess attitudes toward murderers, and wrote down participants' responses.

Although attitudes toward murderers expressed in the laboratory immediately after listening to the interview with James showed only a nonsignificant trend for research participants in the imagine-other (high-empathy) condition to report more positive attitudes toward murderers than participants in the remain-objective (low-empathy) condition, attitudes expressed during the unrelated telephone interview one to two weeks later showed a clearly significant effect. Participants who had been induced to feel empathic concern for James in the lab reported more positive attitudes toward murderers in the telephone interview than did participants who had remained objective. It appeared that when attitudes were assessed immediately, participants in the imagine condition resisted letting the empathic feelings they felt for James influence their attitudes toward murderers in general. Later, with their guard down, an effect on attitudes was apparent. In the laboratory, many participants took the first two steps in the three-step process but balked at the third. By the time of the telephone interview, they had taken the third.

This experiment wasn't the first to provide evidence of an enduring empathy-attitude effect. Clore and Jeffrey (1972) reported a similar effect of empathy on attitudes toward people with physical disabilities. Participants in their experiment were randomly assigned to one of three conditions: (a) be wheeled around campus as if a wheelchair-bound student, (b) follow and observe the wheelchair-bound participant, or (c) walk around campus freely. Measures of thoughts and feelings taken immediately afterward indicated that participants in the first two conditions reported feeling more empathic concern (*compassionate, concerned*) and reported more positive attitudes toward the disabled than did those in the third condition. Further, empathic concern mediated the effect of experimental condition on attitudes. Showing endurance, Clore and Jeffrey found that the effect on attitudes was still present four months later using a disguised measure. It seems that an empathy-attitude effect not only exists, but also that it has some staying power.

Finally, path analyses of data from each of the experiments designed to test the three-step process provided support for it. In response to homeless Harold Mitchell, path analysis revealed that the effect of the perspective manipulation on valuing of Harold was mediated by the effect of the manipulation on empathic concern, and that the effect on valuing in turn mediated the effect of empathic concern on attitudes toward the homeless. In response to the murderer James Stevens, the effect of the perspective manipulation on valuing was again mediated by the effect of the manipulation on empathic concern, and the effect on valuing in turn mediated the effect of empathic concern on attitudes toward murderers measured one to two weeks later.

In response to Jared Briggs, the same path sequence—imagine-other perspective→ empathic concern→valuing of Jared's welfare→improved attitude toward addicts—was found. But there was a complication in this last experiment. Even though the predicted path model fit the data well, a model that also included a direct path from the perspective manipulation to attitude toward addicts fit even better. This direct effect wasn't as strong as the mediated effect, but it pointed to an effect of imagine-other perspective taking on attitudes that was outside the mediation through empathic concern and valuing specified by the three-step process. More about this effect shortly.

Extending the range of the empathy-attitude effect. The three-step process addressed whether, when an imagine-other perspective is used to arouse empathic concern for the needs of a member of a stigmatized group (Step 1 of the three-step process), the increased valuing of the member's welfare produced by this empathic concern (Step 2) will generalize to the group as a whole (Step 3). At least for the stigmatized groups tested, the answer seems to be yes—as long as membership in the stigmatized group is a salient aspect of the member's need for which empathy is induced. In each experiment, adopting an imagine-other perspective had a significant effect (compared to remaining objective) on more positive attitudes. Moreover, this effect was mediated by increased empathic concern and the valuing of the member's welfare that this empathy produced.

Subsequent research has found empathy-attitude effects for a number of other out-groups. Empathic concern (including empathic anger) induced for a member of a racial or ethnic minority has been found to improve attitudes

166 • EMPATHIC CONCERN

toward the minority group (Dovidio, Johnson, Gaertner, Pearson, Saguy, & Ashburn-Nardo, 2010; Dovidio, ten Vergert, Stewart, Gaertner, Johnson, Esses, Rick, & Pearson, 2004; Esses & Dovidio, 2002; Finlay & Stephan, 2000; Vescio, Sechrist, and Paolucci, 2003). Empathic concern induced for a gay man improved attitudes toward homosexuals (Vescio & Hewstone, 2001). The more positive out-group attitudes that result from friendship with an ethnic out-group member have been interpreted as being the result of increased empathic concern (Brown & Hewstone, 2005; Pettigrew, 1998). Suggesting the breadth of applicability of empathy-induced attitude change, Schultz (2000) found that empathic concern felt for animals being harmed by pollution improved attitudes toward protecting the natural environment (also see Berenguer, 2007).

Adding Action

As we've seen in earlier chapters, there's considerable evidence that empathic concern felt for a person in need increases readiness to help that person. This raises the question of whether a fourth step should be added to the three-step sequence: Does empathy felt for a member of a stigmatized group increase readiness to help not only that specific individual but also other members of the group even when doing so doesn't benefit the specific individual? More precisely, will the increased valuing of the group's welfare reflected in the more positive attitude toward the group increase motivation to help the group as a whole, producing an interpersonal-empathy→interpersonal-valuing→intergroup-valuing/attitude→intergroup-action sequence?

Doubt. To propose that empathic concern felt for a member of a stigmatized group increases readiness to help the group may seem contrary to results of an experiment reported by Dovidio, Allen, and Schroeder (1990), described in Chapter 7. As you may recall, that experiment provided support for the need-specific assumption of the empathy-altruism hypothesis by showing that inducing empathic concern in response to one need increased the readiness to help with that need but not with a different need of the same person. If empathy-induced helping doesn't generalize across two needs of the same individual, what reason is there to expect that inducing empathy for one member of a stigmatized group can increase helping of other members of the group in a way that doesn't benefit the individual for whom empathy is felt?

Hope. There are at least three reasons to expect it can. First, research reported in the previous section showed that inducing empathy for a member can improve attitudes toward the group as a whole. If these attitudes produce

Intergroup Benefits • 167

attitude-consistent behavior, they should lead to more action to benefit the group. Second, in an experiment that preceded and helped prompt the Dovidio and colleagues (1990) experiment just mentioned, Matthews, Dovidio, and Schroeder (1987) found that empathy induced for one person led to increased helping of a second person who had a similar need. This finding suggests that as long as other members of the stigmatized group have needs similar to those of the member for whom empathy is induced, the effect of empathy on motivation to help may generalize to them (also see Faulkner, 2018). Third, again reflecting breadth, Shelton and Rogers (1981) found that empathic concern induced while watching a video clip showing whales increased readiness to help save whales in general. It seems that people induced to feel empathic concern for a member of an out-group—stigmatized or not—are willing to act for as well as feel for the group.

A test. The Jared Briggs experiment reported by Batson, Chang, and colleagues (2002) tested the idea that inducing empathic concern for a member of a stigmatized group not only improves attitudes toward but also increases helping of other members of the group. In that experiment, participants were given an opportunity to help addicts in a way that couldn't benefit Jared. Specifically, they could recommend how much, if any, of the Student Senate's $20,000 in community-outreach funds for the next year should be allocated to a new Addiction Counseling Service designed to help hard-drug addicts—with the understanding that any allocation to this program meant reducing the funding of one or more of the currently funded outreach programs, all of which were worthwhile and needed continued support. From listening to the interview with Jared, participants knew that he was in only the second year of his seven-year sentence and planned to leave the area when released. Thus, it was clear that he couldn't benefit from any funds allocated to the Counseling Service.

Consistent with the hypothesized empathy-valuing-attitudes-action four-step process, allocations to the Addiction Counseling Service were significantly higher in the high-empathy condition. On average, high-empathy participants allocated over $1,600 more than low-empathy participants to the Counseling Service.

But was this difference in allocations due to the hypothesized four-step process? As already mentioned, participants instructed to imagine Jared's feelings reported significantly more empathic concern for him than did participants instructed to remain objective (Step 1). Further, these high-empathy participants reported more valuing of his welfare (Step 2) and a more positive attitude toward people addicted to hard drugs (Step 3). Combining

168 • EMPATHIC CONCERN

these findings with the allocations (Step 4), we have significant predicted effects of the perspective manipulation (imagine-other vs. objective) on each of the variables in the four-step empathy-valuing-attitudes-action sequence.

Yet, to find significant effects for each step in the sequence didn't adequately test the specific causal sequence hypothesized. The hypothesized sequence specified that adopting an imagine-other perspective increased empathic concern for Jared (Path 1), which increased caring for Jared's welfare (Path 2), which increased positive attitudes toward drug addicts (Path 3), which increased recommended funding to help hard-drug addicts other than Jared (Path 4). Many other causal sequences were possible.

Batson, Chang, and colleagues (2002) tested this specific sequence and found that it was a good fit to the data. However, analyses also indicated that another path model—one which added a direct path from the perspective manipulation to attitudes toward drug addicts (i.e., the direct path noted earlier)—fit the data even better. In this five-path model, the effect of the direct path from the perspective manipulation to attitudes toward the stigmatized group was smaller than the predicted mediated effect, but it was statistically significant.

Although this best-fitting model still supported the four-step process that extended the empathy-valuing-attitude sequence to action, it also suggested an unpredicted direct effect of an imagine-other perspective on attitudes toward the stigmatized group—an effect that wasn't mediated by empathy and valuing. Apparently, not all effects of perspective taking on improved attitudes toward stigmatized groups are a result of empathic emotion. There also seem to be direct perceptual/cognitive effects.

Perceptual/Cognitive Effects of Perspective Taking

Research has indeed found direct perceptual/cognitive effects of perspective taking on attitudes. Moreover, these effects seem to differ for the two forms of perspective taking identified in Chapters 2 and 3. Imagining how a member of a stigmatized group feels about his or her situation (an imagine-other perspective) has been found to lead to situational rather than dispositional attributions for the member's difficulties, presumably because it enables one to better recognize the situational pressures that out-group members are under. Imagining oneself in the place of a member of a stigmatized group (an imagine-self perspective) has been found to reduce negative stereotyping of the group member and of the group as a whole, presumably because it enables you to better understand why out-group members feel and act the way they do. Each of these perceptual/cognitive effects has, in turn, been associated with more positive attitudes toward the group, independent of the effect mediated by empathic concern. Here's the evidence for each effect.

An Imagine-Other Perspective Increases Situational Attributions

Negative attitudes toward a stigmatized group are often associated with personal rather than situational attributions for the difficulties that group members endure—as when we say or think, "they brought it on themselves" (see Pettigrew, 1979). But research shows that adopting an imagine-other perspective toward a person in need increases situational attributions for the person's plight (e.g., Regan & Totten, 1975).

Building on these two findings, Vescio, Sechrist, and Paolucci (2003) reasoned that if research participants are induced to adopt an imagine-other perspective, this will encourage situational rather than personal explanations for an out-group member's plight—which will in turn improve attitudes toward that group. To test their reasoning, Vescio and colleagues instructed some White U.S. undergraduate research participants to adopt an imagine-other perspective while watching a video interview in which a young Black man described his experiences as a target of racial discrimination. Other participants were instructed to remain objective while watching. After watching the interview, all participants completed questionnaires assessing (a) empathic concern felt in response to the interview, (b) attributions of responsibility for the young man's situation, and (c) attitudes toward Blacks in general (using Katz & Hass's, 1988, pro-Black and anti-Black attitude scales). Compared to participants instructed to remain objective, those who adopted an imagine-other perspective reported feeling more empathic concern, attributed the young man's difficulties more to situational instead of personal factors, and reported more pro-Black attitudes. Mediation analyses indicated that empathic concern and situational attributions were separate mediators of the effect of the imagine-other perspective on more positive attitudes, with situational attributions being at least as strong a mediator as empathic feelings.

An Imagine-Self Perspective Reduces Stereotyping

The perceptual/cognitive effects on out-group attitudes of imagining oneself in the place of a member of a stigmatized group seem to be mediated primarily by increased understanding of why members of the group act as they do

170 • EMPATHIC CONCERN

("If I were treated that way, I'd act angry and suspicious too!"). Such mediation seems especially likely when information about the member's thoughts and feelings is limited.

Specifically, Galinsky and Moskowitz (2000) reasoned that when we adopt an imagine-self perspective toward a member of an out-group, "the self-concept gets activated and applied toward the target" (p. 709). This application is then generalized, leading to reduced stereotyping and more positive evaluation of other members of the out-group. To test their reasoning, Galinsky and Moskowitz showed undergraduates a photograph of an elderly man and asked them to write an essay about a day in his life. Before seeing the photo, the undergraduates were instructed either to imagine themselves in the man's place or to suppress the use of stereotypes about older adults while writing the essay—or they were given no specific instructions about how to go about writing the essay (control condition). Content of the essay, which was used to measure conscious stereotyping, revealed that both the imagine-self and the suppress-stereotypes instructions led research participants to write essays that contained significantly less stereotyping than did the essays written in the control condition. However, on a lexical decision-making task used to measure nonconscious stereotyping, the suppress-stereotypes instructions *increased* accessibility of stereotypes of the elderly, whereas neither the imagine-self instructions nor having no instructions (control) did. Overall, writing about a day in the elderly man's life after "looking at the world through his eyes and walking through the world in his shoes" (Galinsky & Moskowitz, 2000, p. 711) seemed to reduce stereotyping and lead to a more positive evaluation both of the man and of the elderly in general.

In a second experiment, Galinsky and Moskowitz found that an imagine-self perspective led undergraduates' representations of the elderly to became more similar to their representations of themselves, which were positive. Although this finding is consistent with the idea that these undergraduates activated and applied their self-concepts to the elderly, as Galinsky and Moskowitz hypothesized, it wasn't conclusive because, since the undergraduates' representations of themselves tended to be positive, the increased similarity could be an artifact of the more positive evaluation of the elderly induced by the perspective.

In a third experiment, participants who were told that they were a "dot over-estimator" subsequently gave trait ratings of both dot over-estimators and under-estimators. The trait ratings provided a generalized replication of the previous perceptual/cognitive effects of an imagine-self perspective. Participants who adopted an imagine-self perspective while writing about

Intergroup Benefits • 171

a day in the life of an under-estimator (i.e., an out-group member) tended to evaluate under-estimators more positively than did participants (a) who simply rated, or (b) who wrote about similarities between the two groups, or (c) who recalled a time when they underestimated something.

The projection process described by Galinsky and Moskowitz— participants inferring the out-group member's character from their own— implies that a more positive perception of the out-group should occur only when a participant has a positive self-concept. Consistent with this implication, Galinsky and Ku (2004) found that adopting an imagine-self perspective before writing about the elderly man's day improved evaluations of the elderly only among participants with chronically (Experiment 1) or temporarily (Experiment 2) high self-esteem.

It's important to note two features of all five of these experiments by Galinsky and colleagues. First, participants had very little information about the person into whose shoes they were asked to step. Second, the out-group of which the person was a member was always one toward which it was unlikely that participants had entrenched antipathy. Under these conditions, for participants to project their own thoughts and feelings onto the target and evaluate him as they do themselves may be natural—perhaps even necessary. However, as discussed in the next chapter, if someone has entrenched antipathy toward an out-group, or if an out-group's plight has been caused by one's own group, there may be reluctance to imagine oneself in the out-group member's shoes. And even if such imagination occurs, it may highlight differences rather than similarities between one's own response and that of the target, leading to a contrast effect, not assimilation. In such cases, inducing an imagine-self perspective may have precisely the opposite effects from those found by Galinsky and his colleagues. It may blind the imaginer to the unique needs of the out-group (think, e.g., of the Israeli-Palestinian conflict—Shnabel & Nadler, 2008).

Two Questions about These Perceptual/Cognitive Effects

The described perceptual/cognitive effects raise two questions. First, do the effects of the two types of perspective taking (imagine other; imagine self) involve two distinct psychological processes—or are the different effects (attributions, stereotypes) simply tapping distinct components of the same prejudice-reduction process? Vescio and colleagues assessed attributions. Galinsky and colleagues assessed stereotypes. Had either included measures of both attributions and stereotypes, would they have found parallel effects on each? (After all, shouldn't more situational attributions reduce stereotyping, and shouldn't reduced stereotyping increase situational attributions?) Consistent with this single-process possibility is the observation made in Chapter 3 that the two perspectives can work together—adopting an imagine-self perspective can serve as a stepping-stone to adopting an imagine-other perspective. To use an imagine-self perspective as a stepping stone seems especially likely when the perceiver has very limited information about how the out-group member thinks and feels, as was true in the research by Galinsky and colleagues (also see Todd, Bodenhausen, Richerson, & Galinsky, 2011; Todd & Burgmer, 2013; Todd & Galinsky, 2014).

Second, neither the Vescio and colleagues' nor the Galinsky and colleagues' research assessed action on behalf of the stigmatized group. Had they, would the observed perceptual/cognitive effects carry sufficient motivational force to affect behavior, as the effects mediated by empathic concern seem to do? Without behavioral measures in the studies described, this question remained unanswered. But subsequent research has supported a positive answer—that yes, the perceptual/cognitive effects can indeed affect actions as well as attitudes (see Shih, Wang, Bucher, & Stotzer, 2009; Todd, Bodenhausen, & Galinsky, 2012; Wang, Tai, Ku, & Galinsky, 2014).

Empathic Anger as a Response to Out-Group Suffering

To hear about the unfair treatment of members of a stigmatized out-group sometimes evokes feelings of empathic anger, a special case of empathic concern (see Chapter 6). Demonstrating such an effect, Finlay and Stephan (2000) had White U.S. undergraduates read a series of brief essays written by Black students attending a metropolitan college in the United States. The essays described the Black students' personal experiences as targets of discrimination—being falsely accused of wrongdoing, being denied membership in a group, being perceived as a threat, and so on. Although participants who didn't read the essays (control condition) tended to rate Whites more positively than Blacks, participants who read the essays after receiving perspective instructions (either imagine-other or imagine-self) did not. Instead, independent of which imagine perspective instructions participants received, those who read the essays about discrimination reported feeling more *anger*, *annoyance*, *hostility*, *discomfort*, and *disgust* toward Whites than did those not reading the essays. Finley and Stephan (2000) suggested that these feelings reflected anger at the unfair treatment of the Blacks writing the essays (i.e., empathic anger).

To assess possible intergroup benefits of such empathic anger, Esses and Dovidio (2002) instructed White U.S. undergraduates to focus either on their thoughts or on their feelings while watching a video clip from *True Colors*, a news documentary that showed several acts of racial discrimination against a young Black man. The thoughts-focused participants were significantly more likely to minimize or deny the discrimination than were the participants who focused on their feelings. Feelings-focused participants were more likely to report feeling *outraged, appalled,* and *indignant* while watching the clip. Following the lead of Finlay and Stephan (2000), Esses and Dovidio (2002) interpreted this anger as indignation at the injustice (again, empathic anger). Indicative of intergroup benefit, feelings-focused participants also showed greater willingness to have contact with Blacks in the future. A path analysis indicated that reported anger mediated this effect.

Subsequent work by Dovidio, ten Vergert, and colleagues (2004, Study 1) provided further evidence that anger felt in response to witnessing an out-group member suffer discrimination can also improve attitudes toward the out-group. Before watching the *True Colors* video clip, White undergraduates were instructed either to remain objective or to imagine the Black man's feelings—or they were given no specific instructions about how to watch. A significant reduction in prejudice toward Blacks was found only in the imagine-feelings condition. And once again, a mediation analysis indicated that reported feelings of anger at the injustice (*anger, annoyed, alarmed, bothered*) were responsible for this effect.

Conclusion

Empathic concern is an interpersonal emotion felt by one person for an-other in need, not an intergroup emotion. Yet empathic concern, including empathic anger, seems capable of providing important intergroup benefits—most notably, when the valuing of a stigmatized-group member's welfare for whom empathic concern is felt generalizes to other members of the group. Of course, getting people to feel empathy for a member of a stigmatized out-group poses challenges, especially when antipathy exists toward the group. In research to date, the technique most frequently and most successfully used to induce such empathy is to have potential empathizers focus on how a stigmatized group-member feels about his or her plight (an imagine-other perspective). As long as membership in the group is central to the need for which empathy is induced, the resulting valuing of the member's wel-fare seems capable of generalizing to the group as a whole, leading to more positive attitudes and action toward the group. Research supports a four-step sequence: Perspective taking leads to empathic concern for the individual member, which leads to increased valuing of him or her, which leads to a more positive attitude toward the group, which leads to more action on behalf of the group.

Research also indicates that not all intergroup benefits of perspective taking are due to this four-step sequence. There are perceptual/cognitive benefits as well. Adopting an imagine-other perspective toward a member has been found to increase situational attributions for out-group members' behavior. Adopting an imagine-self perspective has been found to reduce stereotyping. Whether these findings reflect two distinct perceptual/cognitive processes or are two different components of the same process is not at present clear. Finally, research suggests that these perceptual/cognitive effects of perspective taking can stimulate action to benefit the group, not just attitudes.

This chapter has focused on intergroup benefits of empathic concern. But, in addition to the described benefits, empathic concern also has intergroup liabilities that shouldn't be ignored. These liabilities are the focus of Chapter 11.

11 BEHAVIORAL CONSEQUENCES

INTERGROUP LIABILITIES

In the previous chapter, I noted that empathic concern is an interpersonal emotion felt for individuals in need, not for groups. I also noted that if membership in a stigmatized group is central to the individual's need for which empathy is felt, then it's possible for empathy to lead to more positive attitudes and action toward the group as a whole.

Despite this possibility, we're more likely to feel empathy for close others, for similar others, and for near rather than distant others—as pointed out in the 18th century by David Hume and Adam Smith (see Chapter 3). Because members of out-groups often lack these qualities, there should be an in-group bias in empathic concern. Without an explicit induction, we should be more likely to feel empathy for an in-group member in need than for an out-group member experiencing the same need. In recent years there has been much talk of such a bias—variously referred to as *parochial empathy*, an *empathy gap*, an *empathy deficit*, or a *failure of empathy* (Bloom, 2016; Bruneau, Cikara, & Saxe, 2015, 2017; Cikara, Bruneau, & Saxe, 2011; Schumann, Zaki, & Dweck, 2014; Zaki, 2019; Zaki & Cikara, 2015).

Evidence of In-Group Bias in Empathic Concern

Although it certainly seems plausible that there would be an in-group bias in empathy, the evidence is actually mixed.

Empathic Concern. C. Daniel Batson, Oxford University Press. © Oxford University Press 2023.
DOI: 10.1093/oso/9780197610923.003.0012

Pro

Consistent with bias, Johnson, Simmons, Jordan, MacLean, Taddei, Thomas, Dovidio, and Reed (2002) found that White undergraduates at a university in the southeastern United States reported feeling significantly more empathic concern (on a five-item index created by averaging responses to *sympathy*, *compassion*, *warmth*, *softhearted*, and *moved*) for a college sophomore guilty of stealing a $6,500 Rolex watch from a jewelry store when the thief was described as White than when he was described as Black. Also consistent, Xu, Zuo, Wang, and Han (2009) reported a study in which they placed both Caucasian and Chinese participants in an fMRI scanner and showed them a series of 3-second video clips of faces with neutral expressions. Half of the faces were Caucasian and half were Chinese. Additionally, in half the clips of each type the person's cheek was pierced with a syringe needle; in the other half, it was touched with a Q-tip. Xu and colleagues found that both Caucasian and Chinese participants had stronger neurological responses in areas associated with empathy for another's pain—the anterior cingulate cortex (significant) and inferior frontal/insula cortex (marginal)—when they saw in-group as opposed to out-group faces pierced with the needle compared to touched with the Q-tip. That is, stronger response when Caucasians saw Caucasian faces as opposed to Chinese faces pierced rather than touched and when Chinese saw Chinese faces as opposed to Caucasian faces pierced rather than touched. Although Xu and colleagues (2009) didn't measure self-reported empathy, they concluded that these neural responses reflected an in-group bias in empathy.

Avenanti, Sirigu, and Aglioti (2010) compared needle pierce versus Q-tip touch on the hand rather than the face. They found that for both White (Italian) and Black (African) participants living in Italy, higher scores on a measure of implicit racial bias (a race version of the Implicit Association Test [IAT]—Greenwald, Nozek, & Banaji, 2003) correlated positively with reduced empathic sensorimotor response to observing other-race pain (pierce of a Black or White hand, respectively) relative to observing same-race pain. Avenanti and colleagues concluded that although humans can react empathically to the pain of strangers, racial bias and stereotypes can reduce this reactivity when the strangers are members of a racial out-group. (Again, no measure of self-reported empathy was taken.)

Hein, Silani, Preuschoff, Batson, and Singer (2010) found that when male soccer fans of the local Zurich soccer team observed another participant who was also a fan of the local team (actually a confederate) endure painful electric shocks, they reported feeling significantly more empathic concern (on the six-item Empathic Concern Index) than when the other participant was a fan of a rival soccer team—an in-group empathy bias. Hein and colleagues also found that the reported empathic concern was significantly positively correlated with more activation in the left anterior insula (AI), a brain region frequently thought to be associated with empathic response to another's pain. (AI activation is most often believed to indicate feeling-as rather than feeling-for the other—e.g., Singer et al., 2004; Singer et al., 2006, but I don't think we yet know which form or forms of empathic feeling AI activation reflects—see Craig, 2009; Lamm & Singer, 2010.)

Moreover, when participants were given a chance to help the fan receiving the shocks by taking half of the shock themselves, helping the in-group fan was best predicted by (a) left-AI activation when seeing him suffer and (b) self-reported empathic concern. In contrast, *declining* to help the out-group fan was best predicted by (a) activation of the right nucleus accumbens (NAcc), a pleasure center, when seeing him suffer and (b) the negativity of their evaluation of him. The NAcc activation seemed to reflect schadenfreude (i.e., pleasure at his pain).

Overall, Hein and colleagues (2010) concluded that the more positive evaluation of the in-group fan relative to the out-group fan produced both in-group bias in empathy-related AI responses and in-group favoritism in helping. But Hein and colleagues also noted that to the degree the out-group fan was evaluated positively, as he was by some participants, his suffering elicited an empathy-related AI response instead of NAcc activation, and he was more likely to receive help despite his out-group membership. This last finding suggests that the observed empathy bias was a product of devaluing the out-group member, not of his out-group membership *per se*.

Finally, Cikara, Bruneau, Van Bavel, and Saxe (2014, Experiments 1 & 2) had groups compete online for a cash bonus. Even though group members never met or saw one another, Cikara and colleagues found less empathy and more schadenfreude for members of the competing out-group relative to members of the in-group.

Con

Three experiments conducted by Stefan Stürmer and his colleagues failed to find an in-group bias in empathy, even though these experiments have often been cited as doing so. In the first, Stürmer, Snyder, and Omoto (2005, Study 2) had heterosexual U.S. university students take part in an instant

178 · EMPATHIC CONCERN

messaging conversation via computer in which they responded to a same-sex student—ostensibly randomly assigned to be the Communicator—who explained being anxious and upset over recently learning that his or her partner had tested positive for hepatitis, meaning that the Communicator was likely infected, too. Reference to the partner as "he" or "she" made it clear that the Communicator was either heterosexual (in-group) or homosexual (out-group). Empathic concern was measured after the conversation by having participants rate how *compassionate* and *moved* they felt (embedded among other emotion adjectives). Subsequently, intention to help the Communicator was measured by how much time (from none to 60 minutes) participants were willing to spend with him or her "helping with personal issues" or "talking on the phone" (among other possible activities). Providing no evidence of an in-group empathy bias, reported empathic concern was not significantly affected by the sexual orientation of the Communicator. Nor was reported willingness to help.

Stürmer and colleagues (2005) did, however, find a significant positive correlation between reported empathy and amount of help offered the in-group Communicator but no such correlation in response to the out-group Communicator. This pattern led them to conclude that although there was no in-group bias in either empathic concern or willingness to help, there was an in-group bias in the empathy-helping relationship. Yet, I don't think this conclusion was justified because, rather than indicating in-group bias, the lack of such a relationship in the out-group condition could easily have been due to individual differences in participants' judgments about their ability to help the homosexual Communicator or about the appropriateness of offering to do so.

In a second experiment, Stürmer, Snyder, Kropp, and Siem (2006, Experiment 1) had both German and Muslim male university students in Keil, Germany, read an e-mail message from a Communicator—ostensibly another participant who was assigned to talk about a personal issue. In his message, the Communicator described being new in town and unable to find a place to live. To manipulate in-group versus out-group membership, the Communicator gave his name as "Markus," a German first name, or "Muhammed," a Muslim first name. Stürmer and colleagues (2006) then measured empathy (by averaging how much *compassion, sympathy*, and *empathic understanding* participants reported feeling after reading the e-mail message), as well as stated willingness to help if the Communicator asked.

Failing to show an in-group bias, participants didn't report feeling significantly less empathy for the out-group Communicator ("Muhammed" for

German participants, "Markus" for Muslim participants) than the in-group Communicator; nor did they report less willingness to help the out-group Communicator. But once again, there was a significant empathy-helping relationship when the Communicator was an in-group member and not when he was an out-group member. And once again, the lack of relationship in the out-group condition could have been due to individual differences in participants' judgments about their ability to help or the appropriateness of offering.

In the third experiment (Stürmer et al., 2006, Experiment 2), introductory psychology students at the University of Minnesota who were ostensibly participating in a study of factors affecting monetary investments—one factor being communication—received an e-mail message from another participant in the session (the Sender) who was either a "detailed" perceiver, as was the participant (in-group condition), or a "global" perceiver (out-group condition). The message described being upset about having lost credit cards, two concert tickets, and some cash the previous night. After reading the Sender's message, participants completed a questionnaire that included a measure of empathic concern (a five-item index created by averaging ratings of *sympathetic, compassionate, tender, softhearted,* and *moved*). Then participants received $5 to invest and were told that they could invest each dollar either for themselves or for another participant in the session, including the Sender. Helping was measured by how many dollars, if any, participants invested for the Sender. Participants were no less likely to feel empathy for or to invest for the global (out-group) Sender than the detailed (in-group) Sender. (Investment for the Sender was low in both conditions.) Once again, reported empathy was significantly positively correlated with investing for the Sender (i.e., helping) in the in-group but not the out-group condition. And yet again, it was unclear why.

Over these three experiments then, the support for an in-group bias in the empathy-helping relationship was unclear, being amenable to alternative explanations. On the other hand, the *lack* of support for an in-group bias in both reported empathic concern and helping was clear.

Who's Right?

How are we to make sense of the apparent contradiction between research supporting and research failing to support an in-group bias in empathy? The most likely conclusion is, I think, that both sets of researchers are right. Both

180 • EMPATHIC CONCERN

are right because their research focused on two different types of out-groups, each of which produces its own form of bias.

Two Sorts of Out-Groups; Two Forms of Bias

Emile Bruneau, Nicholas Dufour, and Rebecca Saxe (2012) made a useful distinction between *distant* out-groups and *conflict* out-groups. Distant out-groups can be ethnic, racial, religious, or national. They can be far away or in the same society as the in-group. The distance at issue is psychological not physical—although physical distance often contributes to psychological distance. Key is that members of the out-group share a common characteristic or characteristics that set them apart from the in-group but without posing a threat. Members of such groups are distant from us in the sense that they don't figure in our lives in any important way. We don't feel negatively toward members of a distant out-group, but unless our attention is called to them as individuals, we're not likely to feel positively either. We know little about them and the specifics of their lives. If, however, we imagine their thoughts, feelings, and how they're affected by their situation (i.e., if we adopt an imagine-other perspective toward them), we can come to care more for their welfare, as research participants cared for Julie with AIDS and homeless Harold in Chapter 10.

Conflict out-groups are different. Whether near or far, their key defining feature is that they pose threats to us and/or to things we care about—our life, our land, our security, natural resources, political power, economic prosperity, social status, and so on. We see the welfare of members of a conflict out-group as being in a zero-sum relationship with the welfare of the in-group, including our own welfare. Their wins are losses for us (and vice versa), leading us to value their welfare negatively (Chapter 4).

As examples of conflict out-groups, Bruneau, Dufour, and Saxe cited the conflicts between Indians and Pakistanis, Bosnians and Serbs, and Israelis and Palestinians. Less extreme but no less real, we can see a rival political party and its supporters—or even a rival sports team and its fans—as a conflict out-group. I said in the previous paragraph that ethnic, racial, religious, and national out-groups can be distant. Such groups can also be in conflict with "us," not just different. Whether and when they are in conflict depends on whether we see their interests and ours at odds—whether we perceive "them" as a threat. Consciously or unconsciously, we decide what and who is an in-group or out-group (of each type) for us. When groups are in conflict, both groups are likely to see the other as an out-group; this is less likely to be true for members of psychologically distant groups.

Looking back at the three Stürmer and colleagues' experiments that failed to find evidence of an in-group empathy bias, each seems to have presented participants with a member of a distant out-group—a gay person for heterosexual undergraduates, a Muslim student for German university students (and the reverse), a global perceiver for detailed perceivers. The out-group member likely posed no threat or source of conflict for most if not all participants. And in each case, information was provided about how the person in need thought and felt about his or her need. Under these circumstances, no in-group empathy bias was found. Empathic concern was as likely to be reported for an out-group member as an in-group member with the same need.

Turning to the five experiments providing evidence of in-group bias, the out-groups seemed to be a mixture. Two of the experiments involved conflict out-groups, one involved distant out-groups, and two involved a mix:

(a) The Hein and colleagues (2010) and Cikara and colleagues (2014) experiments each involved clear conflict. In the former, the out-group member was a fan of a rival soccer team; in the latter, out-group members were on a team with which the participant's team was competing for a cash bonus. In each of these experiments, empathic concern was higher for in-group than for out-group members. Moreover, each found evidence of schadenfreude in response to out-group members' suffering, which suggested not simply an absence of positive valuing of the out-group members' welfare but the presence of negative valuing—at least among most participants.

(b) In contrast, the Chinese and Caucasian out-group targets used by Xu and colleagues (2009) seemed distant but not in conflict with the Caucasian and Chinese participants, respectively. When seeing in-group targets (with neutral expressions) get their cheek pierced without having any information about how the targets felt, participants may have resorted to imagining how they themselves would feel if their cheek were pierced and concluded that, because they would feel pain, so would the in-group target. When seeing out-group targets pierced, participants may have been less confident that those targets would feel as they did.

(c) Suggesting a mix of distance and conflict effects, Avenanti and colleagues (2010) found reduced physiological resonance in both White participants (Italians) and Black participants (Africans living in Italy) when observing a needle pierce the skin of out-group hands (black and white, respectively)

182 • EMPATHIC CONCERN

relative to the resonance found when observing a needle pierce of in-group hands (white and black, respectively). Paralleling the Xu and colleagues results, this in-group bias could have been due at least in part to cultural distance and unfamiliarity. Anenanti and colleagues, however, also found that in-group bias was greater among individuals who exhibited stronger implicit preference for the in-group on a race IAT. These individuals likely perceived the out-group to be more of a threat and source of conflict with the in-group. Similarly, in the Johnson and colleagues (2002) experiment, both distance and conflict likely contributed to the racial in-group bias shown by undergraduates at a university in the southeastern United States (also see Gutsell & Inzlicht, 2010).

Of course, all my interpretations here are post hoc and based on surmise.

A Direct Test of Empathy for Members of Distant and Conflict Out-Groups

Fortunately, Bruneau and colleagues (2012) conducted an experiment to provide a clearer comparison of empathic concern felt for members of distant and conflict out-groups. They had Jewish Israeli, Arab, and South American adult immigrants or visitors to the United States (all fluent in English) read a series of 84 brief stories while lying in an fMRI scanner. Each story described an experience of an individual (the protagonist).

Of the 84 stories, 36 involved experiences of physical pain (e.g., breaking a leg, receiving a bad burn, taking a fall); another 36 involved emotional suffering (e.g., social rejection, becoming homeless, losing one's job); and 12 involved a neutral event with no pain or suffering. Both the physical pain and emotional suffering stories were divided into three sets of 12, which were matched on vividness, familiarity, amount of pain/suffering, and average length. Within these six sets (three physical pain, three emotional suffering), the name of the protagonist and the setting of each story made it clear the protagonist was either Israeli, Arab, or South American. For a seventh set, comprised of the 12 neutral stories, all protagonists were South American. The seven sets produced a 2 (type of need: physical pain, emotional suffering) x 3 (group membership: Israeli, Arab, South American) repeated measures experimental design with a neutral control condition. Table 11.1 shows four stories as examples—one physical pain story, two emotional suffering stories, and one no-pain story (control).

Table 11.1 Examples of Stories of Pain or Suffering Used by Bruneau and Colleagues (2012)

South American/Physical Pain. Viviana lives in a city in Brazil, but works more in rural areas. Viviana was walking with some gifts to her car. She tripped over the curb and turned to avoid crushing the presents. Viviana landed on the curb with her mouth, breaking her two front teeth in half. Viviana dropped the presents and held her bleeding mouth.[a]

Israeli/Emotional Suffering. Moshe moved from the United States to Israel; his father says it is to support the Jewish homeland. At school, Moshe was happy that some of the boys had offered him some candy. When Moshe put some in his mouth, the boys laughed and said that they had peed on the candy. All the other children started laughing and pointing at Moshe.[a]

Arab/Emotional Suffering. Khalil recently began working for the Hamas government in Gaza. Khalil had worked hard to get the job he has now. He can finally take care of his son and has almost saved enough to give him the gifts he wants for his birthday. Today, Khalil was called in to the office and his boss told him that he was fired.[a]

South American/No Pain or Suffering (Control). Maria moved recently to Argentina from Peru. Maria has a young son who loves trains. She takes him to watch them roll by for hours. One day, after preparing a snack near the train tracks, a train whistled in the distance and her son jumped up on top of a hill with a sandwich to watch it.[b]

[a]From Bruneau et al. (2012, Table 2).
[b]From Bruneau et al. (2012, Supplementary Material).

In the scanner, participants read the stories in six trials. A trial consisted of 14 stories, two from each of the seven experimental conditions. (The order of story presentation was counterbalanced across trials and between participants.) Each story was presented for 24 seconds with a variable interval between stories. In the final four seconds of presentation, a prompt appeared below the story that asked the participant to indicate, "How much compassion do you feel?" ($1 = none$, $2 = moderate$, $3 = a lot$, $4 = extreme$). Responses on this four-point scale, averaged across the 12 stories in each experimental condition for the participants in each group, provided the measure of self-reported empathic concern.

Once back outside the scanner, each participant performed an Arab-Israeli Implicit Association Test (IAT) in which Arab-Muslim names were

184 • EMPATHIC CONCERN

paired with good words as quickly as possible and Jewish-Israeli names with bad words, and the reverse.

With Needs Clear, No In-Group Bias Toward Distant Out-Groups

Bruneau and colleagues (2012) reasoned that both Israelis and Arabs would see South Americans as a relatively pure distant out-group, a source of neither threat nor conflict—and that South Americans would see both Israelis and Arabs as relatively pure distant out-groups. Accordingly, Bruneau and colleagues predicted no in-group bias in empathy on the part of either Israelis or Arabs toward South Americans—and no in-group bias in empathy on the part of South Americans toward either Israelis or Arabs. They made these predictions because the need (or lack of need) of the protagonist in each story was salient and easily understood, which should eliminate any perception-of-need bias caused by distance.

Results supported these predictions. First, South American participants reported feeling significantly more compassion for the South American protagonists who experienced physical pain or emotional suffering than for South American protagonists who had neutral experiences, providing evidence of empathy for in-group members in need—as had much previous research (see Chapter 7). More importantly, Israeli and Arab participants also reported feeling significantly more compassion for the South American protagonists who experienced physical pain or emotional suffering than the ones who had neutral experiences, providing evidence of empathic concern for distant out-group members in need. Ratings of South American pain and suffering by both Israeli and Arab participants weren't significantly lower than the ratings by South American participants. Moreover, Israeli and Arab participants didn't report significantly lower compassion for South American pain or suffering than they did for the pain or suffering of protagonists from their own group (Israelis and Arabs, respectively). Similarly, South American participants didn't report significantly lower compassion for either Israeli or Arab pain or suffering than they did for the pain or suffering of South American protagonists. With the protagonists' needs clear, none of the participant groups showed evidence of in-group bias in empathic concern when responding to the needs of members of a distant out-group.

Intergroup Liabilities · 185

Evidence of In-Group Bias Toward Conflict Out-Groups

But there was clear evidence of an in-group empathy bias in response to the needs of members of conflict out-groups. This possibility was tested by comparing Israeli participants' reported compassion for Arab protagonists to their compassion for Israeli protagonists—and comparing Arab participants' reported compassion for Israeli protagonists to their compassion for Arab protagonists. Both for stories involving physical pain and stories involving emotional suffering, Israeli and Arab participants reported significantly less compassion for protagonists from the opposition group than for those from the in-group. Both Israeli and Arab participants also showed a significant in-group bias in their explicit attitudes (assessed by ratings of warmth felt toward each group completed prior to the experiment) and in their implicit attitudes (assessed by the Arab-Israeli IAT). These explicit and implicit attitude measures were highly correlated.

Neuroimaging Results

Neuroimaging scans indicated that participants thought more about in-group protagonists' internal states than about distant out-group protagonists' states. But when Israeli and Arab participants read about protagonists from the conflict out-group (Arabs and Israelis, respectively), both cognitive and affective neural responses were robust and high, much as they were when reading about in-group protagonists. Given that both Israeli and Arab participants reported less compassion for and more negative attitudes toward conflict out-group protagonists than in-group protagonists, it seems likely that even though misfortunes of members of both groups provoked considerable thought and affect, the nature of the thought and affect was quite different for the two groups.

Implications

In sum, the distant versus conflict distinction seems an important one for understanding in-group bias in empathy. Distance can reduce the likelihood of recognizing or having confidence in one's ability to effectively address the needs of members of an out-group. But if the needs are made salient and clear, people seem as ready to feel empathic concern for members of a distant out-group as they feel for members of their in-group. Not so for members of a conflict out-group. For them, even when the need is salient and clear, empathic concern is likely to be stifled. Due to the out-group antipathy that conflict engenders, empathic concern is apt to be replaced by pleasure at a conflict out-group member's distress—schadenfreude.

Sense can be made of this rather complicated pattern of results by looking back at the necessary conditions for feeling empathic concern described in Chapter 4. The welfare of members of distant out-groups isn't valued negatively, but also not especially positively. As a result, we're not vigilant about these out-group members' welfare. And, given that their needs are remote and don't demand our attention, we're unlikely to perceive their needs—at least unlikely to perceive them with sensitivity. Even if we know they're in need, we don't really care. Yet, if we're led to actively imagine how a distant out-group member in need is affected by his or her plight (i.e., if we're led to adopt an imagine-other perspective), the valuing-of-welfare path is activated. We come to care and to feel empathic concern, as depicted in Figure 4.2.

In contrast, the welfare of members of a conflict out-group is likely to be valued negatively. We pay attention to these members' triumphs and travails because their fate has implications for us and our in-group. But far from feeling empathic concern for conflict out-group members when they suffer, we're more apt to feel pleasure. And if we're induced to adopt an imagine-other perspective, imagining how they're thinking and feeling, that may intensify our pleasure.

Two Further Liabilities in Conflict Situations

In-Group Empathy Can Increase Out-Group Harm

Bruneau, Cikara, and Saxe (2017) reported three studies indicating that increased in-group empathy can increase harm to and/or reduce help for conflict out-group members (also see Lickel, Miller, Stenstrom, Denson, & Schmader, 2006):

Study 1: Americans' help for Arabs. The procedure for their first study was adapted from Cikara and colleagues (2014). American participants from an online sample were told they were members of an English-speaking team, whose language read from left to right (the in-group), and that their team was competing in "directional problem-solving" against an Arabic-speaking team, whose language read from right to left (the conflict out-group). Prior to the competition, participants read brief one-sentence descriptions of some event in the life of each of eight English-speaking-team members and eight Arab-speaking-team members. For members of each team, half of the events were positive, and half were negative. To illustrate, here are four of the events:

Bill recovered from an illness.
Hadia made it home safe after a long journey.
Jane tripped down the stairs and hurt herself.
Ahmad came down with a serious illness. (Adapted from Bruneau et al.,
2017, Supplemental Materials)

To make in-group/out-group membership clear, each computer screen showing an event description included the member's language (English, Arabic) and place of origin (U.S. state, Arab country). After reading each description, participants rated how good and how bad it made them feel that the event had happened to the person named.

In-group empathy was assessed by averaging how good participants felt about a positive event that happened to an in-group member and how badly they felt about a negative event that happened to an in-group member. Out-group empathy was assessed in the same way for events that happened to out-group members. Parochial empathy (i.e., in-group empathy bias) was measured by subtracting out-group empathy from in-group empathy.

Neither in-group empathy nor out-group empathy was significantly correlated with a measure of out-group helping taken right after reading and reacting to the event descriptions. But both in-group and out-group empathy were significantly correlated (in-group negatively; out-group positively) with two out-group helping measures taken on a follow-up online survey that participants completed a week later. Further, consistent with previous research, there was a significant in-group empathy bias—more in-group empathy than out-group empathy—and bias scores correlated significantly negatively with all three out-group helping measures.

Study 2: Hungarians help for Muslim refugees. Bruneau and colleagues' (2017) second study focused on a conflict between Hungarian citizens and Muslim immigrants. Early in 2012, the Hungarian government started an anti-immigration campaign using billboards and statements by Hungarian leaders expressing opposition to the large number of Muslim refugees arriving from the Middle East. Bruneau and colleagues arranged for a survey to be completed by a representative sample of Hungarian citizens in November 2015. The survey included measures of in-group (Hungarian) and out-group (refugee) empathy, dispositional empathy, support for antirefugee policies, readiness to grant asylum to refugees, and willingness to sign a petition in support of refugee aid.

In-group and out-group empathy were assessed by asking survey participants to indicate how much empathy they felt (from "none at all" to "a lot") for individuals suffering eight different misfortunes. The misfortunes were presented in two sets of four each. For one set, the suffering individuals were said to be Hungarians; for the other set, refugees. (The misfortunes in each set and the order of sets were counter-balanced across participants.) To illustrate, some participants might be asked to indicate how much empathy they felt for Hungarians in the following situations:

> Parents whose children don't do well in school.
> Parents who cannot buy their children the gift that they want for their birthday.
> Teenagers who get pregnant accidentally.
> Adults who are not able to find a job despite their qualifications.

Then asked how much empathy they felt for refugees in the following situations:

> Children who are bullied at school.
> Grandparents who want and do not have any grandchildren.
> Adults who become addicted to drugs.
> Adults who work for many hours but still their salary is very low.
> (Bruneau et al., 2017, Supplemental Materials)

Other participants might be asked how much empathy they felt for refugees in the first four situations and Hungarians in the last four.

Responses to the four items in the Hungarian set were averaged to provide a measure of in-group empathy, and responses to the items in the refugee set were averaged to provide a measure of out-group empathy. Subtracting the latter measure from the former provided the measure of in-group empathy bias. Dispositional empathy was also measured, using a Hungarian version of the Empathic Concern scale from Mark Davis's Interpersonal Reactivity Index (Davis, 1983).

Even controlling for dispositional empathy, in-group empathy was significantly positively correlated with support for anti-Muslim policies and significantly negatively correlated with readiness to grant asylum to refugees and to sign a petition in support of refugee aid. Thus, for each of the three outcome measures, in-group empathic concern predicted less pro-refugee attitude or action. In-group empathy bias predicted the same. In contrast, for each measure out-group empathy predicted more pro-refugee attitude and action.

Finally, dispositional empathy was significantly positively correlated with both in-group and out-group empathy, as well as with in-group empathy bias.

Study 3: Greeks' help for Germans. Bruneau and colleagues' third study surveyed Greeks—the in-group—in late September 2015 about willingness to help Germany—the out-group. (September 2015 wasn't long after the European Union, and particularly Germany, rejected the Greek appeal for debt relief, a decision that led to harsh austerity measures in Greece and to strong anti-German sentiment.) Except for changing the in-group to Greeks and the out-group to Germans, the measures of in-group empathy, out-group empathy, in-group empathy bias, and dispositional empathy were all the same as in Study 2.

Results of Study 3 provided a generalized replication of the Study 2 results. Again controlling for dispositional empathy, in-group empathy and in-group bias correlated significantly negatively with support for using Greek resources to save German lives by thwarting a (hypothetical) planned terror attack in Germany. In-group empathy and empathy bias correlated significantly positively with endorsement of the following six statements that advocated not helping, or enjoying suffering by, Germans or Germany:

> I would consider refusing service to a German customer.
> What Germany is doing needs to be remembered—if they are in trouble in 100 years, Greece should block any moves to relieve their suffering.
> If Germany were to have a natural disaster, I think Greece should withhold financial support.
> I would support closing the German Institute (Goethe) in Greece.
> I would be happy if a hacker was able to cripple Germany's financial system for a while.
> I would be happy if a cyberattack accessed and publicly revealed embarrassing personal e-mails from Angela Merkel [Chancellor of Germany at the time]. (Bruneau et al., 2017, Supplemental Materials)

Out-group empathy correlated significantly in the opposite direction for each of these measures. Dispositional empathy again correlated significantly positively with both in-group and out-group empathy, but this time, its correlation with in-group bias wasn't significant.

Implications. In sum, each of these three studies provided evidence that when groups are in conflict, in-group empathy can reduce out-group help and/or increase out-group harm. Before leaving this topic, let me suggest a further possibility. Imagine that two distant out-groups are in conflict (as, for example, Israelis and Palestinians were for the South American participants in the Bruneau et al., 2012, experiment). Further, imagine that a member of the in-group (e.g., a South American participant) is induced to feel empathic concern for members of one of the distant out-groups. Just as empathy felt for in-group members can lead a person to harm members of a conflict out-group, it seems likely that empathy felt for members of one of the distant out-groups would increase willingness to harm members of the other distant out-group. If so, we have another possible intergroup liability of empathy.

Dehumanization of Conflict Out-Group Members

How is it possible not to feel empathic concern for other human beings who are suffering, even members of a conflict out-group? The answer given by many researchers studying intergroup conflict is *dehumanization*—it's possible if you think of the out-group sufferers not as human like you and me but instead as dangerous and/or disgusting creatures (see, for example, Bandura, 1999; Bruneau, Jacoby, Kteily, & Saxe, 2018; Haslam, 2006; Kelman, 1973; Kteily & Bruneau, 2017; Kteily, Bruneau, Waytz, & Cotterill, 2015; and Opotow, 1990). Inciting members of one's in-group to dehumanize and denigrate members of a conflict out-group has long been used by those seeking to fan the flames of out-group antipathy to the point of genocide. For example, the Rwandan government's sponsorship of hate radio broadcasts portraying Tutsis as *Invenze* (cockroaches) was widely considered responsible for inciting non-militant Hutu peasants to pick up their machetes and join the slaughter of Tutsis (Berkeley, 1994). In other conflicts, members of the out-group have variously been called "barbaric," "beasts," "animals," "apes," "monkeys," "swine," "cattle," "vermin," "rats," and "lice."

Such dehumanization can turn the negative-value→low-empathy/ schadenfreude→harm sequence described earlier into an escalating spiral. Dehumanization provides justification for the harm, which in turn provides the basis for further devaluing and failing to perceive need as need, thereby activating the sequence once more: What are cockroaches worth? Why pay attention to their needs? Don't feel for them; exterminate!

Although much research points to a positive relationship between dehumanization and harm, research testing the role that lack of empathic concern plays in this relationship is, thus far, limited. But there is some. Bruneau and Kteily (2017) reported that Palestinians' in-group empathy bias against Israelis was moderately (and significantly) positively correlated with a measure of dehumanization of Israelis. Andrighetto, Baldissarri, Lattanzio,

Loughnan, and Volpato (2014) examined the effect of Italian undergraduates' dehumanization of Haitians (seeing them as animalistic and backward) on the undergraduates' willingness to help earthquake victims in Haiti, and, in a second experimental condition, the effect of dehumanization of Japanese (seeing them as mechanistic, cold, and analytic) on willingness to help earthquake victims in Japan. In each case, participants expressing more dehumanization of the out-group were less willing to help. Importantly, Andrighetto and colleagues also measured empathic feelings of being *touched* and *moved* by the earthquake victims' plight and found that, for each out-group, lower empathy mediated the effect of dehumanization on reduced helping—more dehumanization led to less empathy, which in turn led to less helping.

Unfortunately, a time-of-measure confound in the Andrighetto and colleagues experiment clouded interpretation of its results. Dehumanization was measured a week before empathy and helping, which were measured in a single session. The proximity of the empathy and helping measures may have inflated the empathy-helping correlations relative to the dehumanization-helping correlations, producing a spurious appearance of mediation. Given this confound, we need further tests of the idea that dehumanization promotes an escalating spiral of out-group negative-valuing→low-empathy/schadenfreude→harm→dehumanization, and so on.

Conclusion

Empathic concern's most serious liability for intergroup relations is its in-group bias—the likelihood of feeling more empathy for an in-group member in need than for an out-group member experiencing the same need. But there seem to be two sources of in-group bias, each of which applies to a different type of out-group. For members of groups that are psychologically distant from us—that have no direct impact on our lives or welfare—we're less likely to recognize and appreciate their needs and less likely to value their welfare. If, however, we're induced to adopt their perspective and actively imagine how they're affected by the needs, we can recognize and care about their plight—and feel for them much as we do for in-group members in need. (Of course, as noted in Chapter 9, even if we feel for them, distance may lead us to misperceive their need, inadvertently producing more harm than help.)

The effect of in-group bias is more dire for members of conflict out-groups. We may recognize their needs but feel the opposite of empathic concern. Because their welfare and ours are at odds, we're likely to negatively value theirs. As a result, rather than empathy, we're likely to feel schadenfreude when they suffer, and to intentionally harm not help.

Empathic concern can produce two more liabilities for members of conflict out-groups. First, feeling empathy for in-group members in need can, at times, reduce out-group help and/or increase out-group harm, especially if the out-group is seen as responsible for in-group members' needs. Extending this idea, a parallel effect may occur when two distant out-groups are in conflict with each other. To be induced to feel for members of one of the groups may increase the tendency to harm members of the other. Insofar as I know, this possibility awaits a test.

Second, dehumanization of members of a conflict out-group may turn the negative-value→low-empathy/schadenfreude→harm sequence into an escalating spiral. To see members of the out-group as idiots, beasts, swine, vermin, and so on, both justifies allowing them to suffer and intensifies the negative value we place on their welfare. The intensified negative value, in turn, leads to less empathic concern and more schadenfreude, harm, and dehumanization, further intensifying negative value. How to break this spiral is one of the major challenges facing conflict-resolution efforts today.

12 REALIZING THE POTENTIAL OF EMPATHIC CONCERN

Empathy is integral to solving conflict in the family, schoolyard, boardroom, and war room. [It's] the best peace pill we have.

—MARY GORDON *(2005, pp. xvi–xvii)*

When Noa [a Jewish student] spoke about her father's feelings of not being at home in Israel, I could identify with that feeling. For the first time I felt that Jews are not only enemies, but have similar feelings to those I have.

—PALESTINIAN STUDENT *in Jewish-Palestinian workshop at Ben Gurion University, 2000–2001 (Bar-On & Kassem, 2004, p. 300).*

The object of these sketches is to awaken sympathy and feeling for the African race, as they exist among us; to show their wrongs and sorrows, under a system so necessarily cruel and unjust.

—HARRIET BEECHER STOWE, *Uncle Tom's Cabin (1852/2005, p. 1)*

What role can empathic concern play in moving us toward more positive relations with others, especially others who differ from us? To illustrate its potential, let me describe some of the better-known strategies in which empathy has been used to improve interpersonal and intergroup relations.

The strategies fall into four broad classes—efforts designed to address interpersonal, interracial, and interethnic tensions in educational settings, those designed to address protracted political conflicts, those that employ media (books, plays, movies, television, radio), and those that orchestrate empathy-induced altruism with moral motivation. Three of the empathy states discussed in Chapter 3 most frequently appear in these strategies: (a) imagining how the other is thinking and feeling (i.e., an imagine-other perspective); (b) understanding the

---

Empathic Concern. C. Daniel Batson, Oxford University Press. © Oxford University Press 2023.
DOI: 10.1093/oso/9780197610923.003.0013

194 • EMPATHIC CONCERN

other's thoughts and feelings; and (c) feeling for the other (empathic concern). Two other states sometimes appear but seem more ancillary: (d) imagining how you would think and feel in the other's situation (i.e., an imagine-self perspective) and (e) feeling as the other feels. In addition to describing empathy's role in each strategy, I'll report program-evaluation results when available.

At the outset, two points should be emphasized. First, this collection of strategies is far from exhaustive; it simply provides examples of approaches that have been used. Second, even though they say empathy is an important factor, the people employing a given strategy haven't always been precise about the role that various empathy states play. I'll try to specify empathy's role more precisely. By doing so, I hope that future program development and evaluation may be better able to take advantage of what's known about the various empathy states discussed in Chapter 3, including how they relate to one another and to behavior.

Addressing Interpersonal and Intergroup Relations in Educational Settings

I'll profile four strategies used to improve interactions among students in educational settings, starting with a program designed for primary-school children and ending with ones for university students. Some of these strategies involve a one-time intervention; others last a semester or more.

Roots of Empathy

The Roots of Empathy program developed by Mary Gordon (2005) was first implemented in primary-school classrooms (kindergarten through Grade 8) in Canada and has spread to over 10 other countries. The program is explicitly designed to develop empathy, including imagine-other perspective taking and "emotional literacy" (the ability to "find the humanity in one another"). The aim is to increase collaboration and civility and to reduce aggression and bullying (Gordon, 2005, p. 8). Gordon thought such empathy was key to overcoming intergroup conflict at all levels:

> The Roots of Empathy classroom is creating citizens of the world— children who are developing empathic ethics and a sense of social responsibility that takes the position that we all share the same lifeboat.

These are the children who will build a more caring, peaceful and civil society, child by child. (2005, pp. xvii)

At the core of the Roots of Empathy approach are nine visits to the classroom—one every three weeks—by a mother (or father, sometimes both) and infant from the community. Pupils ring a green blanket on which the parent sits with the baby. They observe the infant and its interaction with the parent, interact with the baby themselves, and ask the parent questions about what the child has learned since the last visit. The idea is that "the relationship between the parent and child is a template for positive, empathic human relationships" (Gordon, 2005, p. 6). It's assumed that observing the baby's development and the parent-infant interaction will encourage perspective taking and valuing of the infant's welfare, which will generalize to the children's relations with their peers. Using interaction with a baby to promote empathy in this way is quite congruent with the idea that the biological substrate for empathic concern lies in parental nurturance and tenderness toward offspring, which can be generalized (see Chapter 5).

A trained Roots of Empathy instructor guides the family visits and meets with the class before and after each visit. The instructor provides basic information about infant development, helps pupils imagine what the baby is thinking and feeling, and encourages them to extend this perspective taking to themselves and to peers. When a Roots of Empathy classroom is racially or ethnically diverse, parents and infants from the various groups represented in the class are recruited, providing a basis for intergroup perspective taking and empathic concern.

Empathy states involved in the Roots of Empathy program are (a) imagine-other perspective taking (at times, imagine-self perspective taking serves as a stepping-stone); (b) increased understanding of others' thoughts and feelings (including the infant's, the parent's, and peers'); and (c) empathic concern—feeling for infant, parent, and peers.

Several evaluation projects designed to assess the program's effectiveness suggest that Roots of Empathy increases children's emotional development, perspective-taking skills, and prosocial behavior, as well as reduces aggression (see, for example, Schonert-Reichl, Smith, Zaidman-Zait, & Hertzman, 2012; for an overview of evaluation projects from 2001 to 2018, see https://us.rootsofempathy.org/research/). Children who have experienced a Roots of Empathy classroom are rated by both teachers and peers as more advanced in emotional and social understanding compared to children who have not.

Cooperative Learning

Cooperative learning departs from the individual learning prevalent in most primary and secondary schools, focusing instead on learning by the exchange of information between students organized in small groups. The immediate goal is to reduce competition by making each student's learning dependent on every other member of the group. Thereby, cooperative learning seeks to improve interpersonal relations among students, especially among students from different racial and ethnic groups.

Perhaps the best-known example of using cooperative learning to improve interpersonal and intergroup relations is the *Jigsaw Classroom*, which Elliot Aronson and his colleagues developed in the early 1970s to try to overcome tension and animosity in recently desegregated schools in Austin, Texas (Aronson, 2004; Aronson, Blaney, Stephan, Sikes, & Snapp, 1978; Aronson & Patnoe, 1997). In a jigsaw classroom, students spend part of their school day in racially/ethnically mixed groups (ideally, five to six students per group). Each group is given a learning task. Before the group convenes, every member of the group becomes "expert" on one, but only one, part of the information the group needs to complete the task. As a result, every person in the group must rely on the contribution of every other person to succeed. After about eight weeks, the groups are dissolved, new groups are formed, and each student must learn to work effectively with four to five more students in a new racially/ethnically mixed group. After another eight weeks, groups are formed again, and so on.

Aronson and colleagues (1978) reported that liking for fellow group members increased as a result of the jigsaw experience—as did helping. Unfortunately, Aronson and colleagues (1978) didn't report the effect specifically on interracial liking and helping. In an earlier study, however, Weigel, Wiser, and Cook (1975) did—they reported the effects of interdependent, ethnically mixed (European-, African-, and Mexican-American) student work groups on liking, conflict, and helping across ethnic lines. Results of that study indicated that working together in interdependent groups significantly increased both cross-ethnic liking and helping behavior; it also reduced cross-ethnic conflict. (For further evidence of effectiveness, see Aronson & Patnoe, 1997; Johnson & Johnson, 1987—but also note that Bratt, 2008, reported only limited positive results of a jigsaw method on intergroup attitudes in Norway, suggesting that there may be cultural or other situational limits on positive effects.)

Why does cooperative interaction in jigsaw groups increase liking and helping and reduce conflict? Such groups involve both personalizing contact and superordinate goals, which should lead to increased imagine-other perspective taking (again, imagine-self perspective taking may serve as a stepping-stone) and, thereby, to increased understanding and valuing of out-group members' welfare as well as to out-group friendships and increased empathic concern. Supporting these expectations, Aronson and colleagues (1978) reported that imagine-other perspective taking—which they called empathy—was "one of the crucial mechanisms underlying the effects" (p. 118—also see Aronson & Bridgeman, 1979).

Importantly, perspective-taking abilities learned in the jigsaw groups seem to generalize. Diane Bridgeman (1981), in dissertation research under Aronson's direction, found that students from a jigsaw classroom performed better on a perspective-taking task than did students from a traditional classroom. The task tested students' ability to adopt the perspective of characters in brief stories and to see the story situation from the character's rather than their own point of view. Research also indicates that cooperative learning in racially or ethnically mixed groups, as in a jigsaw classroom, increases cross-group friendships, especially close friendships (see Paluck & Green, 2009, for a review). These effects suggest that the imagine-other perspective taking induces out-group empathic concern. It may also increase situational attributions for out-group behavior (see Chapter 10).

Writing in the wake of the tragic shooting at Columbine High School in Littleton, Colorado, in April 1999, Aronson (2004) affirmed:

> I believe that, if the jigsaw method had been widely used in Littleton, the Columbine massacre might never have occurred, and those 15 people would still be alive. Admittedly, that is a bold statement—one not usually made by academicians. And, of course, it can never be proved. But I have a high degree of confidence because 31 years of research on the jigsaw method have made it undeniably clear: The jigsaw process builds empathy, and students in jigsaw classrooms are more open to one another, more compassionate, and more tolerant of diversity than students in traditional classrooms. (p. 486)

Discrimination Simulations

Exercises designed to simulate the experience of being a target of discrimination have been used in a variety of educational situations—from primary-school classrooms to universities. Perhaps best known is the "Blue Eyes-Brown Eyes" simulation that Jane Elliott developed for use in her classroom in a predominately White rural primary school in Iowa (Peters, 1987). In this simulation, which usually lasts three to six hours, members of one group (typically, blue-eyed individuals) are subjected to discrimination by being excluded from conversations, and deprived of seats, convenient restrooms, and other privileges—and in university settings, being subjected to ridicule. Members of the other group (non-blue-eyed individuals) are given privileges and (in university settings) encouraged to join in the ridicule. Sometimes, the roles are then reversed so that students in each group experience being discriminated against and being privileged. In discussion following the discrimination, members of each group have a chance to express and reflect on how they felt and acted. The goal is to help participants understand the consequences of discrimination—both the feelings it evokes and the behaviors—and thereby to improve attitudes toward its targets.

Positive effects of the Blue Eyes-Brown Eyes simulation have frequently been interpreted as being a result of increased empathy (e.g., Byrnes & Kiger, 1990; Weiner & Wright, 1973). What empathy states are involved? Those who experience the discrimination may feel similar emotions to those felt by the victims of discrimination in society, which may encourage them to imagine how they would feel were they targets of discrimination outside the simulation. This imagine-self experience may, in turn, lead them to imagine and better understand how the targets of discrimination in society feel and act, and, thereby, to have more positive feelings toward them, including feelings of empathic concern. Presumably, this was Elliott's original goal when she developed the simulation to teach her students about prejudice and discrimination after the assassination of Martin Luther King, Jr.

Evidence on the effectiveness of the Blue Eyes-Brown Eyes simulation is generally supportive but not straightforward. Weiner and Wright (1973) found that among third graders in North Carolina, those undergoing an Orange People-Green People simulation (closely modeled on Elliott's original) were more likely than children from a no-simulation comparison class to (a) express less-prejudiced beliefs about Black children and (b) want a picnic with a group of Black children both on the day after the simulation and two weeks later. Weiner and Wright noted, however, that demand characteristics may have played a role in producing these results. Byrnes and Kiger (1990) reported moderate effects of a Blue Eyes-Brown Eyes simulation on racial attitudes among university teacher-education students but no reliable effect on a racial social-distance measure. Once again, demand was a concern.

Stewart, LaDuke, Bracht, Sweet, and Gamarel (2003) reported significantly more positive attitudes toward Asian Americans and Hispanic Americans, and marginally more positive attitudes toward African Americans, among students at a liberal college in the northeastern United States. But in this college-student population, attitudes toward each out-group were strongly positive even among students not taking part in the simulation, clouding interpretation. Both Byrnes and Kiger (1990) and Stewart and colleagues (2003) also noted that their participants and leaders found the simulation experience, which in each case involved ridicule, stressful.

Intergroup-Dialogue Classes

Building on a model developed around 1990 at the University of Michigan, intergroup-dialogue classes have been introduced at a number of universities across the United States (see Zúñiga, Nagada, & Sevig, 2002, for a review). The goal of these classes (typically a semester-long undergraduate course) is to improve student relations across racial, ethnic, religious, and other divides. Students (usually 10-20), drawn in equal numbers from two groups with a history of conflict (e.g., Blacks and Whites), are first taught general dialogue norms and communication skills, then share their experiences relevant to the intergroup difference and conflict, discuss substantive issues of identity and social justice, and, finally, consider actionable steps in their own lives to improve intergroup relations. The dialogue facilitators are often trained students who have previously gone through the class themselves (Stephan & Stephan, 2001).

Most obviously, these classes provide personalized contact with members of the other group. The frank sharing of personal experiences, coupled with norms to understand one another and to respect differences, (a) leads to both hearing and being heard, (b) provides better awareness of out-group needs, and (c) encourages imagine-other perspective taking. These conditions should, in turn, produce more empathic concern (including possible feelings of empathic anger—see Chapters 6 and 10), leading to more positive attitudes toward out-group members and a desire to see discrimination eliminated:

> It is believed that participants benefit from an opportunity to express deeply felt emotions and opinions regarding central issues of contention between groups and that the members of the other group need to hear these concerns expressed in an open and honest way. In the

200 · EMPATHIC CONCERN

process, people come to value the opinions and welfare of people who differ from them.... (Stephan & Stephan, 2001)

An evaluation of the University of Michigan program conducted by Gurin, Peng, Lopez, and Nagada (1999) measured students' attitudes three years after they took part in an intergroup-dialogue class (pretest-posttest design with a matched comparison group). This evaluation revealed that White students who participated in the program perceived greater commonality of interests and values with students of color and more frequently supported affirmative action than did Whites who didn't participate. Highly group-identified students of color showed similar changes in attitudes toward Whites. In addition, students of color who participated in the program reported more positive interactions with Whites compared to students of color who didn't participate. Thus, the program appeared to produce long-term positive effects.

Addressing Protracted Political Conflicts

Understanding how those on the other side of a protracted political conflict are thinking and feeling is a key component of programs developed to improve relations among those on opposite sides of such conflicts. To that end, participants from both sides are brought together and encouraged to speak honestly and openly and to listen to one another's concerns (Kelman, 1990, 1997; Malhotra & Liyange, 2005; Shnabel & Nadler, 2008; Stephan & Findlay, 1999). Frequently, imagine-other perspective taking is encouraged, and personalizing contact is used to produce positive valuing and empathic concern for members of the opposition. Such programs include conflict-resolution workshops, peace workshops/camps, and storytelling.

Conflict-Resolution Workshops

In conflict-resolution workshops, three to six leading figures on each side of a political conflict are brought together in a nonthreatening, neutral location for a workshop that rarely lasts more than a week. There, confidential off-the-record interaction is designed to encourage (a) better understanding of each other's position and (b) finding a path toward a mutually beneficial negotiated settlement. The interaction is guided by trained facilitators who establish ground rules and set the agenda.

Perhaps the best-known examples of such workshops are those organized by Herbert Kelman and his colleagues that brought together Israeli and Palestinian representatives (Kelman, 2005; Kelman & Cohen, 1986; Rouhana & Kelman, 1994; also see Burton, 1986, 1987; Fisher, 1994). Participants were encouraged to express their hopes and fears and to listen to one another—actively adopting the perspective of those on the other side while not losing track of real differences. In Kelman's (1997) words, "Out of these interactions, participants develop increasing degrees of empathy, of sensitivity and responsiveness to the other's concerns, and of working trust, which are essential ingredients of the new relationship to which conflict-resolution efforts aspire" (p. 219).

What empathy states are involved? Adoption of an imagine-other perspective, which then leads to better understanding of the other's thoughts and feelings, seems key. Although mutual respect (and sometimes even friendships) can develop among the adversaries, empathic emotion—whether feeling-as or feeling-for the other—isn't the goal of these workshops. As Kelman (2005) pointed out, becoming too chummy with the other side may lead to being mistrusted by your own side. Rather than producing empathic concern, the imagine-other perspective taking that occurs seems to encourage a shift in attributions for the opposing side's behavior—a recognition that the other side is responding to situational pressures (including pressures from one's own side) and isn't guided by dispositional malevolence (see Chapter 10). "The working trust that we aim for is trust in the other side's seriousness and sincerity in the quest for peace—in its genuine commitment, largely out of its own interests, to finding a mutually acceptable accommodation" (Kelman, 2005, p. 646).

Formal evaluation of these conflict-resolution workshops is rarely possible, but they have achieved some success (although rarely the ultimate goal of a mutually acceptable peace). Participants have developed a more differentiated and sensitive view of the other side and a willingness to recognize and address the opposition's concerns (Stephan & Stephan, 2001). At times, such workshops have contributed in important ways to official negotiations between the two sides—most notably, to the Oslo accords (Kelman, 1997).

Peace Workshops/Camps

Peace workshops and camps are typically designed for teenagers from opposite sides of a protracted political conflict. Workshops often last only three to four days, while camps may last a month or more. In each, participants from the opposing sides live together, engage in structured and unstructured joint activities (e.g., interactive drama, painting, cultural events), spend free time together, and exchange views in dialogue sessions under the direction of trained leaders. These activities provide personalizing contact, awareness of out-group needs, and superordinate goals. The workshops and camps promote imagine-other perspective taking, leading to increased understanding of and sensitivity to the needs of members of the out-group. Cross-group friendships are encouraged.

One well-known example is the workshop program for Jewish and Arab youth at Neve Shalom/Wahat al Salam (the Hebrew and Arabic names for the same community) in Israel (Bargal & Bar, 1992). Less well-known, but quite interesting because of a follow-up assessment of attitudes and behavior toward the out-group, was a four-day peace workshop in Sri Lanka that brought together Sinhalese (majority) and Tamil (minority) youth (Malhotra & Liyanage, 2005). At the follow-up conducted a year later, participants in this workshop expressed more understanding of and concern for the well-being of members of the other group (on a version of Mark Davis's Empathic Concern Scale modified to be specific to the other group) than did either of two comparison groups—(a) youth who were nominated for the workshop but didn't take part due to budget cuts and (b) youth from demographically similar schools not involved in nominating students. Compared to these nonparticipants, workshop participants also voluntarily donated a larger portion of the money that they received for completing the follow-up questionnaires to help poor children of the other group.

Storytelling

An interesting variation on the peace workshop model is the storytelling method used in a year-long class with Jewish and Palestinian students at Ben Gurion University in 2000–2001 (Bar-On & Kassem, 2004). Bar-On had previously used storytelling in Germany to facilitate dialogue between children of survivors of the Holocaust and children of perpetrators (Bar-On, 1995). The method used at Ben Gurion involved having students in the class audiotape interviews with family members from their parents' or grandparents' generation in which the family member told his or her life story. These interviews were then played for the entire class and served as a springboard to reflection and discussion under the guidance of a Jewish and a Palestinian facilitator, who sought to maintain an atmosphere of openness and tolerance. Students also kept personal journals in which they described both what happened in the group during each class meeting, and their reactions. Additionally, Jewish–Palestinian student pairs gave a joint class presentation and wrote a joint final paper.

The sharing of family life stories appeared effective in providing personalizing contact among class members and in increasing awareness of out-group needs. It also seemed to induce imagine-other perspective taking (with an imagine-self perspective sometimes serving as a stepping-stone). No objective measures of effects of the class experience were taken, but based on the facilitators' notes and students' journals, Bar-On and Kassem (2004) concluded that "the sharing of stories contributed to the students' ability to listen to one another and to construct a more complex image of the 'other' than the one usually conveyed through the media" (p. 297). The imagine-other perspective taking that occurred seemed to lead to increased situational attributions for out-group suffering—and perhaps to increased empathic concern (empathy wasn't assessed).

Addressing Interpersonal and Intergroup Relations Via Media

Is it possible to use empathic concern to improve attitudes and action toward others without relying on carefully constructed face-to-face interaction? As noted at the start of Chapter 10, it seems so—through books, movies, television, radio, and other forms of media (including live theater—see Rathji, Hackel, & Zaki, 2021). And for four reasons, improving relations via media is likely to be easier, at least initially, than via face-to-face contact: First, there is ample evidence that a skilled writer can lead us to imagine how a real or fictional protagonist is thinking and feeling (imagine-other perspective) and, as a result, to feel empathic concern for him or her—even for a member of a stigmatized out-group (e.g., Batson, Chang et al., 2002; Harrison, 2008; Keen, 2007: Oatley, 2002; Zillmann, 1991). Second, this concern can be induced in low-cost, low-risk situations. To create positive face-to-face personalizing contact requires elaborate arrangements, but books, movies, television, and radio can lead us to feel empathy for others as we sit comfortably in our own home.

Third, empathy-inducing exposure to individual members of an out-group via audiotaped interviews can lead to more positive attitudes and action toward the out-group as a whole (Batson, Chang et al., 2002; Batson, Polycarpou et al., 1997—see Chapter 10). And there's suggestive evidence that other forms of media can have similar effects (Graves, 1999; Hayes & Conklin, 1953; Paluck, 2009a; Rathji et al., 2021; Slater, 2002; and Strange, 2002). Fourth, as long as out-group membership is a salient feature of the need for which empathy is induced, the resulting improvement in attitudes and action doesn't seem vulnerable to subtyping (i.e., improvement toward only one or a small subset of exceptional members of the out-group). In Chapter 10 I noted that subtyping has been found to plague cognitive approaches to attitude change—such as learning stereotype-inconsistent information about an individual out-group member (Brewer, 1988; Pettigrew, 1998).

For these four reasons, using media to induce empathy looks promising as a first step toward more positive interpersonal and intergroup relations. But lest we come to understand and feel only for imagined others and not those with whom we interact, this first step should be followed with direct, personalizing contact using approaches such as those described in the first two sections of this chapter.

To illustrate the potential of media-induced empathic concern, let me present two examples—one old, one new:

Uncle Tom's Cabin

A decade before the American Civil War, Harriet Beecher Stowe wrote her famous novel seeking to galvanize opposition to slavery (Stowe, 1852/2005). It isn't clear that when she met Abraham Lincoln at the White House in 1862, he actually said, "So this is the little woman who made this big war," but there's little doubt that *Uncle Tom's Cabin* contributed importantly to the abolition of slavery in the United States (Morris, 2007).

How did Stowe, who wasn't exempt from the racial stereotypes of her day, manage to inspire effective opposition to so deeply ingrained and profitable a practice as slavery? Her strategy was, as quoted at the start of this chapter, "to awaken sympathy and feeling," which she did by taking her readers into the lives and minds of slaves (i.e., providing an imagine-other perspective), thereby humanizing the dehumanized and evoking strong empathic concern. At the same time, she hammered home with examples and dialogue the clear immorality of one human owning another, appealing to principles of fairness, justice, care, personal dignity, human rights, and sanctity of the family—all moral principles her readers held dear but withheld from slaves.

Stowe first has us follow the runaways George and Eliza Harris, and their little son Harry, on a harrowing but successful flight to Canada, where they can rest free at last. She summarizes:

> Who can speak the blessings of that rest which comes down on the free man's pillow, under laws which insure to him the rights that God has given to man? How fair and precious to that mother was that sleeping child's face, endeared by the memory of a thousand dangers! How impossible was it to sleep, in the exuberant possession of such blessedness! And yet, these two had not one acre of ground,—not a roof that they could call their own,—they had spent their all, to the last dollar. They had nothing more than the birds of the air, or the flowers of the field,—yet they could not sleep for joy. "O ye who take freedom from man, with what words shall ye answer it to God?" (p. 328)

Then she has us accompany devout, loyal Tom after he is sold away from his home, wife, and children, down the river to New Orleans. There, he first serves kind but feckless Augustine St. Clare and his angelic daughter Evangeline. But with St. Clare's sudden death, Tom is sold to vicious Simon Legree, who eventually has him beaten to death for refusing to betray other slaves.

Stowe reflects on Tom's fate:

> It is one of the bitterest apportionments of the lot of slavery, that the negro, sympathetic and assimilative, after acquiring, in a refined family, the tastes and feelings which form the atmosphere of such a place, is not the less liable to become the bond-slave of the coarsest and most brutal,—just as a chair or table, which once decorated the superb saloon, comes, at last, battered and defaced, to the bar-room of some filthy tavern, or some low haunt of vulgar debauchery. The great difference is, that the table and chair cannot feel, and the *man* can; for even a legal enactment that he shall be "taken, reputed, adjudged in law, to be chattel personal," cannot blot out his soul, with its own private little world of memories, hopes, loves, fears, and desires. (p. 285, italics in original)

Stowe's flowery yet unflinching call to men and women, North and South, to act for the abolition of slavery outsold every book except the Bible in the

EMPATHIC CONCERN

19th century (Morris, 2007). Arguably, It had more impact on public policy and social reform than has any other piece of fiction written in English.

But it's not alone. Dickens's novels, such as *Oliver Twist* (1838/2001), used empathic concern to help transform treatment of the poor in Victorian England. And many other books and movies since have used empathic concern to improve attitudes and actions toward other stigmatized groups. I cited a few at the start of Chapter 10.

New Dawn

In the 1994 Rwanda genocide, Hutu militia killed from 500,000 to 800,000 Tutsi—and raped an estimated 250,000 to 500,000 women. A decade later, Elizabeth Paluck (2009a) conducted an ambitious year-long field experiment to test the effect of a radio soap opera, *New Dawn*, designed to promote reconciliation between Tutsi and Hutu. Along with didactic messages about the roots and prevention of prejudice, the soap opera presented characters wrestling with problems known to all Rwandans—cross-group friendships, overbearing leaders, poverty, and memories of violence. The program featured the struggles of a young cross-group couple who pursue their love in the face of community disapproval, and work together to start a youth coalition for peace and cooperation.

The drama, especially the young couple's struggles, seemed to produce both imagine-other perspective taking and empathic concern for the lovers. Follow-up measures indicated that these effects generalized, producing increased perspective taking and feelings of concern for a range of people in Rwandan society. Compared to individuals who listened to a soap opera focused on health issues, those hearing the reconciliation soap opera were more accepting of cross-group marriage and more willing to trust and to cooperate with others in their community, including members of the out-group. Paluck (2009a) concluded:

> The dramatic narrative form of the radio program may have provoked emotional and imaginative processes critical to the changes observed . . . . Listeners' emotional empathic reactions to the soap opera characters may have transferred onto the real-life counterparts of the groups the characters represented (measured by the increased empathy for real-life Rwandans—prisoners, genocide survivors, the poor, and leaders). (p. 584)

For a commentary on Paluck's research, and her response, see Staub & Pearlman (2009) and Paluck (2009b).

Orchestrating Empathy-Induced Altruism and Moral Motivation

Research indicates that empathy-induced altruistic motivation and moral motivation are two distinct prosocial motives (see Batson, 2011, 2016; Batson, Klein et al., 1995). Specifically, altruism is directed toward the ultimate goal of increasing the welfare of one or more other individuals (see Chapter 7). Moral motivation is directed toward the ultimate goal of upholding one or more moral standards, principles, or ideals (Batson, 2016). Either can motivate prosocial behavior—behavior that benefits other individuals or society.

Moreover, each has its own set of strengths and weaknesses. As documented in previous chapters, empathy-induced altruism has a strong emotional base in feelings of sympathy, compassion, and tenderness for others in need. Its major weakness is that we don't care for all others to the same degree. Moral motivation is more inclusive. Think of moral principles such as fairness, justice, the Golden Rule, and "the greatest good for the greatest number." These principles and the moral motivation they produce apply to everyone, even enemies (at least in theory).

But, in addition to this virtue, moral motivation has a serious vice. Because universal principles are general, abstract, and reason based, they're vulnerable to rationalization. When our own interests are best served by compromising our principles, we often find ways to do just that—yet still reason our way to seeing ourselves as moral (Batson, 2016; Sedikides & Strube, 1997; Van Lange, 1991): We manage to convince ourselves that it's right for us to use a disproportionate share of the world's resources. That attacks by our enemies are atrocities but attacks by our allies, necessities. That storing our toxic waste in someone else's backyard is fair. That foregoing the extra effort to recycle isn't wrong. The abstractness and multiplicity of moral principles make it easy to follow those that just happen to serve our interests at the time.

Empathy-induced altruism and moral motivation can—and often do— co-occur. And when they do, they don't always work in harmony. As we saw in Chapter 9, empathy-induced altruism can undercut and oppose moral motivation. But these two motives can also cooperate. One way to promote a more just and caring society may be to orchestrate empathy-induced altruism and moral motivation so that the strengths of one motive can overcome the weaknesses of the other.

Consider the widely held moral principle, "Be fair." It's universal and impartial, but our motivation to be fair is often self-interested. That is, our ultimate goal isn't to uphold the principle but to avoid guilt or enhance

208 • EMPATHIC CONCERN

self-esteem. If we can do so without having to be fair—either by convincing ourselves that we've been fair when we haven't or that fairness doesn't apply here—so much the better for us. We can get the self-benefits that come with seeing ourselves and being seen by others as fair without paying the price of actually being fair.

In contrast, empathy-induced altruism is based on emotion not reason, so it isn't as vulnerable to rationalization as is moral motivation. But it's limited in scope. It produces special concern for special people.

If, through orchestration, we can be induced to feel empathy for the victims of injustice, the unique strengths of the two motives can be combined. Universal principles of justice and care can provide reason and a sense of obligation, even if in the service of self-interest. Empathy-induced altruism can provide a potent desire to see the victims' suffering end—a *want* to accompany the moral *ought*. The orchestrated combination of the two motives can both discourage rationalization and extend our empathic emotion beyond its normal limits, creating what philosopher Robert Solomon called "a passion for justice" (Solomon, 1990).

Unfortunately, I know of no research that evaluates the potential of such orchestration. All I can do is cite some cases in which orchestration seems to have occurred and been effective. At times, the orchestration was unplanned; at other times, planned.

Unplanned Orchestration

Data collected by Samuel and Pearl Oliner and their colleagues suggest that such orchestration occurred in the lives of many rescuers of Jews in Nazi Europe (Oliner & Oliner, 1988). Involvement in rescue activity often began with helping a specific individual or individuals for whom empathic concern was felt—neighbors, friends, a fleeing child. This initial involvement seemed to be motivated by empathy-induced altruism, not moral principle. But, over time, that involvement led to other contacts and rescue activity, and to a moral commitment that extended the rescuer's efforts well beyond the bounds of the initial empathic concern.

Such orchestration also seems to have occurred during the civil rights demonstrations in Birmingham, Alabama, in 1963. The sight on TV news of a small Black child being washed head-over-heels down the street by water from a fire hose under the direction of local police—and the empathic concern this sight evoked—seemed to do more to promote racial equality and justice than had hours of reasoned moral argument about civil rights.

Planned

In the two examples just cited, the orchestration wasn't planned. It occurred as a result of unfolding events. But sometimes the orchestra has a human conductor. Both Mahatma Gandhi in India and Martin Luther King, Jr., in the United States organized nonviolent protest and civil disobedience in the face of entrenched injustice. The protests, and the harsh response to them by authorities, evoked empathic concern for the mistreated and motivation to right the wrong. A passion for justice.

Planned orchestration of empathy-induced altruism and a concern for fairness can also be found in the writing of Jonathan Kozol. Deeply troubled by what he called the "savage inequalities" in public education between rich and poor communities in the United States, Kozol documented the disparities and injustice. But he did more. He took us into the lives of individual children so that we came to care about their welfare and, as a result, to care about the injustice (Kozol, 1991). Kozol's goal wasn't simply to get us to feel. He wanted us involved in action to improve funding for schools in poor communities. He pursued this goal by orchestrating empathy-induced altruism and moral motivation. A non-fiction echo of Stowe's and Dickens's strategy.

Conclusion

After their 2009 review of 985 studies of prejudice-reduction programs, Paluck and Green lamented: "In order to formulate policies that reduce prejudice, one currently must extrapolate well beyond the data, using theoretical presuppositions to fill in the empirical blanks" (Paluck & Green, 2009, p. 357). Taking their lament to heart, I've tried to be as explicit as possible about the role played by different empathy states in the various programs described. My hope is that doing so has provided a conceptual framework for developing future programs and evaluation studies that will attend to and assess the role played by empathic concern and other empathy states. Both program development and program evaluation at this more precise level seems essential if we're to identify the building blocks from which to create more effective programs.

To think in terms of building blocks suggests the potential benefit of bringing together aspects of different programs when creating new approaches. Rather than choosing one "peace pill" (to borrow Mary Gordon's, 2005, metaphor quoted at the start of this chapter), a combination of ingredients may be more effective. For example, one might consider using media experiences to induce an imagine-other perspective—and thereby increased empathic concern for out-group members—prior to participation in any of the various face-to-face, personal contact programs such as cooperative learning, intergroup dialogue, or peace workshops/camps. In this combination, media experiences could set the stage in a low-threat situation for increased understanding of and feeling for out-group members. Direct face-to-face contact could, in turn, channel the media-produced attitude change into concrete action. Another example: Imagine the potential benefits of having children experience a Roots of Empathy program when five to eight years old before entering a cooperative learning (jigsaw) classroom when 10 to 12. These are only two combinations worth considering. I hope you can think of others.

As this chapter shows, empathic concern has been put to good use. Still, we're far from exhausting its potential.

EPILOGUE

Before closing, it may be useful to review the current understanding of what empathic concern is and why it's important—as well as to think about possible sources of further understanding.

What Empathic Concern Is . . . and Isn't

Empathic concern involves feeling for another in need. More formally, it's an other-oriented emotional state elicited by and congruent with the perceived welfare of someone in need (Chapter 1). Rather than using the term to refer to one specific emotional state, I use it as an umbrella term that covers a variety of other-oriented feelings—not only feelings labeled empathy and concern but also those described as sympathy, compassion, tenderness, and more. To provide a measure of empathic concern, a brief self-report index was developed based on induced-state validity.

The specific character of empathic concern depends on the character of the need eliciting the empathy (Chapter 6). Current need evokes sympathy; vulnerability evokes tenderness. If the other is struggling to cope with a difficult situation, empathic concern may be felt as distress. (This other-focused empathic distress is different from self-focused personal distress felt on witnessing another's suffering—Chapter 2.) If the other has experienced a loss, we may feel sorry for him or her (empathic sadness). If the other has been unjustly harmed by someone, we may feel anger toward the harm doer (empathic anger). Additional types of need will evoke their own shades of empathic concern.

Perception of the other as in need is a necessary condition for feeling empathic concern, but we don't feel empathy for every need we perceive. In addition to perceiving need, we must care that the other is in need (i.e., value his or her welfare). I think these two conditions—perceiving the other's need and

212 • Epilogue

valuing the other's welfare—are necessary and sufficient to lead us to feel empathic concern (Chapter 4). Other conditions are sometimes claimed necessary (e.g., similarity to the other; having previously experienced the need; taking the perspective of the other), but each seems to affect empathic concern through its effect on perception of need, valuing the other's welfare, or both.

Other Psychological States Called Empathy

Various scholars and researchers have used the term empathy to refer to one or more psychological states other than the state I'm calling empathic concern. To get the conceptual and empirical clarity necessary to make progress in science, it's essential to distinguish each of these states from empathic concern, and from one another. If we don't, we can't learn what role(s) each plays in our lives—how the different states relate to one another and how each affects behavior. And without such knowledge, we're shooting blind in developing empathy-based programs to improve social relations.

In recent years, the other psychological state most frequently called empathy (especially by developmental psychologists and neuroscientists) is feeling as another feels. Researchers have suggested that we can come to feel as the other through contagion, mimicry, or neural matching. As noted in Chapter 3, two qualifications are usually put on what's necessary for feeling-as to be called empathy. First, the empathizer need not feel exactly the same emotion as the target, only a similar one (how similar is unspecified). Second, the empathizer's emotion needs to be caught from the target, not simply a parallel response to the same situation.

To feel as another feels is different from empathic concern as I've defined it. At the start of Chapter 3, I illustrated empathic concern with the sorrow you felt for your friend who was scared about losing her job. Your sorrow and her fear are two different emotions; you felt *for* her, not *as* she felt. I also noted that we can feel empathic concern for someone who's feeling nothing at all, such as the man who fell among thieves in the Parable.

Knowing what another person is thinking and feeling is another psychological state often called empathy. This use of the term is common among psychiatrists, clinical psychologists, and other therapists—as well as among philosophers interested in the puzzle of how we know the internal states of others. Accurate knowledge of what a client is thinking and feeling is often essential in therapy, but it's not necessary in order to feel empathic concern. We can feel empathic concern based on an erroneous perception of need. Moreover, there are perceived needs in which the other's thoughts and feelings play no role—as when we see a need of which the cared-for other is unaware (e.g., the young nephew playing happily at the start of Chapter 1).

Perspective taking is an act of imagination that's also often called empathy. In Chapter 3, I distinguished two forms of perspective taking that are frequently confused or conflated—(a) taking an other-focused perspective and imagining how the other is affected by his or her situation and (b) taking a self-focused perspective and imagining how you would be affected if you were in the other's situation. Each of these cognitive/perceptual states is distinct from empathic concern, which is an emotional state. But each can, under specifiable circumstances, evoke empathic concern.

For example, an imagine-other perspective can lead to empathic concern by both sharpening the perception of need and increasing valuing of the other's welfare, the two necessary conditions noted earlier. But, reflecting the priority of valuing over perspective taking, evidence indicates that when we encounter a needy other whose welfare we value, we're apt to spontaneously adopt an imagine-other perspective. We don't need perspective instructions (Chapter 4).

An imagine-self perspective can contribute to empathic concern in two ways. First, if the other's need is unclear or ambiguous, then to imagine being in his or her situation may enable us to recognize the need. Second, if we imagine that we would react like the other is reacting in the situation, an imagine-self perspective may serve as a stepping-stone to adopting an imagine-other perspective and, thereby, to empathic concern.

But an imagine-self perspective doesn't always facilitate empathic concern. We may get so caught up in thinking about how we would feel in the other's situation that we lose sight of the other and his or her need. Or, if we imagine we would react to the situation differently from the way the other is reacting, we may find ourselves taking an objective, evaluative perspective toward the other, which is likely to inhibit empathic concern (Chapter 3).

Dispositional Empathy

In addition to these psychological states called empathy, the term empathic concern has been applied to a disposition or trait to feel for others in need— that is, to a trait to feel the emotional state I've called empathic concern. Indeed, this is the most frequent use of the term empathic concern in recent psychological research articles, as an online search of databases will show.

I noted in Chapter 3 that there doubtless are dispositional differences in the ability and inclination to feel empathic concern, but it's doubtful that

214 • Epilogue

self-report questionnaires can provide a valid measure of these differences. Self-reports of a general disposition to be caring are too likely to be affected by self-presentation and social desirability. Reflecting this problem, colleagues and I (Batson, Bolen et al., 1986) found that it was only the part of self-reported situational empathy—empathy for a specific person in a specific situation—that *wasn't* correlated with self-reported dispositional empathy that seemed to provide a valid measure of empathic concern.

Possible Next Steps

The existing research on what empathic concern is and isn't points to several directions for future research:

1. We need physiological, including neurophysiological, measures that can validly differentiate empathic concern from personal distress—and from the other psychological states called empathy.
2. We need more tests of the causal relations among the different states called empathy, tests that reveal what affects what and why. Are some states necessary for others? Sufficient? Do some states mediate or moderate the relations between others?

   For example, in Chapter 4, I provided evidence that valuing the other's welfare is a necessary condition for feeling empathic concern—and that an imagine-other perspective can be either a consequence or a source of valuing. It would be good to have further research on exactly how these two antecedents interact to affect empathic concern.
3. In Chapter 6, I identified five different types of need, each of which evokes a different form of empathic concern. Further research should test the proposed distinctions and relations—as well as the downstream consequences of each form for motivation and behavior. Additionally, there's no reason to think that the five forms I identified exhaust the possibilities. Other forms of empathic concern likely exist.
4. The idea that the genetic basis of empathic concern lies in parental nurturance (Chapter 5) needs more direct tests—if possible, tests including genetic data. Also, the role oxytocin that plays in emotional, motivational, and behavioral responses to the needs of various cared-for others deserves more focused and theoretically based attention. Such research won't be easy but could be extremely valuable.

Why Empathic Concern Is Important

The importance of empathic concern is most apparent when we consider its motivational consequences (Chapter 7). There's much evidence that empathic concern produces altruistic motivation—motivation with the ultimate goal of increasing another's welfare by removing the empathy-inducing need. Such motivation has important behavioral consequences, negative as well as positive, at both the interpersonal and the intergroup levels.

Interpersonal Benefits and Liabilities

At the interpersonal level, there's evidence that empathic concern and the altruistic motivation it produces can lead not only to more caring response by parents to their child's needs but also to more caring responses in romantic relationships, in friendships, and in response to strangers in need (Chapter 8). Empathic concern has been shown to provide more sensitive and less fickle help, less aggression toward the person for whom empathy is felt, and reduced derogation of the victims of injustice.

But there's also evidence of interpersonal liabilities (Chapter 9). Consistent with the idea that empathic concern is an extension of parental care, it can lead to paternalism/maternalism toward others in need. It can make helping harder when what's needed is an objective, unemotional approach to the problem. Knowledge that empathic concern is likely to evoke altruistic motivation can produce an egoistic motive to avoid empathy in order to avoid the costs of acting on the empathy-induced altruistic motive. Further, empathic concern is less likely to be felt for some needs—needs of nonpersonalized others and needs that are abstract or chronic. And it can produce partiality toward its targets, leading us to violate our moral principles of fairness and what's best for all. Finally, empathic concern can at times hurt the empathizer, causing him or her to risk harm and experience stress—as well as to give ground in competitive situations.

Intergroup Benefits and Liabilities

Although empathic concern is an interpersonal emotion, it can provide intergroup benefits when induced for a member of a stigmatized group through positive personalizing contact—whether the contact is face-to-face, via media, or induced by imagine-other perspective instructions (Chapter 8). And, as long as the member's need is clearly linked to membership in the

216 • Epilogue

group, it seems that the positive effects of empathy can generalize, improving attitudes and action toward other members of the group (Chapter 10).

Turning to intergroup liabilities (Chapter 11), the most obvious obstacle to using empathic concern to improve attitudes and action toward an out-group is *in-group empathy bias*—the oft-cited claim that we're more likely to feel empathic concern for members of our in-group than for members of an out-group. But evidence of such bias is mixed, suggesting the need for a more nuanced analysis.

Meeting this need, recent research differentiates between two types of out-groups—distant and conflict—and suggests that a distinct form of empathy bias occurs for each type. For members of distant out-groups, that is, out-groups with no direct impact on our lives or welfare, we're unlikely to be aware of or care about their plight. If, however, we're induced to adopt their perspective, we can come to recognize and care about their need, leading us to feel much as we do for in-group members. Unfortunately, even when we feel for members of a distant out-group, we may fail to fully understand their needs, inadvertently producing more harm than help.

The effect of empathy bias is more dire for members of conflict out-groups. We may recognize their needs yet feel the opposite of empathic concern. Because their welfare and ours are in conflict, we're likely to negatively value theirs. As a result, rather than empathy, we feel schadenfreude (malicious glee) when they suffer, and we want to harm not help. We can also dehumanize, leading us to further negatively value them, turning the negative-value→low-empathy/schadenfreude→harm sequence into an escalating spiral.

Programs Using Empathic Concern to Improve Social Relations

Theory and research on empathic concern has been put to use in a variety of programs designed to improve interpersonal and/or intergroup relations (Chapter 12). In educational settings, programs have reduced conflict, bullying, and discrimination, as well as increased cooperation and helping. Designed for students from kindergarten to college, the programs have used a range of strategies—from observing and interacting with an infant (Roots of Empathy), to cooperative learning (the Jigsaw Classroom), discrimination simulations (the Blue Eyes–Brown Eyes simulation), and intergroup-dialogue classes.

Programs have also been developed to address protracted political conflicts. Conflict-resolution workshops bring together leaders from opposing sides in a political conflict. Peace workshops and camps bring together teens. Storytelling involves, for example, having university students from both sides of a conflict share and reflect on audiotaped interviews in which the students' parents or grandparents (or other relatives) tell how the conflict affected their lives.

In addition to positive face-to-face contact, media (books, movies, plays, TV, radio) have been used to induce empathic concern for those who are disadvantaged, downtrodden, or stigmatized. Both fiction and nonfiction can evoke empathy by personalizing the lives and suffering of out-group members (distant or conflict)—and can do so without the complexities and uncertainties of creating positive face-to-face intergroup contact.

Finally, orchestration of empathy-induced altruistic motivation and moral motivation has served to extend the scope of empathic concern to victims of injustice outside our normal circle of care. Orchestration enables the unique strength of each motive to overcome the weakness of the other.

Possible Next Steps

Research on the benefits and liabilities of empathic concern highlights many issues needing more attention. For example:

1. Further research is needed on the benefits—and liabilities—of empathic concern in friendships and romantic relationships, especially longitudinal research.
2. Research indicates that there can be negative effects of adopting an imagine-other perspective when interacting directly with a member of a stigmatized group. Are these negative effects due to empathic concern being overridden by self-concern about how the member thinks and feels about the empathizer, as I suggested, or due to empathy being inhibited?
3. Are the prosocial effects of meditation practices mediated by empathic concern?
4. Can increased accuracy in perception of a cared-for other's need reduce paternalism/maternalism? If so, how can accuracy best be increased?
5. When and why does dissimilarity inhibit empathic concern? Does it reduce perception of need, reduce valuing the other's welfare, both, or neither?
6. What are the long-term effects of empathic concern on outcomes when negotiations are repeated, as in business and politics?

218 • Epilogue

7. Is punishment of someone who harms a cared-for other motivated by concern for the other's welfare (i.e., empathy-induced altruism) or by a desire for justice (i.e., retribution)?
8. Does lack of empathic concern mediate the relationship between dehumanization and harm?
9. Research is needed to directly test the idea that evoking empathic concern for victims of injustice can overcome the respective weaknesses of both empathy-induced altruistic motivation (limited scope) and moral motivation (rationalization).
10. Most research evaluating the effectiveness of programs that employ empathy to improve interpersonal and intergroup relations has been conducted by researchers with vested interests in the programs' success. We also need evaluation by—or at least in collaboration with—independent researchers.

Looking back, our understanding of empathic concern and the role it plays in our lives has grown substantially over recent decades. But looking forward, it's clear that more growth is needed.

ACKNOWLEDGMENTS

Many people provided valuable assistance, insights, and suggestions over the almost 50 years I've been studying and conducting research on empathic concern. They include students, colleagues, and friends. Naming them here doesn't do justice to their various contributions, and doubtless I've failed to think of everyone who should be listed. Apologies.

With those provisos, sincere thanks to the following graduate and post-doctoral students: Nadia Ahmad, Michael Bayly, Beverly Brummett, Chris Burris, Jay Coke, Karen Dawson, Bruce Duncan, Janine Dyck, Jim Fultz, Rick Gibbons, Eddie Harmon-Jones, David Lishner, Kevin McCaul, Kathrine McDavis, Rosalie McMaster, Karen O'Quin, Suzanne Pate, Adam Powell, Patricia Schoenrade, Laura Shaw, Eric Stocks, Miho Toi, Jo-Ann Tsang, Mary Vanderplas, and Joy Weeks.

Sincere thanks also to undergraduates Paula Ackerman, Carlo Aldeguer, Steve Bedell, Sergio Barrientos, Lori Bednar, Kimberly Birch, Michelle Bolen, Randy Brandt, Terese Buckley, Johee Chang, Valerie Chermok, Jennifer Cook, Julie Cross, Chris Cowles, Peter Decruz, Shannon Early, Victoria Fortenbach, Cari Griffitt, Eric Garst, Kevin Harrell, Jess Heidrich, Lori Highberger, Jennifer Hindman, Jennifer Hoyt, Heidi Imhoff, Geoffrey Jennings, Jennifer Johnson, Misook Kang, Tricia Klein, Missy McCarthy, Erin Mitchener, Tecia Moran, Helen Neuringer-Benefiel, Kathy Oleson, Ryan Orr, Biaggio Ortiz, Marina Polycarpou, Heli Peekna, Anne Powell, Jennifer Rowland, Kostia Rubschinsky, Giovanni Salvarani, Karen Sager, Stacey Sawyer, Suzie Sympson, Jacque Slingsby, Peter Springelmeyer, Christie Templin, Matt Todd, Laurie Varney, Aaron Whiteside, and Jodi Yin.

Colleagues and friends contributed in many different ways. Among them are Rick Archer, Elliot Aronson, Donn Baumann, Monica Biernat,

220 • Acknowledgments

James Blair, Paul Bloom, Mark Barnett, Jack Brehm, Sharon Brehm, Sarah Brosnan, Stephanie Brown, Emile Bruneau, Daryl Cameron, Sue Carter, Bob Cialdini, Mina Cikara, Russ Clark, Nancy Collins, Chris Crandall, John Darley, Mark Davis, Richard Dawkins, Jean Decety, Bella DePaulo, Frans de Waal, Antoine Dijker, Jack Dovidio, Nancy Eisenberg, Jakob Eklund, Nick Epley, Mark Fagiano, Ernst Fehr, Lowell Gaertner, Adam Galinsky, Omri Gillath, Jen Goetz, Mary Gordon, Bill Graziano, Maria Guibert, Paul Gump, Jodi Halpern, Mary Harris, Fritz Heider, Grace Heider, Grit Hein, Miles Hewstone, Sara Hodges, Marty Hoffman, Tom Insel, Alice Isen, Aleksandra Kostic, Dennis Krebs, Claus Lamm, Mel Lerner, Belén López-Peréz, Sam McFarland, Heidi Maibom, Jon Maner, Karen Matthews, Josh May, Mario Mikulincer, Christian Miller, Jason Mitchell, Arie Nadler, Lidewij Niezink, Martha Nusbaum, Luis Oceja, Allen Omoto, Michael Olson, Betsy Paluck, Keith Payne, Lou Penner, Alicia Pérez-Albéniz, Jane Piliavin, Stephen Post, Daniel Povinelli, Stephanie Preston, Jesse Prinz, Dennis Regan, Matthieu Ricard, Bunker Roy, Pete Richerson, Philippe Rushton, Roberta Saxe, Mark Schaller, Dave Schroeder, Phil Shaver, Pete Sherrard, Garriy Shteynberg, Joan Silk, Tania Singer, Walter Sinnott-Armstrong, Kyle Smith, Mark Snyder, Elliott Sober, Ervin Staub, Steve Stich, Ezra Stotland, Karsten Stueber, Abraham Tesser, Michael Tomasello, Paul Van Lange, Terri Vescio, Guy Vitagliano, Jacquie Vorauer, Felix Warneken, Bob Wicklund, Lauren Wispé, Rex Wright, Carolyn Zahn-Waxler, and Jamil Zaki.

For about 10 years, my research on empathic concern and altruistic motivation benefited greatly from National Science Foundation support.

As for this book, many thanks to Abby Gross, Psychology Editor-in-Chief, and to Nadina Persaud, Social Psychology and Neuropsychology Editor, at Oxford University Press. They provided enthusiastic support throughout the publication process. Others at OUP provided valuable assistance as well. Among them, Katie Pratt deserves special mention.

Finally, enduring thanks to my wife Judy for her involvement from start to finish—for her readiness to talk empathy and altruism over drinks again and again, her exceptional insight as a pilot participant in many experiments, her care and dedication assisting with data collection, her comments on chapter drafts, her editorial skill, and her overall patience, understanding, and care. Who could ask for more?

REFERENCES

Adams, F. (2001). Empathy, neural imaging, and the theory versus simulation debate. *Mind and Language, 16*, 368–392.

Aderman, D., & Berkowitz, L. (1983). Self-concern and the unwillingness to be helpful. *Social Psychology Quarterly, 46*, 293–301.

Aderman, D., Brehm, S. S., & Katz, L. B. (1974). Empathic observation of an innocent victim: The just world revisited. *Journal of Personality and Social Psychology, 29*, 342–347.

Allman, J. M., Watson, K. K., Tetreault, N. A., & Hakeem, A. Y. (2005). Intuition and autism: A possible role for Von Economo neurons. *Trends in Cognitive Sciences, 9*, 367–373.

Allport, F. H. (1924). *Social psychology*. Boston: Houghton Mifflin.

Allport, G. W. (1937). *Personality: A psychological interpretation*. New York: Holt.

Andrighetto, L., Baldissarri, C., Lattanzio, S., Loughnan, S., & Volpato, C. (2014). Human-itarian aid? Two forms of dehumanization and willingness to help after natural disasters. *British Journal of Social Psychology, 53*, 573–584.

Aquinas, T. (1917). *The summa theologica*, Vol. 2, Part II. (Fathers of the English Dominican Province, Trans.). New York: Benziger Bros. (Original work produced 1270)

Archer, R. L., Diaz-Loving, R., Gollwitzer, P. M., Davis, M. H., & Foushee, H. C. (1981). The role of dispositional empathy and social evaluation in the empathic mediation of helping. *Journal of Personality and Social Psychology, 40*, 786–796.

Arnold, M. B. (1960). *Emotion and personality* (2 vols.). New York: Columbia University Press.

Aronson, E. (2004). Reducing hostility and building compassion: Lessons from the jigsaw classroom. In A. G. Miller (Ed.), *The social psychology of good and evil* (pp. 469–488). New York: Guilford Press.

Aronson, E., Blaney, N., Stephan, C., Sikes, J., & Snapp, M. (1978). *The jigsaw classroom*. Beverly Hills, CA: Sage.

Aronson, E., & Bridgeman, D. (1979). Jigsaw groups and the desegregated classroom: In pursuit of common goals. *Personality and Social Psychology Bulletin, 5*, 438–446.

222 • References

Aronson, E., & Carlsmith, J. M. (1963). Effects of the severity of threat on the devaluation of forbidden behavior. *Journal of Abnormal and Social Psychology, 66*, 584–588.

Aronson, E., & Patnoe, S. (1997). *The jigsaw classroom: Building cooperation in the classroom* (2nd ed.), New York: Longman.

Ashar, Y. K., Andrews-Hanna, J. R., Dimidjian, S., & Wager, T. D. (2017). Empathic care and distress: Predictive brain markers and dissociable brain systems. *Neuron, 94*, 1263–1273.

Atzil, S., Hendler, T., & Feldman, R. (2011). Specifying the neurobiological basis of human attachment: Brain, hormones, and behavior in synchronous and intrusive mothers. *Neuropsychopharmacology, 36*, 2603–2615.

Avenanti, A., Sirigu, A., & Aglioti, S. M. (2010). Racial bias reduces empathic sensorimotor resonance with other-race pain. *Current Biology, 20*, 1018–1022.

Balzac, H. de (1962). *Pere Goriot* (H. Reed, Trans.). New York: New American Library. (Original work published 1834)

Bandura, A. (1969). *Principles of behavior modification*. New York: Holt, Rinehart & Winston.

Bandura, A. (1999). Moral disengagement in the perpetuation of inhumanities. *Personality and Social Psychology Review, 3*, 193–209.

Bandura, A., & Rosenthal, L. (1966). Vicarious classical conditioning as a function of arousal level. *Journal of Personality and Social Psychology, 3*, 54–62.

Bard, K. A. (1995). Parenting in primates. In M. H. Bornstein (Ed.), *Handbook of parenting: Vol. 2, Biology and ecology of parenting* (pp. 27–58). Mahwah, NJ: Erlbaum.

Bargal, D., & Bar, H. (1992). A Lewinian approach to intergroup workshops for Arab-Palestinian and Jewish youth. *Journal of Social Issues, 48*, 139–154.

Bar-On, D. (1995). Encounters between descendants of Nazi perpetrators and descendants of Holocaust survivors. *Psychiatry, 58*, 225–245.

Bar-On, D., & Kassem, F. (2004). Storytelling as a way to work through intractable conflicts: The German-Jewish experience and its relevance to the Palestinian-Israeli context. *Journal of Social Issues, 60*, 289–306.

Barraza, J. A., & Zak, P. J. (2009). Empathy toward strangers triggers oxytocin release and subsequent generosity. *Annals of the New York Academy of Science, 1167*, 182–189.

Barrett-Lennard, G. T. (1981). The empathy cycle: Refinement of a nuclear concept. *Journal of Counseling Psychology, 28*, 91–100.

Bartal, I. B.-A., Decety, J., & Mason, P. (2011). Empathy and pro-social behavior in rats. *Science, 334*, 1427–1430.

Bartels, A., & Zeki, S. (2000). The neural basis of romantic love. *NeuroReport, 11*, 3829–3834.

Bartels, A., & Zeki, S. (2004). The neural correlates of maternal and romantic love. *NeuroImage, 21*, 1155–1166.

Batson, C. D. (1983). Sociobiology and the role of religion in promoting prosocial behavior: An alternative view. *Journal of Personality and Social Psychology, 45*, 1380–1385.

Batson, C. D. (1987). Prosocial motivation: Is it ever truly altruistic? In L. Berkowitz (Ed.), *Advances in experimental social psychology* (Vol. 20, pp. 65–122). New York: Academic Press.

Batson, C. D. (1989). Personal values, moral principles, and a three-path model of prosocial motivation. In N. Eisenberg et al. (Eds.), *Social and moral values: Individual and societal perspectives* (pp. 213–228). Hillsdale, NJ: Erlbaum Associates.

Batson, C. D. (1991). *The altruism question: Toward a social-psychological answer.* Hillsdale, NJ: Erlbaum Associates.

Batson, C. D. (2009). These things called empathy: Eight related but distinct phenomena. In J. Decety & W. Ickes (Eds.), *The social neuroscience of empathy* (pp. 3–15). Cambridge, MA: MIT Press.

Batson, C. D. (2011). *Altruism in humans.* New York: Oxford University Press.

Batson, C. D. (2016). *What's wrong with morality?: A social-psychological perspective.* New York: Oxford University Press.

Batson, C. D. (2019). *A scientific search for altruism: Do we care only about ourselves?* New York: Oxford University Press.

Batson, C. D., & Ahmad, N. (2001). Empathy-induced altruism in a Prisoner's Dilemma II: What if the target of empathy has defected? *European Journal of Social Psychology, 31*, 25–36.

Batson, C. D., Ahmad, N., Yin, J., Bedell, S. J., Johnson, J. W., Templin, C. M., & Whiteside, A. (1999). Two threats to the common good: Self-interested egoism and empathy-induced altruism. *Personality and Social Psychology Bulletin, 25*, 3–16.

Batson, C. D., Batson, J. G., Griffitt, C. A., Barrientos, S., Brandt, J. R., Sprengelmeyer, P., & Bayly, M. J. (1989). Negative-state relief and the empathy-altruism hypothesis. *Journal of Personality and Social Psychology, 56*, 922–933.

Batson, C. D., Batson, J. G., Slingsby, J. K., Harrell, K. L., Peekna, H. M., & Todd, R. M. (1991). Empathic joy and the empathy-altruism hypothesis. *Journal of Personality and Social Psychology, 61*, 413–426.

Batson, C. D., Batson, J. G., Todd, R. M., Brummett, B. H., Shaw, L. L., & Aldeguer, C. M. R. (1995). Empathy and the collective good: Caring for one of the others in a social dilemma. *Journal of Personality and Social Psychology, 68*, 619–631.

Batson, C. D., Bolen, M. H., Cross, J. A., & Neuringer-Benefiel, H. (1986). Where is the altruism in the altruistic personality? *Journal of Personality and Social Psychology, 50*, 212–220.

Batson, C. D., Chang, J., Orr, R., & Rowland, J. (2002). Empathy, attitudes, and action: Can feeling for a member of a stigmatized group motivate one to help the group? *Personality and Social Psychology Bulletin, 28*, 1656–1666.

Batson, C. D., Cowles, C., & Coke, J. S. (1979). *Empathic mediation of the response to a lady in distress: Egoistic or altruistic?* Unpublished manuscript. University of Kansas.

Batson, C. D., Denton, D. M., & Vollmecke, J. T. (2008). Quest religion, anti-fundamentalism, and limited versus universal compassion. *Journal for the Scientific Study of Religion, 47*, 135–145.

224 · References

Batson, C. D., Duncan, B., Ackerman, P., Buckley, T., & Birch, K. (1981). Is empathic emotion a source of altruistic motivation? *Journal of Personality and Social Psychology, 40*, 290–302.

Batson, C. D., Dyck, J. L., Brandt, J. R., Batson, J. G., Powell, A. L., McMaster, M. R., & Griffitt, C. (1988). Five studies testing two new egoistic alternatives to the empathy-altruism hypothesis. *Journal of Personality and Social Psychology, 55*, 52–77.

Batson, C. D., Early, S., & Salvarani, G. (1997). Perspective taking: Imagining how another feels versus imagining how you would feel. *Personality and Social Psychology Bulletin, 23*, 751–758.

Batson, C. D., Eklund, J. H., Chermok, V. L., Hoyt, J. L., & Ortiz, B. G. (2007). An additional antecedent of empathic concern: Valuing the welfare of the person in need. *Journal of Personality and Social Psychology, 93*, 65–74.

Batson, C. D., Floyd, R. B., Meyer, J. M., & Winner, A. L. (1999). "And who is my neighbor?" Intrinsic religion as a source of universal compassion. *Journal for the Scientific Study of Religion, 38*, 445–457.

Batson, C. D., Fultz, J., & Schoenrade, P. A. (1987). Distress and empathy: Two qualitatively distinct vicarious emotions with different motivational consequences. *Journal of Personality, 55*, 19–39.

Batson, C. D., Klein, T. R., Highberger, L., & Shaw, L. L. (1995). Immorality from empathy-induced altruism: When compassion and justice conflict. *Journal of Personality and Social Psychology, 68*, 1042–1054.

Batson, C. D., Lishner, D. A., Carpenter, A., Dulin, L., Harjusola-Webb, S., Stocks, E. L., Gale, S., Hassan, O., & Sampat, B. (2003). "As you would have them do unto you": Does imagining yourself in the other's place stimulate moral action? *Personality and Social Psychology Bulletin, 29*, 1190–1201.

Batson, C. D., Lishner, D. A., Cook, J., & Sawyer, S. (2005). Similarity and nurturance: Two possible sources of empathy for strangers. *Basic and Applied Social Psychology, 27*, 15–25.

Batson, C. D., & Moran, T. (1999). Empathy-induced altruism in a Prisoner's Dilemma. *European Journal of Social Psychology, 29*, 909–924.

Batson, C. D., O'Quin, K., Fultz, J., Vanderplas, M., & Isen, A. (1983). Self-reported distress and empathy and egoistic versus altruistic motivation for helping. *Journal of Personality and Social Psychology, 45*, 706–718.

Batson, C. D., Polycarpou, M. P., Harmon-Jones, E., Imhoff, H. J., Mitchener, E. C., Bednar, L. L., Klein, T. R., & Highberger, L. (1997). Empathy and attitudes: Can feeling for a member of a stigmatized group improve feelings toward the group? *Journal of Personality and Social Psychology, 72*, 105–118.

Batson, C. D., Sager, K., Garst, E., Kang, M., Rubchinsky, K., & Dawson, K. (1997). Is empathy-induced helping due to self-other merging? *Journal of Personality and Social Psychology, 73*, 495–509.

Batson, C. D., Schoenrade, P., & Ventis, W. L. (1993). *Religion and the individual: A social-psychological perspective.* New York: Oxford University Press.

Batson, C. D., & Shaw, L. L. (1991). Evidence for altruism: Toward a pluralism of pro-social motives. *Psychological Inquiry, 2,* 107–122.

Batson, C. D., Shaw, L. L., & Oleson, K. C. (1992). Differentiating affect, mood, and emotion: Toward functionally based conceptual distinctions. In M. S. Clark (Ed.), *Emotion: Review of personality and social psychology* (Vol. 13, pp. 294–326). Newbury Park, CA: Sage Publications.

Batson, C. D., Sympson, S. C., Hindman, J. L., Decruz, P., Todd, R. M., Weeks, J. L., Jennings, G., & Burris, C. T. (1996). "I've been there, too": Effect on empathy of prior experience with a need. *Personality and Social Psychology Bulletin, 22,* 474–482.

Batson, C. D., Turk, C. L., Shaw, L. L., & Klein, T. R. (1995). Information function of empathic emotion: Learning that we value the other's welfare. *Journal of Personality and Social Psychology, 68,* 300–313.

Batson, C. D., & Weeks, J. L. (1996). Mood effects of unsuccessful helping: Another test of the empathy-altruism hypothesis. *Personality and Social Psychology Bulletin, 22,* 148–157.

Bavelas, J. B., Black, A., Lemery, C. R., & Mullett, J. (1986). "I show you how you feel": Motor mimicry as a communicative act. *Journal of Personality and Social Psychology, 50,* 322–329.

Bavelas, J. B., Black, A., Lemery, C. R., & Mullett, J. (1987). Motor mimicry as primitive empathy. In N. Eisenberg & J. Strayer (Eds.), *Empathy and its development* (pp. 317–338). New York: Cambridge University Press.

Bell, D. C. (2001). Evolution of parental caregiving. *Personality and Social Psychology Review, 5,* 216–229.

Berenguer, J. (2007). The effect of empathy in proenvironmental attitudes and behaviors. *Environment and Behavior, 39,* 269–283.

Berger, S. (1962). Conditioning through vicarious instigation. *Psychological Review, 69,* 450–466.

Berkeley, B. (1994). Sounds of violence: Rwanda's killer radio. *The New Republic, 211* (8/9), 18–19.

Berry, D. R., Cairo, A. H., Goodman, R. J., Quaglia, J. T., Green, J. D., & Brown, K. W. (2018). Mindfulness increases prosocial responses toward ostracized strangers through empathic concern. *Journal of Experimental Psychology: General, 147,* 93–112.

Berry, D. R., Hoerr, J. P., Cesko, S., Alayoubi, A., Carpio, K., Zirzow, H., Wslters, W., Scram, G., Rodriguez, K., & Beaver, V. (2020). Does mindfulness training without explicit ethics-based instruction promote prosocial behaviors? A meta-analysis. *Personality and Social Psychology Bulletin, 46,* 1247–1269.

Berscheid, E. (1983). Emotion. In H. H. Kelley, E. Berscheid, A. Christiansen, J. H. Harvey, T. L. Houston, G. Levinger, E. McClintock, L. A. Peplau, & D. L. Peterson (Eds.), *Close relationships* (pp. 110–168). New York: W. H. Freeman.

226 • References

Berscheid, E., & Reis, H. T. (1998). Attraction and close relationships. In D. T. Gilbert, S. T. Fiske, & G. Lindzey (Eds.), *The handbook of social psychology* (4th ed.), (Vol. 2, pp. 193–281). Boston: McGraw-Hill.

Blair, R. J. R. (2007). The amygdala and ventromedial prefrontal cortex in morality and psychopathy. *Trends in Cognitive Sciences, 11*, 387–392.

Blake, J. A. (1978). Death by hand grenade: Altruistic suicide in combat. *Suicide and Life-Threatening Behavior, 8*, 46–59.

Bloom, P. (2016). *Against empathy: The case for rational compassion.* London: Bodley Head.

Boehm, C. (1999). The natural selection of altruistic traits. *Human Nature, 10*, 205–252.

Bowlby, J. (1969). *Attachment and loss*: Vol 1. Attachment. New York: Basic Books.

Bowles, S. (2008). Policies designed for self-interested citizens may undermine "the moral sentiments": Evidence from economic experiments. *Science, 320*, 1605–1609.

Bratt, C. (2008). The jigsaw classroom under test: No effects on inter-group relations evident. *Journal of Community and Applied Social Psychology, 18*, 403–419.

Brewer, M. B. (1988). A dual process model of impression formation. In T. K. Srull & R. S. Wyer, Jr. (Eds.), *Advances in social cognition* (Vol. 1, pp. 1–36). Hillsdale, NJ: Erlbaum.

Bridgeman, D. L. (1981). Enhanced role-taking through cooperative interdependence: A field study. *Child Development, 52*, 1231–1238.

Brothers, L. (1989). A biological perspective on empathy. *American Journal of Psychiatry, 146*, 10–19.

Brown, C. (1965). *Manchild in the promised land.* New York: Macmillan.

Brown, R., & Hewstone, M. (2005). An integrative theory of intergroup contact. In M. Zanna (Ed.), *Advances in experimental social psychology* (Vol. 37, pp. 255–343). San Diego, CA: Academic Press.

Bruneau, E., Cikara, M., & Saxe, R. (2015). Minding the gap: Narrative descriptions about mental states attenuate parochial empathy. *PLOS One, 10*, e0140838.

Bruneau, E., Cikara, M., & Saxe, R. (2017). Parochial empathy predicts reduced altruism and the endorsement of passive harm. *Social Psychological and Personality Science, 8*, 934–942.

Bruneau, E., Dufour, N., & Saxe, R. (2012). Social cognition in members of conflict groups: Behavioral and neural responses in Arabs, Israelis, and South Americans to each other's misfortunes. *Philosophical Transactions of the Royal Society B, 367*, 717–730.

Bruneau, E., Dufour, N., & Saxe, R. (2013). How we know it hurts: Item analysis of written narratives reveals distinct neural responses to others' physical pain and emotional suffering. *PLoS One, 8*(4), e63085.

Bruneau, E., Jacoby, N., Kteily, N., & Saxe, R. (2018). Denying humanity: The distinct neural correlates of blatant dehumanization. *Journal of Experimental Psychology: General, 147*, 1078–1093.

Bruneau, E., & Kteily, N. (2017). The enemy as animal: Symmetric dehumanization during asymmetric warfare. *PLOS One,* July 26, e0181422.

Buck, R., & Ginsburg, B. (1991). Spontaneous communication and altruism: The communicative gene hypothesis. In M. S. Clark (Ed.), *Review of personality and social psychology: Vol. 12. Prosocial behavior* (pp. 149–175). Newbury Park, CA: Sage.

Buffone, A. E. K., & Poulin, M. J. (2014). Empathy, target distress, and neurohormone genes interact to predict aggression for others—even without provocation. *Personality and Social Psychology Bulletin, 40,* 1406–1422.

Buffone, A. E. K., Poulin, M. J., DeLury, S., Ministero, L., Morrison, C., & Scalco, M. (2017). Don't walk in her shoes! Different forms of perspective taking affect stress physiology. *Journal of Experimental Social Psychology, 72,* 161–168.

Burton, J. W. (1986). The procedures of conflict resolution. In E. E. Azar & J. W. Burton (Eds.), *International conflict resolution: Theory and practice* (pp. 92–116). Boulder, CO: Lynne Reiner.

Burton, J. W. (1987). *Resolving deep-rooted conflict.* Lanham, MD: University Press of America.

Byrnes, D. A., & Kiger, G. (1990). The effect of a prejudice-reduction simulation on attitude change. *Journal of Applied Social Psychology, 20,* 341–356.

Caldwell, M. C., & Caldwell, D. K. (1966). Epimeletic (care-giving) behavior in Cetacea. In K. S. Norris (Ed.), *Whales, dolphins, and porpoises* (pp. 755–789). Berkeley: University of California Press.

Call, J., & Tomasello, M. (2008). Does the chimpanzee have a theory of mind? 30 years later. *Trends in Cognitive Sciences, 12,* 187–192.

Cameron, C. D., & Payne, B. K. (2011). Escaping affect: How motivated emotion regulation creates insensitivity to mass suffering. *Journal of Personality and Social Psychology, 100,* 1–15.

Caporeal, L. R., Dawes, R., Orbell, J. M., & van de Kragt, A. J. C. (1989). Selfishness examined: Cooperation in the absence of egoistic incentives. *Behavioral and Brain Sciences, 12,* 683–739.

Carter, C. S. (1998). Neuroendocrine perspectives on social attachment and love. *Psychoneuroendocrinology, 23,* 779–818.

Carter, C. S. (2014). Oxytocin pathways and the evolution of human behavior. *Annual Review of Psychology, 65,* 17–39.

Chartrand, T. L., & Bargh, J. A. (1999). The Chameleon Effect: The perception-behavior link and social interaction. *Journal of Personality and Social Psychology, 76,* 893–910.

Churchland, P., & Winkielman, P. (2012). Modulating social behavior with oxytocin: How does it work: What does it mean? *Hormones and Behavior, 61,* 392–399.

Cialdini, R. B., Brown, S. L., Lewis, B. P., Luce, C., & Neuberg, S. L. (1997). Reinterpreting the empathy-altruism relationship: When one into one equals oneness. *Journal of Personality and Social Psychology, 73,* 481–494.

228 • References

Cialdini, R. B., Schaller, M., Houlihan, D., Arps, K., Fultz, J., & Beaman, A. L. (1987). Empathy-based helping: Is it selflessly or selfishly motivated? *Journal of Personality and Social Psychology, 52*, 749–758.

Cikara, M., Bruneau, E., & Saxe, R. R. (2011). Us and them: Intergroup failures of empathy. *Current Directions in Psychological Science, 20*, 149–153.

Cikara, M., Bruneau, E., Van Bavel, J. J., & Saxe, R. (2014). Their pain gives us pleasure: How intergroup dynamics shape empathic failures and counter-empathic responses. *Journal of Experimental Social Psychology, 55*, 110–125.

Clark, R. D., & Word, L. E. (1972). Why don't bystanders help? Because of ambiguity? *Journal of Personality and Social Psychology, 24*, 392–401.

Clark, R. D., & Word, L. E. (1974). Where is the apathetic bystander? Situational characteristics of the emergency. *Journal of Personality and Social Psychology, 29*, 279–288.

Clore, G. L., & Jeffrey, K. M. (1972). Emotional role playing, attitude change, and attraction toward a disabled person. *Journal of Personality and Social Psychology, 23*, 105–111.

Coke, J. S. (1980). Empathic mediation of helping: Egoistic or altruistic? (Doctoral dissertation, University of Kansas, 1979). *Dissertation Abstracts International, 41B*, 405. (University Microfilms No. 8014371)

Coke, J. S., Batson, C. D., & McDavis, K. (1978). Empathic mediation of helping: A two-stage model. *Journal of Personality and Social Psychology, 36*, 752–766.

Collins, N. L., Ford, M. B., Guichard, A. C., Kane, H. S., & Feeney, B. C. (2010). Responding to need in intimate relationships: Social support and care-giving processes in couples. In M. Mikulincer & P. R. Shaver (Eds.), *Prosocial motives, emotions, and behavior: The better angels of our nature* (pp. 367–389). Washington, DC: American Psychological Association.

Condon, P., Desbordes, G., Miller, W. B., & DeSteno, D. (2013). Meditation increases compassionate responses to suffering, *Psychological Science, 24*, 2125–2127.

Connor, R. C., & Norris, K. S. (1982). Are dolphins reciprocal altruists? *American Naturalist, 119*, 358–374.

Craig, A. D. (2005). Forebrain emotional asymmetry: A neuroanatomical basis? *Trends in Cognitive Sciences, 9*, 566–571.

Craig, A. D. (2009). How do you feel—now? The anterior insula and human awareness. *Nature Reviews Neuroscience, 10*, 59–70.

Craig, K. D., & Lowery, J. H. (1969). Heart-rate components of conditioned vicarious autonomic responses. *Journal of Personality and Social Psychology, 11*, 381–387.

Craig, K. D., & Wood, K. (1969). Psychophysiological differentiation of direct and vicarious affective arousal. *Canadian Journal of Behavioral Science, 1*, 98–105.

Crocker, J., & Canevello, A. (2008). Creating and undermining social support in communal relationships: The role of compassionate and self-image goals. *Journal of Personality and Social Psychology, 95*, 555–575.

Cuff, B. M. P., Brown, S. J., Taylor, L., & Howat, D. J. (2016). Empathy: A review of the concept. *Emotion Review, 8*, 144–153.

Curtis, J. T., & Wang, Z. (2003). The neurochemistry of pair bonding. *Current Directions in Psychological Science, 12*, 49–53.

Custance, D., & Mayer, J. (2012). Empathy-like responding by domestic dogs (*Canis familiaris*) to distress in humans: An exploratory study. *Animal Cognition, 15*, 851–859.

Damasio, A. R. (1994). *Descartes' error: Emotion, reason, and the human brain*. New York: Avon Books.

Damasio, A. R. (1999). *The feeling of what happens: Body and emotion in the making of consciousness*. New York: Harcourt Brace & Company.

Damasio, A. R. (2002). A note on the neurobiology of emotions. In S. G. Post, L. G. Underwood, J. P. Schloss, & W. B. Hurlbut (Eds.), *Altruism and altruistic love: Science, philosophy, and religion in dialogue* (pp. 264–271). New York: Oxford University Press.

Damasio, A. R. (2003). *Looking for Spinoza: Joy, sorrow, and the feeling brain*. Orlando, FL: Harcourt.

Damasio, H. (2002). Impairment of interpersonal social behavior caused by acquired brain damage. In S. G. Post, L. G. Underwood, J. P. Schloss, & W. B. Hurlbut (Eds.), *Altruism and altruistic love: Science, philosophy, and religion in dialogue* (pp. 272–283). New York: Oxford University Press.

Danziger, N., Faillenot, I., & Peyron, R. (2009). Can we share a pain we never felt? Neural correlates of empathy in patients with congenital insensitivity to pain. *Neuron, 61*, 203–212.

Darwall, S. (1998). Empathy, sympathy, care. *Philosophical Studies, 89*, 261–282.

Darwin, C. (1871). *The descent of man and selection in relation to sex*. New York: Appleton.

Davidov, M., Paz, Y., Roth-Hanania, R., Uzefovsky, F., Orlitsky, T., Mankuta, D., & Zahn-Waxler, C. (2021). Caring babies: Concern for others in distress during infancy. *Developmental Science, 24*(2), 1–17.

Davidov, M., Zahn-Waxler, C., Roth-Hanania, R., & Knafo, A. (2013). Concern for others in the first year of life: Theory, evidence, and avenues for research. *Child Development Perspectives, 7*, 126–131.

Davis, M. H. (1983). Measuring individual differences in empathy: Evidence for a multidimensional approach. *Journal of Personality and Social Psychology, 44*, 113–126.

Davis, M. H. (1994). *Empathy: A social psychological approach*. Madison, WI: Brown & Benchmark.

Davis, M. H., Conklin, L., Smith, A., & Luce, C. (1996). The effect of perspective taking on the cognitive representation of persons: A merging of self and other. *Journal of Personality and Social Psychology, 70*, 713–726.

Davis, M. H., Soderlund, T., Cole, J., Gadol, E., Kute, M., Myers, M., & Wiehing, J. (2004). Cognitions associated with attempts to empathize: How *do* we imagine the perspective of another? *Personality and Social Psychology Bulletin, 30*, 1625–1635.

230 • References

Decety, J. (2010). To what extent is the experience of empathy mediated by shared neural circuits? *Emotion Review, 2*, 204–207.

Decety, J., & Chaminade, T. (2003). Neural correlates of feeling sympathy. *Neuropsychologia, 41*, 127–138.

Decety, J., Echols, S., & Correll, J. (2010). The blame game: The effect of responsibility and social stigma on empathy for pain. *Journal of Cognitive Neuroscience, 22*(5), 985–997.

Decety, J., & Lamm, C. (2009). Empathy versus personal distress: Recent evidence from social neuroscience. In J. Decety & W. Ickes (Eds.), *The social neuroscience of empathy* (pp. 199–213). Cambridge, MA: MIT Press.

de Paúl, J., & Guibert, M. (2008). Empathy and child neglect: A theoretical model. *Child Abuse and Neglect, 32*, 1063–1071.

de Paúl, J., Pérez-Albéniz, A., Guibert, M., Asla, N., & Ormaechea, A. (2008). Dispositional empathy in neglectful mothers and mothers at high risk for child physical abuse. *Journal of Interpersonal Violence, 23*, 670–684.

Des Pres, T. (1976). *The survivor: An anatomy of life in the death camps*. New York: Oxford University Press.

DeSteno, D. (2015). Compassion and altruism: How our minds determine who is worthy of help. *Current Directions in Behavioral Sciences, 3*, 80–83.

de Vignemont, F., & Singer, T. (2006). The empathic brain: How, when, and why? *Trends in Cognitive Sciences, 10*, 435–441.

de Waal, F. B. M. (1996). *Good natured: The origins of right and wrong in humans and other animals*. Cambridge, MA: Harvard University Press.

de Waal, F. B. M. (2006). *Primates and philosophers: How morality evolved*. Princeton, NJ: Princeton University Press.

de Waal, F. B. M. (2008). Putting the altruism back into altruism: The evolution of empathy. *Annual Review of Psychology, 59*, 279–300.

de Waal, F. B. M. (2009). *The age of empathy: Nature's lessons for a kinder society*. New York: Harmony Books.

de Waal, F. B. M., & Preston, S. D. (2017). Mammalian empathy: behavioral manifestations and neural basis. *Nature Reviews/Neuroscience, 18*(8), 498–509.

Dickens, C. (2001). *Oliver Twist, or, the Parish Boy's Progress*. London: Penguin. (Original work published 1838)

Dijker, A. J. (2001). The influence of perceived suffering and vulnerability on the experience of pity. *European Journal of Social Psychology, 31*, 659–676.

Dijker, A. J. (2010). Perceived vulnerability as common basis of moral emotions. *British Journal of Social Psychology, 49*, 415–423.

Dimberg, U., Thunberg, M., & Elmehed, K. (2000). Unconscious facial reactions to emotional facial expressions. *Psychological Science, 11*, 86–89.

Dixon, M. L., & Dweck, C. S. (2022). The amygdala and the prefrontal cortex: The co-communication of intelligent decision-making. *Psychological Review, 129*(6), 1414–1441.

Donaldson, Z. R., & Young, L. J. (2008). Oxytocin, vasopressin, and the neurogenetics of sociality. *Science, 322*, 900–904.

Dondi, M., Simion, F., & Caltran, G. (1999). Can newborns discriminate between their own cry and the cry of another newborn infant? *Developmental Psychology, 35*, 418–426.

Dovidio, J. F. (1984). Helping behavior and altruism: An empirical and conceptual overview. In L. Berkowitz (Ed.), *Advances in experimental social psychology* (Vol. 17, pp. 361–427). New York: Academic Press.

Dovidio, J. F., Allen, J. L., & Schroeder, D. A. (1990). The specificity of empathy-induced helping: Evidence for altruistic motivation. *Journal of Personality and Social Psychology, 59*, 249–260.

Dovidio, J. F., Gaertner, S. L., & Saguy, T. (2009). Commonality and the complexity of "we": Social attitudes and social change. *Personality and Social Psychology Review, 13*, 3–20.

Dovidio, J. F., Johnson, J. D., Gaertner, S. L., Pearson, A. R., Saguy, T., & Ashburn-Nardo, L. (2010). Empathy and intergroup relations. In M. Mikulincer & P. R. Shaver (Eds.), *Prosocial motives, emotions, and behavior: The better angels of our nature* (pp. 393–408). Washington, DC: American Psychological Association.

Dovidio, J. F., Piliavin, J. A., Schroeder, D. A., & Penner, L. A. (2006). *The social psychology of prosocial behavior*. Mahawan, NJ: Lawrence Erlbaum Associates.

Dovidio, J. F., ten Vergert, M., Stewart, T. L., Gaertner, S. L., Johnson, J. D., Esses, V. M., Rick, B. M., & Pearson, A. R. (2004). Perspective and prejudice: Antecedents and mediating mechanisms. *Personality and Social Psychology Bulletin, 30*, 1537–1549.

Doyle, A. C. (1890). *The sign of four*. London: Spencer Blackett.

Dymond, R. F. (1950). Personality and empathy. *Journal of Consulting Psychology, 14*, 343–350.

Eibl-Eibesfeldt, I. (1970). *Ethology: The biology of behavior*. New York: Holt, Rinehart, & Winston.

Eisenberg, N. (2000). Emotion, regulation, and moral development. *Annual review of psychology, 51*, 665–697.

Eisenberg, N., Fabes, R. A., Miller, P. A., Fultz, J., Shell, R., Mathy, R. M., & Reno, R. R. (1989). Relation of sympathy and personal distress to prosocial behavior: A multimethod study. *Journal of Personality and Social Psychology, 57*, 55–66.

Eisenberg, N., Fabes, R. A., Schaller, M., Miller, P., Carlo, G., Poulin, R., Shea, C., & Shell, R. (1991). Personality and socialization correlated of vicarious emotional responding. *Journal of Personality and Social Psychology, 61*, 459–470.

Eisenberg, N., & Miller, P. A. (1987). Empathy and prosocial behavior. *Psychological Bulletin, 101*, 91–119.

Eisenberg, N., & Strayer, J. (1987). Critical issues in the study of empathy. In N. Eisenberg & J. Strayer (Eds.), *Empathy and its development* (pp. 3–13). New York: Cambridge University Press.

232 • References

Eliasz, H. (1980). The effect of empathy, reactivity, and anxiety on interpersonal aggression intensity. *Polish Psychological Bulletin, 11*, 169–178.

Englis, B. G., Vaughan, K. B., & Lanzetta, J. T. (1982). Conditioning of counter-empathetic emotional responses. *Journal of Experimental Social Psychology, 18*, 375–391.

Epley, N., Keysar, B., Van Boven, L., & Gilovich, T. (2004). Perspective taking as egocentric anchoring and adjustment. *Journal of Personality and Social Psychology, 87*, 327–339.

Eslinger, P. J. (1998). Neurological and neuropsychological bases of empathy. *European Neurology, 1998*, 193–199.

Esses, V. M., & Dovidio, J. F. (2002). The role of emotions in determining willingness to engage in intergroup contact. *Personality and Social Psychology Bulletin, 28*, 1202–1214.

Fabi, S., Weber, L. A., & Leuthold, H. (2019). Empathic concern and personal distress depend on situational but not dispositional factors. *PLoS One, 14*(11), e0225102.

Faulkner, N. (2018). "Put yourself in their shoes": Testing empathy's ability to motivate cosmopolitan behavior. *Political Psychology, 39*, 217–228.

Feeney, B. C., & Collins, N. L. (2001). Predictors of care-giving in adult intimate relationships: An attachment theoretical perspective. *Journal of Personality and Social Psychology, 80*, 972–994.

Feeney, B. C., & Collins, N. L. (2003). Motivations for care-giving in adult intimate relationships: Influences on care-giving behavior and relationship functioning. *Personality and Social Psychology Bulletin, 29*, 950–968.

Feldman, R. (2012). Oxytocin and social affiliation in humans. *Hormones and Behavior, 61*, 380–391.

Feldman, R. (2017). The neurobiology of human attachments. *Trends in Cognitive Sciences, 21*, 80–99.

Feldman, R., Weller, A., Zagoory-Sharon, O., & Levine, A. (2007). Evidence for a neuroendocrinological foundation of human affiliation: Plasma oxytocin levels across pregnancy and the postpartum period predict mother-infant bonding. *Psychological Science, 18*, 965–970.

Feldman, R., Zagoory-Sharon, O., Weisman, O., Scheniderman, I., Gordon, I., Maoz, R., Shalev, I., & Ebstein, R. P. (2012). Sensitive parenting is associated with plasma oxytocin and polymorphisms in the *OXTR* and *CD38* genes. *Biological Psychiatry, 72*, 175–181.

Feshbach, N. D., & Roe, K. (1968). Empathy in six- and seven-year-olds. *Child Development, 39*, 133–145.

Figley, C. R. (2002). Compassion fatigue: Psychotherapists' chronic lack of self-care. *Journal of Clinical Psychology* (Special Issue: *Chronic Illness*), *58*, 1433–1441.

Fincham, F. D., Paleari, F. G., & Regalia, C. (2002). Forgiveness in marriage: The role of relationship quality, attributions, and empathy. *Personal Relationships, 9*, 27–37.

References • **233**

Finlay, K. A., & Stephan, W. G. (2000). Improving intergroup relations: The effects of empathy on intergroup attitudes. *Journal of Applied Social Psychology, 30*, 1720–1737.

Fisher, J. D., Nadler, A., & DePaulo, B. M. (Eds.) (1983). *New directions in helping: Vol. 1. Recipient reactions to aid.* New York: Academic Press.

Fisher, R. (1994). General principles for resolving intergroup conflict. *Journal of Social Issues, 50*, 47–66.

Freud, S. (1922). *Group psychology and the analysis of the ego.* London: International Psycho-Analytic Press.

Frijda, N. H. (1988). The laws of emotion. *American Psychologist, 43*, 349–358.

Frodi, A. M., & Lamb, M. E. (1980). Child abusers' responses to infant smiles and cries. *Child Development, 51*, 238–241.

Fultz, J. (1982). *Influence of potential for self-reward on egoistically and altruistically motivated helping.* Unpublished M. A. thesis. University of Kansas.

Fultz, J., Batson, C. D., Fortenbach, V. A., McCarthy, P. M., & Varney, L. L. (1986). Social evaluation and the empathy-altruism hypothesis. *Journal of Personality and Social Psychology, 50*, 761–769.

Fultz, J., Schaller, M., & Cialdini, R. B. (1988). Empathy, sadness, and distress: Three related but distinct vicarious affective responses to another's suffering. *Personality and Social Psychology Bulletin, 14*, 312–325.

Gaines, T., Kirwin, P. M., & Gentry, W. D. (1977). The effect of descriptive anger expression, insult, and no feedback on interpersonal aggression, hostility, and empathy motivation. *Genetic Psychology Monographs, 95*, 349–367.

Galinsky, A. D., & Ku, G. (2004). The effects of perspective-taking on prejudice. *Personality and Social Psychology Bulletin, 30*, 594–604.

Galinsky, A. D., Ku, G., & Wang, C. S. (2005). Perspective-taking and self-other overlap: Fostering social bonds and facilitating social coordination. *Group Processes and Intergroup Relations, 8*. 109–124.

Galinsky, A. D., Maddux, W. W., Gilin, D., & White, J. B. (2008). Why it pays to get inside the head of your opponent: The differential effects of perspective taking and empathy in negotiations. *Psychological Science, 19*, 378–384.

Galinsky, A. D., & Moskowitz, G. B. (2000). Perspective-taking: Decreasing stereotype expression, stereotype accessibility, and in-group favoritism. *Journal of Personality and Social Psychology, 78*, 708–724.

Galinsky, A. D., Wang, C. S., & Ku, G. (2008). Perspective-takers behave more stereotypically. *Journal of Personality and Social Psychology, 95*, 404–419.

Gallese, V., Gernsbacher, M. A., Heyes, C., Hickok, G., & Iacoboni, M. (2011). Mirror neuron forum. *Perspectives on Psychological Science, 6*(4), 369–407.

George, C., & Solomon, J. (1999). Attachment and caregiving: The caregiving behavioral system. In J. Cassidy & P. R. Shaver, *Handbook of attachment: Theory, research, and clinical applications* (pp. 649–670). New York: Guilford.

234 • References

Gibbons, F. X., & Wicklund, R. A. (1982). Self-focused attention and helping behavior. *Journal of Personality and Social Psychology, 43*, 462–474.

Gilbert, D. (2007, March). Compassionate commercialism. *New York Times*, Op-Ed Contribution, March 25, 2007.

Glenberg, A. M. (2011). Introduction to the mirror neuron forum. *Perspectives on Psychological Science, 6*(4), 363–368.

Goetz, J. L., Keltner, D., & Simon-Thomas, E. (2010). Compassion: An evolutionary analysis and empirical review. *Psychological Bulletin, 136*, 351–374.

Goldman, A. I. (1992). Empathy, mind, and morals. *Proceedings from the American Philosophical Association, 66*, 17–41.

Goldman, A. I. (1993). Ethics and cognitive science. *Ethics, 103*, 337–360.

Goodall, J. (1990). *Through a window: My thirty years with the chimpanzees of Gombe*. Boston: Houghton Mifflin.

Gordon, I., Zagoory-Sharon, O., Leckman, J. F., & Feldman, R. (2010). Oxytocin and the development of parenting in humans. *Biological Psychiatry, 68*, 377–382.

Gordon, M. (2005). *Roots of empathy: Changing the world child by child*. Markham, ON: Thomas Allen & Son.

Gordon, R. M. (1995). Sympathy, simulation, and the impartial spectator. *Ethics, 105*, 727–742.

Graves, S. B. (1999). Television and prejudice reduction: When does television as a vicarious experience make a difference? *Journal of Social Issues, 55*, 707–725.

Greenwald, A. G., Nozek, B. A., & Banaji, M. R. (2003). Understanding and using the Implicit Association Test: I. An improved scoring algorithm. *Journal of Personality and Social Psychology, 85*, 197–216.

Grewen, K. M., Girdler, S. S., Amico, J., & Light, K. C. (2005). Effects of partner support on resting oxytocin, cortisol, norepinephrine, and blood pressure before and after warm partner contact. *Psychosomatic Medicine, 67*, 531–538.

Gruen, R. J., & Mendelsohn, G. (1986). Emotional responses to affective displays in others: The distinction between empathy and sympathy. *Journal of Personality and Social Psychology, 51*, 609–614.

Gurin, P., Peng, T., Lopez, G., & Nagada, B. R. (1999). Context, identity, and intergroup relations. In D. Prentice & D. T. Miller (Eds.), *Cultural divides: The social psychology of intergroup contact* (pp. 133–170). New York: Russell Sage Foundation.

Gutsell, J. N., & Inzlicht, M. (2010). Empathy constrained: Prejudice predicts reduced mental simulation of actions during observation of outgroups. *Journal of Experimental Social Psychology, 46*, 841–845.

Halpern, J. (2001). *From detached concern to empathy: Humanizing medical practice*. New York: Oxford University Press.

Hardin, G. (1977). *The limits of altruism: An ecologist's view of survival*. Bloomington: Indiana University Press.

References · 235

Harlow, H. K., Harlow, M. K., Dodsworth, R. O., & Arling, G. L. (1966). Maternal behavior of rhesus monkeys deprived of mothering and peer association in infancy. *Proceedings of the American Philosophical Society, 110,* 58–66.

Harmon-Jones, E., Vaughn-Scott, K., Mohr, S., Sigelman, J., & Harmon-Jones, C. (2004). The effect of manipulated sympathy and anger on left and right frontal cortical activity. *Emotion, 4,* 95–101.

Harrison, M.-C. (2008). The paradox of fiction and the ethics of empathy: Reconceiving Dickens's realism. *Narrative, 16,* 256–278.

Haslam, N. (2006). Dehumanization: An integrative review. *Personality and Social Psychology Review, 10,* 252–264.

Hatfield, E., Cacioppo, J. T., & Rapson, R. L. (1994). *Emotional contagion.* New York: Cambridge University Press.

Hayes, M. L., & Conklin, M. E. (1953). Intergroup attitudes and experimental change. *Journal of Experimental Education, 22,* 19–36.

Hein, G., Morishima, Y., Leiberg, S., Sul, S., & Fehr, E. (2016). The brain's functional network architecture reveals human motives. *Science, 351*(6277), 1074–1078.

Hein, G., Silani, G., Preuschoff, K, Batson, C. D., & Singer, T. (2010). Neural responses to ingroup and outgroup members' suffering predict individual differences in costly helping. *Neuron, 68,* 149–160.

Hepach, R., Vaish, A., & Tomasello, M. (2013). A new look at children's prosocial motivation. *Infancy, 18,* 67–90.

Hickok, G. (2014). *The myth of mirror neurons: The real neuroscience of communication and cognition.* New York: W. W. Norton.

Hodges, S. D. (2005). Is how much you understand me in your head or mine? In B. F. Malle & S. D. Hodges (Eds.), *Other minds: How humans bridge the divide between self and others* (pp. 298–309). New York: Guilford Press.

Hodges, S. D., Kiel, K. J., Kramer, A. D. I., Veach, D., & Villanueva, B. R. (2010). Giving birth to empathy: The effects of similar experience on empathic accuracy, empathic concern, and perceived empathy. *Personality and Social Psychology Bulletin, 36,* 398–409.

Hoess, R. (1959). *Commandant at Auschwitz: Autobiography.* London: Weidenfeld and Nicholson.

Hoffman, M. L. (1981a). The development of empathy. In J. P. Rushton & R. M. Sorrentino (Eds.), *Altruism and helping behavior: Social, personality, and developmental perspectives* (pp. 41–63). Hillsdale, NJ: Erlbaum.

Hoffman, M. L. (1981b). Is altruism part of human nature? *Journal of Personality and Social Psychology, 40,* 121–137.

Hoffman, M. L. (1991). Is empathy altruistic? *Psychological Inquiry, 2,* 131–133.

Hoffman, M. L. (2000). *Empathy and moral development: Implications for caring and justice.* New York: Cambridge University Press.

Hornstein, H. A. (1991). Empathic distress and altruism: Still inseparable. *Psychological Inquiry, 2,* 133–135.

236 • References

Hrdy, S. B. (2009). *Mothers and others: The evolutionary origins of mutual understanding*. Cambridge, MA: Harvard University Press.

Hrdy, S. B., & Burkart, J. M. (2020). The emergence of emotionally modern humans: Implications for language and learning. *Philosophical Transactions of the Royal Society B: Biological Sciences, 375*(1803), 20190499.

Hume, D. (1896). *A treatise of human nature*. (L. A. Selby-Bigge, Ed.). Oxford: Oxford University Press. (Original work published 1739–1740)

Hutcherson, C. A., Seppala, E. M., & Gross, J. J. (2008). Loving-kindness meditation increases social connectedness. *Emotion, 8*, 720–724.

Hygge, S. (1976). Information about the model's unconditioned stimulus and response in vicarious classical conditioning. *Journal of Personality and Social Psychology, 33*, 764–771.

Ickes, W. (1993). Empathic accuracy. *Journal of Personality, 61*, 587–610.

Ilyes, I. (2017). Empathy in Hume and Smith. In H. L. Maibom (Ed.), *The Routledge handbook of philosophy of empathy* (pp. 98–109). New York: Routledge.

Immordino-Yang, M. H., McColl, A., Damasio, H., & Damasio, A. (2009). Neural correlates of admiration and compassion. *Proceedings of the National Academy of Sciences, USA, 106*(19), 8021–8026.

Insel, T. R. (1997). A neurobiological basis of social attachment. *American Journal of Psychiatry, 154*, 726–735.

Insel, T. R. (2000). Toward a neurobiology of attachment. *Review of General Psychology, 4*, 176–185.

Insel, T. R. (2002). Implications for the neurobiology of love. In S. G. Post, L. G. Underwood, J. P. Schloss, & W. B. Hurlbut (Eds.), *Altruism and altruistic love: Science, philosophy, and religion in dialogue* (pp. 254–263). New York: Oxford University Press.

Isaacson, W. (1992, December 21). Sometimes, right makes might. *Time* (p. 82).

Israelashvili, J., Sauter, D. A., & Fischer, A. H. (2020). Different faces of empathy: Feelings of similarity disrupt recognition of negative emotion. *Journal of Experimental Social Psychology, 87*, 103912.

Jackson, P. L., Brunet, E., Meltzoff, A. N., & Decety, J. (2006). Empathy examined through the neural mechanisms involved in imagining how I feel versus how you feel pain. *Neuropsychologia, 44*, 752–761.

Jacob, P. (2008). What do mirror neurons contribute to human social cognition? *Mind and Language, 23*, 190–223.

Jahoda, G. (2005). Theodor Lipps and the shift from "sympathy" to "empathy." *Journal of the History of the Behavioral Sciences, 41*, 151–163.

Jansen, L. A. (2009). The ethics of altruism in clinical research. *Hastings Center Report, 39*(4), 26–36.

Jarymowicz, M. (1992). Self, we, and other(s): Schemata, distinctiveness, and altruism. In P. M. Oliner, S. P. Oliner, L. Baron, L. A. Blum, D. L. Krebs, & M. Z. Smolenska

(Eds.), *Embracing the other: Philosophical, psychological, and historical perspectives on altruism* (pp. 194–212). New York: New York University Press.

Johnson, D. W., & Johnson, R. T. (1987). *Learning together and alone: Cooperative, competitive, and individualistic learning.* Englewood Cliffs, NJ: Prentice-Hall.

Johnson, J. D., Simmons, C. H., Jordan, A., MacLean, L., Taddei, J., Thomas, D., Dovidio, J. F., & Reed, W. (2002). Rodney King and O. J. Simpson revisited: The impact of race and defendant empathy induction on judicial decisions. *Journal of Applied Social Psychology, 32,* 1206–1223.

Kahneman, D., & Ritov, I. (1994). Determinants of stated willingness to pay for public goods: A study in the headline method. *Journal of Risk and Uncertainty, 9,* 5–38.

Kahneman, D., Slovic, P., & Tversky, A. (Eds.) (1982). *Judgment under uncertainty: Heuristics and biases.* New York: Cambridge University Press.

Kalawski, J. P. (2010). Is tenderness a basic emotion? *Motivation and Emotion, 34,* 158–167.

Kameda, T., Murata, A., Sasaki, C., Higuchi, S., & Inukai, K. (2012). Empathizing with a dissimilar other: The role of self-other distinction in sympathetic responding. *Personality and Social Psychology Bulletin, 38,* 997–1003.

Kang, Y., Gray, J. R., & Dovidio, J. F. (2014). The non-discriminating heart: Loving-kindness meditation training decreases implicit intergroup bias. *Journal of Experimental Psychology: General, 143,* 1306–1313.

Katz, I., & Haas, R. G. (1988). Racial ambivalence and American value conflict: Correlational and priming studies of dual cognitive structures. *Journal of Personality and Social Psychology, 55,* 893–905.

Keen, S. (2007). *Empathy and the novel.* Oxford, UK: Oxford University Press.

Kelley, H. H. (1979). *Personal relationships: Their structures and processes.* Hillsdale, NJ: Erlbaum.

Kelley, H. H. (1983). Love and commitment. In H. H. Kelley, E., Berscheid, A. Christiansen, J. H. Harvey, T. L. Houston, G. Levinger, E. McClintock, L. A. Peplau, & D. L. Peterson, *Close relationships* (pp. 265–314). New York: Freeman.

Kelman, H. C. (1973). Violence without moral restraint: Reflections on the dehumanization of victims and victimizers. *Journal of Social Issues, 29,* 25–61.

Kelman, H. C. (1990). Interactive problem-solving: A social psychological approach to conflict resolution. In J. W. Burton & F. Dukes (Eds.), *Conflict: Readings in management and resolution* (pp. 199–215). New York: St. Martin's Press.

Kelman, H. C. (1997). Group processes in the resolution of international conflicts: Experiences from the Israeli-Palestinian case. *American Psychologist, 52,* 212–220.

Kelman, H. C. (2005). Building trust among enemies: The central challenge for international conflict resolution. *International Journal of Intercultural Relations, 29,* 639–650.

238 • References

Kelman, H. C., & Cohen, S. P. (1986). Resolution of international conflict: An interactional approach. In S. Worchel & W. G. Austin (Eds.), *Psychology of intergroup relations* (pp. 323–432). Chicago: Nelson Hall.

Keltner, D., & Haidt, J. (1999). Social functions of emotions at multiple levels of analysis. *Cognition and Emotion, 13*, 505–522.

Keltner, D., & Haidt, J. (2001). Social function of emotions. In T. J. Mayne & G. A. Bonanno (Eds.), *Emotions: Current issues and directions* (pp. 192–213). New York: Guilford Press.

Kendrick, K. M. (2000). Oxytocin, motherhood, and bonding. *Experimental Physiology, 85s*, 111s–124s.

Kerr, N. L. (1995). Norms in social dilemmas. In D. A. Schroeder (Ed.), *Social dilemmas: Perspectives on individuals and groups* (pp. 31–47). Westport, CT: Praeger.

Kesey, K. (1962). *One flew over the cuckoo's nest*. New York: Viking.

Kidder, T. (2003). *Mountains beyond mountains*. New York: Random House.

Kim, J-W., Kim, S-E., Kim, J-J., Jeong, B., Park, C-H., Son, A. R., Song, J. E., & Ki, S. W. (2009). Compassionate attitude toward others' suffering activates the mesolimbic neural system. *Neuropsychologia, 47*, 2073–2081.

Klimecki, O. M., Leiberg, S., Ricard, M., & Singer, T. (2014). Differential pattern of functioning brain plasticity after compassion and empathy training. *Social Cognitive and Affective Neuroscience, 9*, 873–879.

Knafo, A., Zahn-Waxler, C., Van Hulle, C., Robinson, J. L., & Rhee, S. H. (2008). The developmental origins of a disposition toward empathy: Genetic and environmental contributions. *Emotion, 8*, 737–752.

Kogut, T., & Ritov, I. (2005a). The "identified victim" effect: An identified group, or just a single individual? *Journal of Behavioral Decision Making, 18*, 157–167.

Kogut, T., & Ritov, I. (2005b). The singularity effect of identified victims in separate and joint evaluations. *Organizational Behavior and Human Decision Processes, 97*, 106–116.

Kohlberg, L. (1976). Moral stages and moralization: The cognitive-developmental approach. In T. Lickona (Ed.), *Moral development and behavior: Theory, research, and social issues* (pp. 31–53). New York: Holt, Rinehart, & Winston.

Kohler, W. (1929). *Gestalt psychology*. New York: Liveright.

Kohut, H. (1959). Introspection, empathy, and psychoanalysis. An examination of the relationship between mode of observation and theory. *Journal of the American Psychoanalytic Association, 7*, 459–483.

Köster, M., Ohmer, X., Nguyen, T. D., & Kärtner, J. (2016). Infants understand others' needs. *Psychological Science, 27*, 542–548.

Kozol, J. (1991). *Savage inequalities: Children in America's schools*. New York: Crown.

Krebs, D. L. (1975). Empathy and altruism. *Journal of Personality and Social Psychology, 32*, 1134–1146.

Krebs, D. L., & Russell, C. (1981). Role-taking and altruism: When you put yourself in the shoes of another, will they take you to their owner's aid? In J. P. Rushton & R.

M. Sorrentino (Eds.), *Altruism and helping behavior: Social, personality, and developmental perspectives* (pp. 137–165). Hillsdale, NJ: Erlbaum.

Kreplin, U., Farias, M., & Brazil, I. A. (2018). The limited prosocial effects of meditation: A systematic review and meta-analysis. *Scientific Reports, 8:2403*. doi:10.1038/s41598-108-20299-z.

Kteily, N. S., & Bruneau, E. (2017). Darker demons of our nature: The need to (re)focus attention on blatant forms of dehumanization. *Current Directions in Psychological Science, 26*, 487–494.

Kteily, N. S., Bruneau, E., Waytz, A., & Cotterill, S. (2015). The ascent of man: Theoretical and empirical evidence for blatant dehumanization. *Journal of Personality and Social Psychology, 109*, 901–931.

Lakin, J. L., & Chartrand, T. L. (2003). Using nonconscious behavioral mimicry to create affiliation and rapport. *Psychological Science, 14*, 334–339.

Lamm, C., Batson, C. D., & Decety, J. (2007). The neural substrate of human empathy: Effects of perspective-taking and cognitive appraisal. *Journal of Cognitive Neuroscience, 19*, 1–17.

Lamm, C., Decety, J., & Singer, T. (2011). Meta-analytic evidence for common and distinct neural networks associated with directly experienced pain and empathy for pain. *Neuroimage, 54*, 2492–2502.

Lamm, C., Meltzoff, A. N., & Decety, J. (2010). How do we empathize with someone who is not like us? A functional magnetic resonance imaging study. *Journal of Cognitive Neuroscience, 22*, 362–376.

Lamm, C., & Singer, T. (2010). The role of anterior insular cortex in social emotions. *Brain Structure and Function, 214*, 579–591.

La Rochefoucauld, F., Duke de (1691). *Moral maxims and reflections, in four parts.* London: Gillyflower, Sare, & Everingham.

Latané, B., & Darley, J. M. (1970). *The unresponsive bystander: Why doesn't he help?* New York: Appleton-Century-Crofts.

Leibenluft, E., Gobbini, I., Harrison, T., & Haxby, J. V. (2004). Mothers' neural activation in response to pictures of their children and other children. *Biological Psychiatry, 56*, 225–232.

Lepper, M. R. (1983). Social-control processes and the internalization of social values: An attributional perspective. In E. T. Higgins, D. N. Ruble, & W. W. Hartup (Eds.), *Social cognition and social development* (pp. 294–330). New York: Cambridge University Press.

Lerner, M. J. (1980). *The belief in a just world: A fundamental delusion.* New York: Plenum.

Levenson, R. W., & Ruef, A. M. (1992). Empathy: A physiological substrate. *Journal of Personality and Social Psychology, 63*, 234–246.

Lewin, K. (1938). The conceptual representation and the measurement of psychological forces. *Contributions to psychological theory, 1*(4), Whole Issue (pp. 1–247). Durham, NC: Duke University Press.

240 • References

Lewin, K. (1944/1951). Constructs in psychology and psychological ecology. *University of Iowa Studies in Child Welfare, 20,* 1–29. Reprinted in Lewin, K. (1951). *Field theory in social science: Selected Theoretical Papers,* as Chapter 2, "Constructs in Field Theory," pp. 30–42. New York: Harper.

Lickel, B., Miller, N., Stenstrom, D. M., Denson, T. F., & Schmader, T. (2006). Vicarious retribution: The role of collective blame in intergroup aggression. *Personality and Social Psychology Review, 10,* 372–390.

Lipps, T. (1903). Einfühlung, inner Nachahmung, und Organ-empfindungen. *Archiv für die gesamte Psychologie, 2,* 185–204.

Lishner, D. A., Batson, C. D., & Huss, E. (2011). Tenderness and sympathy: Distinct empathic emotions elicited by different forms of need. *Personality and Social Psychology Bulletin, 37,* 614–625.

Lishner, D. A., Oceja, L. V., Stocks, E. L., & Zaspel, K. (2008). The effect of infant-like characteristics on empathic concern for adults in need. *Motivation and Emotion, 32,* 270–277.

Liu, J., Gong, P., Li, H., & Zhou, X. (2017). A field study of the association between *CD38* gene and altruistic behavior: Empathic response as a mediator. *Psychoneuroendocrinology, 85,* 165–171.

López-Pérez, B., Ambrona, T., Gregory, J., Stocks, E., & Oceja, L. (2013). Feeling at hospitals: Perspective-taking, empathy, and personal distress among professional nurses and nursing students. *Nurse Education Today, 33,* 334–338.

Lorenz, K. Z. (1981). *The foundations of ethology: The principal ideas and discoveries in animal behavior.* New York: Springer-Verlag.

McAuliffe, W. H. B., Carter, E. C., Berhane, J., Snihur, A. C., & MiCullough, M. E. (2020). Is empathy the default response to suffering? A meta-analytic evaluation of perspective taking's effect on empathic concern. *Personality and Social Psychology Review, 24,* 141–162.

McAuliffe, W. H. B., Forster, D. E., Philippe, J., & McCullough, M. E. (2018). Digital altruists: Resolving key questions about the empathy-altruism hypothesis in an internet sample. *Emotion, 18,* 493–506.

McConahay, J. B. (1986). Modern racism, ambivalence, and the Modern Racism Scale. In J. F. Dovidio & S. L. Gaertner (Eds.), *Prejudice, discrimination, and racism* (pp. 91–125). Orlando, FL: Academic Press.

McCullough, M. E., Rachal, K. C., Sandage, S. J., Worthington, E. L., Jr., Brown, S. W., & Hight, T. L. (1998). Interpersonal forgiving in close relationships: II. Theoretical elaboration and measurement. *Journal of Personality and Social Psychology, 75,* 1586–1603.

McCullough, M. E., Worhington, E. L., Jr., & Rachal, K. C. (1997). Interpersonal forgiving in close relationships. *Journal of Personality and Social Psychology, 73,* 321–336.

McDougall, W. (1908). *An introduction to social psychology.* London: Methuen.

MacLean, P. D. (1967). The brain in relation to empathy and medical education. *Journal of Nervous and Mental Disease, 144*, 374–382.

MacLean, P. D. (1990). *The triune brain in evolution: Role in paleocerebral functions.* New York: Plenum Press.

Maibom, H. L. (2018). Self-simulation and empathy. In N. Roughley & T. Schramme (Eds.), *Forms of fellow-feeling: Empathy, sympathy, concern, and moral agency* (pp. 109–132). Cambridge: Cambridge University Press.

Maisel, N. C., & Gable, S. L. (2009). The paradox of received social support: The importance of responsiveness. *Psychological Science, 20*, 928–932.

Majdandžić, J., Amaschufer, S., Hummer, A., Windischberger, C., & Lamm, C. (2016). The selfless mind: How prefrontal involvement in mentalizing with similar and dissimilar others shapes empathy and prosocial behavior. *Cognition, 157*, 24–38.

Malhotra, D., & Liyanage, S. (2005). Long-term effects of peace workshops in protracted conflicts. *Journal of Conflict Resolution, 49*, 908–924.

Maner, J. K., Luce, C. L., Neuberg, S. L., Cialdini, R. B., Brown, S., & Sagarin, B. J. (2002). The effects of perspective taking on motivations for helping: Still no evidence for altruism. *Personality and Social Psychology Bulletin, 28*, 1601–1610.

Marsh, A. A. (2016). Neural, cognitive, and evolutionary foundations of human altruism. *Wiley Interdisciplinary Reviews: Cognitive Science, 7*, 59–71.

Marsh, A. A. (2019). The caring continuum: Evolved hormonal and proximal mechanisms explain prosocial and antisocial extremes. *Annual Review of Psychology, 70*, 347–371.

Martin, G. B., & Clark, R. D., III (1982). Distress crying in neonates: Species and peer specificity. *Developmental Psychology, 18*, 3–9.

Maslach, C. (1982). *Burnout: The cost of caring.* Englewood Cliffs, NJ: Prentice-Hall.

Masten, C. L., Morelli, S. A., & Eisenberg, N. I. (2011). An fMRI investigation of empathy for "social pain" and subsequent prosocial behavior. *Neuroimage, 55*, 381–388.

Matthews, L. L., Dovidio, J. F., & Schroeder, D. A. (1987, May). *Does empathic concern motivate egoistic or altruistic helping?* Paper read at the annual convention of the Midwestern Psychological Association, Chicago.

Mauss, I. B., & Robinson, M. D. (2009). Measures of emotion: A review. *Cognition and Emotion, 23*, 209–237.

Mead, G. H. (1934). *Mind, self, and society.* Chicago: University of Chicago Press.

Medina, E. (2022, July 19). Dog helps owner who fell 70 feet in California forest. *The New York Times.* https://www.nytimes.com/2022/07/19/us/dog-saves-owner-tahoe-california.html

Meindl, J. R., & Lerner, M. J. (1983). The heroic motive: Some experimental demonstrations. *Journal of Experimental Social Psychology, 19*, 1–20.

Meltzoff, A. N., & Decety, J. (2003). What imitation tells us about social cognition: A rapprochement between developmental psychology and cognitive neuroscience. *Philosophical Transactions of the Royal Society of London: Biological Sciences, 358*, 491–500.

Meltzoff, A. N., & Moore, M. K. (1997). Explaining facial imitation: A theoretical model. *Early Development and Parenting, 6*, 179–192.

Mikulincer, M., & Shaver, P. R. (2003). The attachment behavioral system in adulthood: Activation, psychodynamics, and interpersonal processes. In M. P. Zanna (Ed.), *Advances in experimental social psychology* (Vol. 35, pp. 53–152). San Diego, CA: Academic Press.

Milgram, S. (1970). The experience of living in cities. *Science, 167*, 1461–1468.

Miller, N. (2002). Personalization and the promise of contact theory. *Journal of Social Issues, 58*, 387–410.

Miller, P. A., & Eisenberg, N. (1988). The relation of empathy to aggressive and externalizing/antisocial behavior. *Psychological Bulletin, 103*, 324–344.

Miller, R. S. (1987). Empathic embarrassment: Situational and personal determinants of reactions to the embarrassment of another. *Journal of Personality and Social Psychology, 53*, 1061–1069.

Milner, J. S., Halsey, L. B., & Fultz, J. (1995). Empathic responsiveness and affective reactivity to infant stimuli in high- and low-risk for physical child abuse mothers. *Child Abuse and Neglect, 19*, 767–780.

Ministero, L. M., Poulin, M. J., Buffone, A. E. K., & DeLury, S. (2018). Empathic concern and the desire to help as separate components of compassionate responding. *Personality and Social Psychology Bulletin, 44*, 475–491.

Momaday, N. S. (1968). *House made of dawn*. New York: Harper & Row.

Monette, P. (1988). *Borrowed time: An AIDS memoir*. San Diego, CA: Harcourt Brace Jovanovich.

Morelli, S. A., & Lieberman, M. D. (2013). The role of automaticity and attention in neural processes underlying empathy for happiness, sadness, and anxiety. *Frontiers in Human Neuroscience, 7*, Article 160.

Morris, R. (2007). Introduction. In D. B. Sachsman, S. K. Rushing, & R. Morris (Eds.), *Memory and myth: The Civil War in fiction and film from* Uncle Tom's Cabin *to* Cold Mountain (pp. 1–8). West Lafayette, IN: Purdue University Press.

Morrison, I., & Downing, P. E. (2007). Organization of felt and seen pain responses in the anterior cingulated cortex. *NeuroImage, 37*, 642–651.

Moss, C. (2000). *Elephant memories: Thirteen years in the life of an elephant family* (2nd ed.). Chicago: University of Chicago Press.

Myers, M. W., Laurent, S. M., & Hodges, S. D. (2014). Perspective taking instructions and self-other overlap: Different motives for helping. *Motivation and Emotion, 38*, 224–234.

Nadler, A., Fisher, J. D., & DePaulo, B. M. (Eds.) (1983). *New directions in helping: Vol. 3. Applied perspectives on help-seeking and -receiving*. New York: Academic Press.

Nadler, A., & Halabi, S. (2006). Intergroup helping as status relations: Effects of status stability, identification, and type of help on receptivity to high-status group's help. *Journal of Personality and Social Psychology, 91*, 97–110.

Nelson, E. E., & Panksepp, J. (1998). Brain substrates of infant-mother attachment: Contributions of opioids, oxytocin, and norepinephrine. *Neuroscience and Biobehavioral Reviews, 22*, 437–452.

Neyer, F. J., Banse, R., & Asendorpf, J. B. (1999). The role of projection and empathic accuracy in dyadic perception between older twins. *Journal of Social and Personal Relationships, 16*, 419–442.

Nichols, S. (2001). Mindreading and the cognitive architecture underlying altruistic motivation. *Mind & Language, 16*, 425–455.

Nichols, S. (2004). *Sentimental rules: On the natural foundations of moral judgment.* New York: Oxford University Press.

Nickerson, R. S. (1999). How we know—and sometimes misjudge—what others know: Imputing one's own knowledge to others. *Psychological Bulletin, 125*, 737–759.

Niedenthal, P. M. (2007). Embodying emotion. *Science, 316*, 1002–1005.

Niedenthal, P. M., Winkielman, P., Mondillon, L., & Vermeulen, N. (2009). Embodiment of emotion concepts. *Journal of Personality and Social Psychology, 96*, 1120–1136.

Niezink, L. W., Siero, F. W., Dijkstra, P., Buunk, A. P., & Barelds, D. P. H. (2012). Empathic concern: Distinguishing between tenderness and sympathy. *Motivation and Emotion, 36*, 544–549.

Nussbaum, M. C. (2001). *Upheavals of thought: The intelligence of emotions.* New York: Cambridge University Press.

Oakley, B., Knafo, A., Madhavan, G., & Wilson, D. S. (Eds.) (2012). *Pathological altruism.* New York: Oxford University Press.

Oatley, K. (2002). Emotions and the story worlds of fiction. In M. C. Green, J. J. Strange, & T. C. Brock (Eds.), *Narrative impact: Social and cognitive foundations* (pp. 39–69). Mahwah, NJ: Lawrence Erlbaum Associates.

Oceja, L. V., & Jiménez, I. (2007). Beyond egoism and group identity. Empathy toward the other and awareness of others in a social dilemma. *The Spanish Journal of Psychology, 10*, 369–379.

O'Connell, S. M. (1995). Empathy in chimpanzees: Evidence for theory of mind? *Primates, 36*, 397–410.

Odendaal, J. S. J., & Meintjes, R. A. (2003). Neurophysiological correlates of affiliative behavior between humans and dogs. *The Veterinary Journal, 165*, 296–301.

Öhman, A. (2002). Automaticity and the amygdala: Nonconscious responses to emotional faces. *Current Directions in Psychological Science, 11*, 62–66.

Olazábal, D. E., & Young, L. J. (2006). Species and individual differences in juvenile female alloparental care are associated with oxytocin receptor density in the striatum and the lateral septum. *Hormones and Behavior, 49*, 681–687.

Oliner, S. P., & Oliner, P. M. (1988). *The altruistic personality: Rescuers of Jews in Nazi Europe.* New York: The Free Press.

244 • References

Olson, M., Jr. (1971). *The logic of collective action: Public goods and the theory of groups.* Cambridge, MA: Harvard University Press.

Omoto, A. M., & Snyder, M. (2002). Considerations of community: The context and process of volunteerism. *American Behavioral Scientist, 45,* 400–404.

Opotow, S. (1990). Moral exclusion and injustice: An introduction. *Journal of Social Issues, 46,* 1–20.

Orne, M. (1962). On the social psychology of the psychological experiment: With particular reference to demand characteristics and their implications. *American Psychologist, 17,* 776–783.

Paluck, E. L. (2009a). Reducing intergroup prejudice and conflict using the media: A field experiment in Rwanda. *Journal of Personality and Social Psychology, 96,* 574–587.

Paluck, E. L. (2009b). What's in a norm? Sources and processes of norm change. *Journal of Personality and Social Psychology, 96,* 594–600.

Paluck, E. L., & Green, D. P. (2009). Prejudice reduction: What works? A review and assessment of research and practice. *Annual Review of Psychology, 60,* 339–367.

Panksepp, J. (1998). *Affective neuroscience: The foundations of human and animal emotions.* New York: Oxford University Press.

Panksepp, J. (2011). Empathy and the laws of affect. *Science, 334* (December 9), 1358–1359.

Patel, V. (2022, January 6). Dog is hailed as "real-life Lassie" after leading police to truck crash. *The New York Times.* https://www.nytimes.com/2022/01/06/us/dog-tins ley-rescues-owner.html

Penn, D. C., Holyoak, K. J., & Povinelli, D. J. (2008). Darwin's mistake: Explaining the discontinuity between human and nonhuman minds. *Behavioral and Brain Sciences, 31,* 109–178.

Penner, L. A., Cline, R. J. W., Albrecht, T. L., Harper, F. W. K., Peterson, A. M., Taub, J. M., & Ruckdeschel, J. C. (2008). Parents' empathic responses and pain and distress in pediatric patients. *Basic and Applied Social Psychology, 30,* 102–114.

Persson, I., & Savulescu, J. (2018). The moral importance of reflective empathy. *Neuroethics, 11,* 183–193.

Peters, W. (1987). *A class divided: Then and now.* New Haven, CT: Yale University Press.

Pettigrew, T. F. (1979). The ultimate attribution error: Extending Allport's cognitive analysis of prejudice. *Personality and Social Psychology Bulletin, 5,* 461–476.

Pettigrew, T. F. (1998). Intergroup contact theory. *Annual Review of Psychology, 49,* 65–85.

Pfattheicher, S., Sassenrath, C., & Keller, J. (2019). Compassion magnifies third-party punishment. *Journal of Personality and Social Psychology, 117,* 124–141.

Piaget, J. (1965). *The moral judgment of the child.* New York: Free Press. (Original work published 1932.)

Piliavin, I. M., Rodin. J., & Piliavin, J. (1969). Good Samaritanism: An underground phenomenon? *Journal of Personality and Social Psychology, 13,* 289–299.

Piliavin, J. A., Dovidio, J. F., Gaertner, S. L., & Clark, R. D., III (1981). *Emergency intervention*. New York: Academic Press.

Piliavin, J. A., Dovidio, J. F., Gaertner, S. L., & Clark, R. D., III (1982). Responsive bystanders: The process of intervention. In V. J. Derlega and J. Grzelak (Eds.), *Cooperation and helping behavior: Theories and research* (pp. 279–304). New York: Academic Press.

Poole, J. (1997). *Coming of age with elephants*. New York: Hyperion.

Povinelli, D. J., Bering, J. M., & Giambrone, S. (2000). Toward a science of other minds: Escaping the argument by analogy. *Cognitive Science, 24*, 509–541.

Povinelli, D. J., & Vonk, J. (2004). We don't need a microscope to explore the chimpanzee's mind. *Mind & Language, 19*, 1–28.

Premack, D., & Woodruff, G. (1978). Does the chimpanzee have a theory of mind? *Behavioral and Brain Sciences, 1*, 515–526.

Preston, S. D. (2013). The origins of altruism in offspring care. *Psychological Bulletin, 139*, 1305–1341.

Preston, S. D. (2022). *The altruistic urge: Why we're driven to help others*. New York: Columbia University Press.

Preston, S. D., & de Waal, F. B. M. (2002). Empathy: Its ultimate and proximate bases. *Behavioral and Brain Sciences, 25*, 1–72.

Prinz, J. (2011a). Against empathy. *The Southern Journal of Philosophy, 49*, 214–233.

Prinz, J. (2011b). Is empathy necessary for morality? In P. Goldie & A. Coplan (Eds.), *Empathy: Philosophical and psychological perspectives* (pp. 211–229). New York: Oxford University Press.

Prinz, J. (2014, August). Forum: Against empathy, *Boston Review*.

Prinz, W. (1987). Ideo-motor action. In H. Heuer & A. F. Sanders (Eds.), *Perspectives on perception and action* (pp. 47–76). Hillsdale, NJ: Lawrence Erlbaum Associates.

Prinz, W. (1997). Perception and action planning. *European Journal of Cognitive Psychology, 9*, 129–154.

Rainer, J. P. (2000). Compassion fatigue: When caregiving begins to hurt. In L. Vandecreek & T. L. Jackson (Eds.), *Innovations in clinical practice: A source book* (Vol. 18, pp. 441–453). Sarasota, FL: Professional Resource Exchange.

Rapoport, A., & Chammah, A. M. (1965). *Prisoner's dilemma*. Ann Arbor: University of Michigan Press.

Rathje, S., Hackel, L., & Zaki, J. (2021). Attending live theatre improves empathy, changes attitudes, and leads to pro-social behavior. *Journal of Experimental Social Psychology, 95*, 104138.

Ravenscroft, I. (1998). What is it like to be someone else? Simulation and empathy. *Ratio, XI*, 170–185.

Regan, D., & Totten, J. (1975). Empathy and attribution: Turning observers into actors. *Journal of Personality and Social Psychology, 32*, 850–856.

Ribar, D. C., & Wilhelm, M. O. (2002). Altruistic and joy-of-giving motivations in charitable behavior. *Journal of Political Economy, 110*, 425–457.

246 • References

Ricard, M. (2006). *Happiness: A guide to developing life's most important skill* (J. Browner, Trans.). New York: Little, Brown & Co.

Ricard, M. (2015). *Altruism: The power of compassion to change yourself and the world.* New York: Little, Brown.

Richardson, D. R., Hammock, G. S., Smith, S. M., Gardner, W., & Signo, M. (1994). Empathy as a cognitive inhibitor of interpersonal aggression. *Aggressive Behavior, 20,* 275–289.

Rogers, C. R. (1961). *On becoming a person: A therapist's view of psychotherapy.* Boston: Houghton Mifflin.

Rogers, C. R. (1975). Empathic: An unappreciated way of being. *The Counseling Psychologist, 5,* 2–10.

Romero, T., Castellanos, M. A., & de Waal, F. B. M. (2010). Consolation as possible expression of sympathetic concern among chimpanzees. *Proceedings of the National Academy of Science, 107,* 12110–12115.

Rosenman, I. J. (1984). Cognitive determinants of emotions: A structural theory. In P. Shaver (Ed.), *Review of Personality and Social Psychology* (Vol. 5, pp. 11–36). Newbury Park, CA: SAGE Publications.

Roughley, N., & Schramme, T. (2018). Empathy, sympathy, concern, and moral agency. In N. Roughley & T. Schramme (Eds.), *Forms of fellow-feeling: Empathy, sympathy, concern, and moral agency* (pp. 3–55). Cambridge: Cambridge University Press.

Rouhana, N. N., & Kelman, H. C. (1994). Promoting joint thinking in international conflicts: An Israeli-Palestinian continuing workshop. *Journal of Social Issues, 50,* 157–178.

Ruby, P., & Decety, J. (2004). How would you feel versus how do you think she would feel? A neuroimaging study of perspective taking with social emotions. *Journal of Cognitive Neuroscience, 16,* 988–999.

Rusbult, C. (1980). Commitment and satisfaction in romantic associations: A test of the investment model. *Journal of Experimental Social Psychology, 16,* 172–186.

Rushton, J. P. (1980). *Altruism, socialization and society.* Englewood Cliffs, NJ: Prentice-Hall.

Ruttan, R. L., McDonnell, M-H., & Nordgren, L. F. (2015). Having "been there" doesn't mean I care: When prior experience reduces compassion for emotional distress. *Journal of Personality and Social Psychology, 108,* 610–622.

Ryan, W. (1971). *Blaming the victim.* New York: Random House.

Sagi, A., & Hoffman, M. L. (1976). Empathic distress in the newborn. *Developmental Psychology, 12,* 175–176.

Schaller, M., & Cialdini, R. B. (1988). The economics of empathic helping: Support for a mood management motive. *Journal of Experimental Social Psychology, 24,* 163–181.

Scherer, K. R. (1984). On the nature and function of emotion: A component process approach. In K. R. Scherer & P. Ekman (Eds.), *Approaches to emotion* (pp. 293–317). Hillsdale, NJ: Erlbaum Associates.

Schlenker, B. R., & Britt, T. W. (1997). Beneficial impression management: Strategically controlling information to help friends. *Journal of Personality and Social Psychology, 76*, 559–573.

Schonert-Reichl, K. A., Smith, V., Zaidman-Zait, & Hertzman, C. (2012). Promoting children's prosocial behaviors in school. Impact of the "Roots of Empathy" program on the social and emotional competence of school-aged children. *School Mental Health, 4*, 1–21.

Schultz, P. W. (2000). Empathizing with nature: The effects of perspective taking on concern for environmental issues. *Journal of Social Issues, 56*, 391–406.

Schultz, R., & Beach, S. (1999). Caregiving as a risk factor for mortality: The Caregiver Health Effects study. *Journal of the American Medical Association, 282*, 2215–2219.

Schultz, R., Williamson, G. M., Morycz, R. K., & Biegel, D. E. (1991). Costs and benefits of providing care to Alzheimer's patients. In S. Spacapan & S. Oskamp (Eds.), *Helping and being helped: Naturalistic Studies* (pp. 153–181). Newbury Park, CA: Sage.

Schumann, K., Zaki, J., & Dweck, C. S. (2014). Addressing the empathy deficit: Beliefs about the malleability of empathy predict effortful responses when empathy is challenging. *Journal of Personality and Social Psychology, 107*, 475–493.

Schwartz, S. H., & Howard, J. (1984). Internalized values as motivators of altruism. In E. Staub, D. Bar–Tal, J. Karylowski, & J. Reykowski (Eds.), *Development and maintenance of prosocial behavior* (pp. 229–255). New York: Plenum.

Sedikides, C., & Strube, M. J. (1997). Self-evaluation: To thine own self be good, to thine own self be sure, to thine own self be true, and to thine own self be better. In M. P. Zanna (Ed.), *Advances in experimental social psychology* (Vol. 29, pp. 209–269). New York: Academic Press.

Shaver, P., Schwartz, J., Kirson, D., & O'Connor, C. (1987). Emotion knowledge: Further exploration of the prototype approach. *Journal of Personality and Social Psychology, 52*, 1061–1086.

Shaw, L. L., Batson, C. D., & Todd, R. M. (1994). Empathy avoidance: Forestalling feeling for another in order to escape the motivational consequences. *Journal of Personality and Social Psychology, 67*, 879–887.

Shelton, M. L., & Rogers, R. W. (1981). Fear-arousing and empathy-arousing appeals to help: The pathos of persuasion. *Journal of Applied Social Psychology, 11*, 366–378.

Sherif, M., Harvey, O. J., White, B. J., Hood, W. E., & Sherif, C. W. (1961). *Intergroup conflict and cooperation: The Robber's Cave experiment.* Norman: University of Oklahoma Book Exchange.

Shih, M., Wang, E., Bucher, A. T., & Stotzer, R. (2009). Perspective taking: Reducing prejudice towards general outgroups and specific individuals. *Group Processes & Intergroup Relations, 12*, 565–577.

Shnabel, N., & Nadler, A. (2008). A needs-based model of reconciliation: Satisfying the differential emotional needs of victim and perpetrator as a key to promoting reconciliation. *Journal of Personality and Social Psychology, 94*, 116–132.

248 • References

Sibicky, M. E., Schroeder, D. A., & Dovidio, J. F. (1995). Empathy and helping: Considering the consequences of intervention. *Basic and Applied Social Psychology, 16,* 435–453.

Silk, J. B. (2009). Social preferences in primates. In P. W. Glimcher, C. F. Camerer, E. Fehr, & R. A. Poldrack (Eds.), *Neuroeconomics: Decision making and the brain* (pp. 269–284). Boston, MA: Elsevier/Academic Press.

Simpson, J. A., Rholes, W. S., & Nelligan, J. S. (1992). Support seeking and support giving within couples in an anxiety-provoking situation: The role of attachment styles. *Journal of Personality and Social Psychology, 62,* 434–446.

Singer, P. (2015). *The most good you can do: How effective altruism is changing ideas about living ethically.* New Haven, CT: Yale University Press.

Singer, T., & Klimecki, O. M. (2014). Empathy and compassion. *Current Biology, 24,* R875–R878.

Singer, T., & Lamm, C. (2009). The social neuroscience of empathy. *Annals of the New York Academy of Sciences, 1156,* 81–96.

Singer, T., Seymour, B., O'Doherty, J., Kaube, H., Dolan, R. J., & Frith, C. D. (2004). Empathy for pain involves the affective but not sensory components of pain. *Science, 303,* 1157–1162.

Singer, T., Seymour, B., O'Doherty, J. P., Stephan, K. E., Dolan, R. J., & Frith, C. D. (2006). Empathic neural responses are modulated by the perceived fairness of others. *Nature, 439,* 466–469.

Slater, M. D. (2002). Entertainment education and the persuasive impact of narratives. In M. C. Green, J. J. Strange, & T. C. Brock (Eds.), *Narrative impact: Social and cognitive foundations* (pp. 157–181). Mahwah, NJ: Lawrence Erlbaum Associates.

Slovic, P. (2007). "If I look at the mass I will never act": Psychic numbing and genocide. *Judgment and Decision Making, 2,* 1–17.

Slovic, P., Västfjäll, D., Erlandsson, A., & Gregory, R. (2017). Iconic photographs and the ebb and flow of empathic response to humanitarian disasters. *Proceedings of the National Academy of Sciences, 114*(4), 640–644.

Small, D. A., Lowenstein, G., & Slovic, P. (2007). Sympathy and callousness: The impact of deliberative thought on donations to identifiable and statistical victims. *Organizational Behavior and Human Decision Processes, 102,* 143–153.

Smith, A. (1976). *The theory of moral sentiments.* (D. D. Raphael & A. L. MacFie, Eds.). Oxford: Oxford University Press. (Original work published 1759.)

Smith, C. A., & Ellsworth, P. C. (1985). Patterns of cognitive appraisal in emotion. *Journal of Personality and Social Psychology, 48,* 813–838.

Smith, K. D., Keating, J. P., & Stotland, E. (1989). Altruism reconsidered: The effect of denying feedback on a victim's status to empathic witnesses. *Journal of Personality and Social Psychology, 57,* 641–650.

Sober, E. (1991). The logic of the empathy-altruism hypothesis. *Psychological Inquiry, 2,* 144–147.

References • 249

Sober, E., & Wilson, D. S. (1998). *Unto others: The evolution and psychology of unselfish behavior*. Cambridge, MA: Harvard University Press.

Solomon, R. C. (1990). *A passion for justice: Emotions and the origins of the social contract*. Reading, MA: Addison-Wesley.

Soltis, J. (2004). The signal functions of early infant crying. *Behavioral and Brain Sciences, 27,* 443–490.

Staub, E. (1974). Helping a distressed person: Social, personality, and stimulus determinants. In L. Berkowitz (Ed.), *Advances in experimental social psychology* (Vol. 7, pp. 293–341). New York: Academic Press.

Staub, E. (1989). Individual and societal (group) values in a motivational perspective and their role in benevolence and harmdoing. In N. Eisenberg, J. Reykowski, & E. Staub (Eds.), *Social and moral values: Individual and societal perspectives* (pp. 45–61). Hillsdale, NJ: Erlbaum.

Staub, E., & Perlman, L. A. (2009). Reducing intergroup prejudice and conflict: A commentary. *Journal of Personality and Social Psychology, 96,* 588–593.

Steins, G., & Wicklund, R. A. (1996). Perspective-taking, conflict, and press: Drawing an *E* on your forehead. *Basic and Applied Social Psychology, 18,* 319–346.

Stellar, J. E., Cohen, A., Oveis, C., & Keltner, D. (2015). Affective and physiological responses to the suffering of others: Compassion and vagal activity. *Journal of Personality and Social Psychology, 108,* 572–585.

Stephan, W. G., & Finlay, K. (1999). The role of empathy in improving intergroup relations. *Journal of Social Issues, 55,* 729–743.

Stephan, W. G., & Stephan, C. W. (2001). *Improving intergroup relations*. Thousand Oaks, CA: Sage.

Stewart, T. L., LaDuke, J. R., Bracht, C., Sweet, B. A. M., & Gamarel, K. E. (2003). Do the "Eyes" have it? A program evaluation of Jane Elliott's "Blue-Eyes/Brown-Eyes" diversity training exercise. *Journal of Applied Social Psychology, 33,* 1898–1921.

Stich, S., Doris, J. M., & Roedder, E. (2010). Altruism. In J. M., Doris and the Moral Psychology Research Group (Eds.), *The moral psychology handbook* (pp. 147–205). Oxford, U.K.: Oxford University Press.

Stocks, E. L., & Lishner, D. A. (2010). The empathy-altruism hypothesis: A critical analysis of current alternative explanations. In A. M. Columbus (Ed.), *Advances in Psychological Research* (Vol. 69, Chapter 12, pp. 1–28). Hauptauge, NY: Nova Science Publishers.

Stocks, E. L., Lishner, D. A., & Decker, S. K. (2009). Altruism or psychological escape: Why does empathy promote prosocial behavior? *European Journal of Social Psychology, 39,* 649–665.

Stocks, E. L., Lishner, D. A., Waits, B. L., & Downum, E. M. (2011). I'm embarrassed for you: The effect of valuing and perspective taking on empathic embarrassment and empathic concern. *Journal of Applied Social Psychology, 41,* 1–26.

250 • References

Stotland, E. (1969). Exploratory investigations of empathy. In L. Berkowitz (Ed.), *Advances in experimental social psychology* (Vol. 4, pp. 271–313). New York: Academic Press.

Stotland, E., Mathews, K. E., Sherman, S. E., Hansson, R. O., & Richardson, B. Z. (1978). *Empathy, fantasy, and helping.* Beverly Hills, CA: Sage.

Stowe, H. B. (2005). *Uncle Tom's cabin.* Mineola, NY: Dover. (Original work published 1852.)

Strange, J. J. (2002). How fictional tales wag real-world beliefs: Models and mechanisms of narrative influence. In M. C. Green, J. J. Strange, & T. C. Brock (Eds.), *Narrative impact: Social and cognitive foundations* (pp. 263–286). Mahwah, NJ: Lawrence Erlbaum Associates.

Stroop, J. R. (1938). Factors affecting speed in serial verbal reactions. *Psychological Monographs, 50,* 38–48.

Stueber, K. R. (2006). *Rediscovering empathy: Agency, folk psychology, and the human sciences.* Cambridge, MA: MIT Press.

Stueber, K. (2018). Empathy. In E. N. Zalta (Ed.), *The Stanford Encyclopedia of Philosophy* (Spring 2018 Edition). https://plato.stanford.edu/archives/spr2018/entries/empathy/

Stürmer, S., Snyder, M., Kropp, A., & Siem, B. (2006). Empathy-motivated helping: The moderating role of group membership. *Personality and Social Psychology Bulletin, 32,* 943–956.

Stürmer, S., Snyder, M., & Omoto, A. M. (2005). Prosocial emotions and helping: The moderating role of group membership. *Journal of Personality and Social Psychology, 88,* 532–546.

Tamir, M., Robinson, M. D., Clore, G. L., Martin, L. L., & Whitaker, D. J. (2004). Are we puppets on a string? The contextual meaning of unconscious expressive cues. *Personality and Social Psychology Bulletin, 30,* 237–249.

Taylor, S. E. (2002). *The tending instinct: How nurturing is essential to who we are and how we live.* New York: Time Books.

Thomas, G., & Fletcher, G. J. O. (1997). Empathic accuracy in close relationships. In W. Ickes (Ed.), *Empathic accuracy* (pp. 194–217). New York: Guilford.

Thompson, W. C., Cowan, C. L., & Rosenhan, D. L. (1980). Focus of attention mediates the impact of negative affect on altruism. *Journal of Personality and Social Psychology, 38,* 291–300.

Titchener, E. B. (1909). *Lectures on the experimental psychology of the thought processes.* New York: Macmillan.

Todd, A. R., Bodenhausen, G. V., & Galinsky, A. D. (2012). Perspective taking combats the denial of intergroup discrimination. *Journal of Experimental Social Psychology, 48,* 738–745.

Todd, A. R., Bodenhausen, G. V., Richeson, J. A., & Galinsky, A. D. (2011). Perspective taking combats automatic expressions of racial bias. *Journal of Personality and Social Psychology, 100,* 1027–1042.

Todd, A. R., & Burgmer, P. (2013). Perspective taking and automatic intergroup evaluation change: Testing an associative self-anchoring account. *Journal of Personality and Social Psychology, 104*, 786–802.

Todd, A. R., & Galinsky, A. D. (2014). Perspective-taking as a strategy for improving intergroup relations: Evidence, mechanisms, and qualifications. *Social and Personality Psychology Compass, 8/7*, 374–387.

Toi, M., & Batson, C. D. (1982). More evidence that empathy is a source of altruistic motivation. *Journal of Personality and Social Psychology, 43*, 281–292.

Tomasello, M. (1999). *The cultural origins of human cognition.* Cambridge, MA: Harvard University Press.

Tomasello, M. (2014). The ultra-social animal. *European Journal of Social Psychology, 44*, 187–194.

Tomasello, M. (2020). The adaptive origins of uniquely human society. *Philosophical Transactions of the Royal Society B: Biological Sciences, 375*(1803), 20190493.

Tomasello, M., & Call, J. (1997). *Primate cognition.* New York: Oxford University Press.

Tomasello, M., Call, J., & Hare, B. (2003). Chimpanzees understand psychological states—the question is which ones and to what extent. *Trends in Cognitive Sciences, 7*, 153–156.

Trötschel, R., Hüffmeier, J., Loschelder, D. D., Schwartz. K., & Gollwitzer, P. M, (2011). Perspective taking as a means to overcome motivational barriers in negotiations: When putting oneself into the opponent's shoes helps to walk toward agreement. *Journal of Personality and Social Psychology, 101*, 771–790.

Turner, R. A., Altemus, M., Enos, T., Cooper, B., & McGuinness, T. (1999). Preliminary research on plasma oxytocin in normal cycling women: Investigating emotion and interpersonal distress. *Psychiatry, 62*, 97–113.

Tusche, A., Böckler, A., Kanske, P., Trautwein, F.-M., & Singer, T. (2016). Decoding the charitable brain: Empathy, perspective taking, and attention shifts differentially predict altruistic giving. *Journal of Neuroscience, 36*, 4719–4732.

Van Boven, L., Loewenstein, G., Dunning, D., & Nordgren, L. F. (2013). Changing places: A dual judgment model of empathy gaps in emotional perspective taking. *Advances in Experimental Social Psychology, 48*, 117–171.

Van Lange, P. A. M. (1991). Being better but not smarter than others: The Muhammad Ali effect at work in interpersonal situations. *Personality and Social Psychology Bulletin, 17*, 689–693.

Vaughan, K. B., & Lanzetta, J. T. (1981). The effect of modification of expressive displays on vicarious emotional arousal. *Journal of Experimental Social Psychology, 17*, 16–30.

Vescio, T. K., & Hewstone, M. (2001). Empathy arousal as a means of improving intergroup attitudes: An examination of the affective supercedent hypothesis. Unpublished manuscript, Pennsylvania State University, State College, Pennsylvania.

Vescio, T. K., Sechrist, G. B., & Paolucci, M. P. (2003). Perspective taking and prejudice reduction: The mediational role of empathy arousal and situational attributions. *European Journal of Social Psychology, 33*, 455–472.

Vitaglione, G. D., & Barnett, M. A. (2003). Assessing a new dimension of empathy: Empathic anger as a predictor of helping and punishing desires. *Motivation and Emotion, 27*, 301–325.

Vollmer, P. J. (1977). Do mischievous dogs reveal their "guilt"? *Veterinary Medicine Small Animal Clinician, 72*, 1002–1005.

Von Neumann, J., & Morgenstern, O. (1944). *Theory of games and economic behavior*. Princeton, NJ: Princeton University Press.

Vorauer, J. (2013). The case for and against perspective-taking. In J. Olson & M. Zanna (Eds.), *Advances in Experimental Social Psychology* (Volume 48, pages 59–115). San Diego, CA: Elsevier.

Vorauer, J., Quesnel, M., & St. Germain, S. L. (2016). Reductions in goal-directed cognition as a consequence of being a target of empathy. *Personality and Social Psychology Bulletin, 42*, 130–141.

Vorauer, J., & Sasaki, S. J. (2009). Helpful only in the abstract? Ironic effects of empathy in intergroup relations. *Psychological Science, 20*, 191–197.

Vorauer, J., & Sasaki, S. J. (2012). The pitfalls of empathy as a default intergroup interaction strategy: Distinct effects of trying to empathize with a lower status outgroup member who does versus does not express distress. *Journal of Experimental Social Psychology, 48*, 519–524.

Walker, A. (1982). *The color purple*. New York: Harcourt Brace Jovanovich.

Wallach, L., & Wallach, M. A. (1991). Why altruism, even though it exists, cannot be demonstrated by social psychological experiments. *Psychological Inquiry, 2*, 153–155.

Wang, C. S., Tai, K., Ku, G., & Galinsky, A. D. (2014). Perspective-taking increases willingness to engage in intergroup contact. *PLOS ONE, 9*, e85681.

Warneken, F. (2015). Precocious prosociality: Why do young children help? *Child Development Perspectives, 9*, 1–6.

Weigel, R. H., Wiser, P. L., & Cook, S. W. (1975). The impact of cooperative learning experiences on cross-ethnic relations and attitudes. *Journal of Social Issues, 31*, 219–244.

Weiner, F. H. (1976). Altruism, ambiance, and action: The effect of rural and urban rearing on helping behavior. *Journal of Personality and Social Psychology, 34*, 112–124.

Weiner, M. J., & Wright, F. E. (1973). Effects of undergoing arbitrary discrimination upon subsequent attitudes toward a minority group. *Journal of Applied Social Psychology, 3*, 94–102.

Weisman, O., Zagoory-Sharon, O., & Feldman, R. (2011, May). Oxytocin improves the hormonal, autonomic, and behavioral basis of fatherhood. Presented at the Biennial Meeting of the European Association for Biological Psychiatry, Prague.

Weng. H. Y., Fox, A. S., Shackman, A. J., Stodola, D. E., Caldwell, J. Z. K., Olson, M. C., Rogers, G. M., & Davidson, R. J. (2013). Compassion training alters altruism and neural response to suffering. *Psychological Science, 24*, 1171–1180.

Wicklund, R. A. (1975). Objective self awareness. In L. Berkowitz (Ed.), *Advances in experimental social psychology* (Vol. 8, pp. 233–275). New York: Academic Press.

Wiesenfeld, A. R., Whitman, P. B., & Malatesta, C. Z. (1984). Individual differences among adult women in sensitivity to infants: Evidence in support of an empathy concept. *Journal of Personality and Social Psychology, 46*, 118–124.

Wispé, L. (1986). The distinction between sympathy and empathy: To call forth a concept a word is needed. *Journal of Personality and Social Psychology, 50*, 314–321.

Wispé, L. (1991). *The psychology of sympathy*. New York: Plenum.

Witvliet, C. V. O., Ludwig, T. E., & Vander Laan, K. L. (2001). Granting forgiveness or harboring grudges: Implications for emotion, physiology, and health. *Psychological Science, 12*, 117–123.

Wondra, J. D., & Ellsworth, P. C. (2015). An appraisal theory of empathy and other vicarious emotional experiences. *Psychological Review, 122*, 411–428.

Worchel, S., & Andreoli, V. (1978). Facilitation of social interaction through deindividuation of the target. *Journal of Personality and Social Psychology, 36*, 549–556.

Worthington, E. L., Jr. (1998). An empathy-humility-commitment model of forgiveness applied within family dyads. *Journal of Family Therapy, 20*, 59–76.

Xu, X., Zuo, X., Wang, X., & Han, S. (2009). Do you feel my pain? Racial group membership modulates empathic neural responses. *Journal of Neuroscience, 29*, 8525–8529.

Yamamoto, S., Humle, T., & Tanaka, M. (2012). Chimpanzees' flexible target helping based on an understanding of conspecifics' goals. *Proceedings of the National Academy of Sciences, 109*, 3588–3592.

Zahavi, D., & Overgaard, S. (2012). Empathy without isomorphism: A phenomenological account. In J. Decety (Ed.), *Empathy: From bench to bedside* (pp. 3–20). Cambridge, MA: MIT Press.

Zahn-Waxler, C., & Radke-Yarrow, M. (1990). The origins of empathic concern. *Motivation and Emotion, 14*, 107–130.

Zahn-Waxler, C., Radke-Yarrow, M., Wagner, E., & Chapman, M. (1992). Development of concern for others. *Developmental Psychology, 28*, 126–136.

Zahn-Waxler, C., Schoen, A., & Decety, J. (2018). An interdisciplinary perspective on the origins of concern for others. In N. Roughley & T. Schramme (Eds.), *Forms of fellow feeling: Empathy, sympathy, concern, and moral agency* (pp. 184–215). Cambridge, U.K.: Cambridge University Press.

Zak, P. J., Stanton, A. A., & Ahmadi, S. (2007). Oxytocin increases generosity in humans. *PLoS ONE, November 7, 2007*(11), e1128, 1–5.

Zaki, J. (2016). Room for Debate: Does empathy guide or hinder moral action? *The New York Times*, December 29, 2016.

254 • References

Zaki, J. (2019). *The war for kindness: Building empathy in a fractured world.* New York: Crown.

Zaki, J., & Cikara, M. (2015). Addressing empathic failures. *Current Directions in Psychological Science, 24,* 471–476.

Zaki, J., Ochsner, K. N., Hanelin, J., Wager, T. D., & Mackey, S. C. (2007). Different circuits for different pain: Patterns of functional connectivity reveal distinct networks for processing pain in self and others. *Social Neuroscience, 2,* 276–291.

Zaki, J., Wager, T. D., Singer, T., Keysers, C., & Gazzola, V. (2016). The anatomy of suffering: Understanding the relationship between nociceptive and empathic pain. *Trends in Cognitive Sciences, 20,* 249–259.

Zeifman, D. M. (2001). An ethological analysis of human infant crying: Answering Tinbergen's four questions. *Developmental Psychobiology, 39,* 265–285.

Zentall, T. R. (2003). Imitation by animals: How do they do it? *Current Directions in Psychological Science, 12,* 91–95.

Zillmann, D. (1991). Empathy: Affect from bearing witness to the emotions of others. In J. Bryant & D. Zillmann (Eds.), *Responding to the screen: Reception and reaction processes* (pp. 135–167). Hillsdale, NJ: Lawrence Erlbaum Associates.

Zimbardo, P. G., Banks, W. C., Haney, C., & Jaffe, D. (1973, April 8). The mind is a formidable jailer: A Prandelian prison. *New York Times Magazine* (Section 6), 38–60.

Zúñiga, X., Nagada, B. A., & Sevig. T. D. (2002). Intergroup dialogues: An educational model for cultivating engagement across differences. *Equity and Excellence in Education, 35,* 7–17.

INDEX

For the benefit of digital users, indexed terms that span two pages (e.g., 52–53) may, on occasion, appear on only one of those pages.

Tables and figures are indicated by *t* and *f* following the page number

aesthetic empathy (Wispé), 52
affectionate parenting, 83–84
Against Empathy (Bloom), 2, 10, 153–54
Age of Empathy, The (de Waal), 1
aggression
  altruistic, 132
  empathic concern can reduce, 132–35
  See also empathy and aggression
AIDS
  empathic concern for people with, 137–38, 157
  volunteering to help people with, 150
alloparenting, 84
altruism, 110, 207
  egoism and, 110, 155–56
altruistic aggression, 132
altruistic personality, 122
anger, 82
animate being, 65
anterior cingulate cortex (ACC), 22
appraisal theories of emotion, 93
Aquinas, Thomas, 109
Aronson, Elliot, 196–97

arousal: cost-reward model, 26–27
  reducing aversive arousal, 26–27
  tension-reduction analysis, 26
attachment theory, 79–80, 129
attitude
  concept of, 71–72
  toward stigmatized groups, improving, 162–66
Auschwitz, Rudolf Hoess of, 147

Balzac, Honoré de, 143
Banks, Bryan, 74, 103
Banks, Katie, 18, 21, 88, 98
  imagine-other perspective, 53
  could results be due to demand, 39–40
  measuring emotional response to need of, 38
  measuring empathic concern for, 18–20
  measuring nature of distress felt for, 36–39
  News from the Personal Side broadcast, 35
  perspective instructions for, 37

256 • Index

Bard, Kim, 82
Barnett, Mark, 99–100
Barrett-Lennard, G.T., 53
Bell, David, 82
Berger, Seymour, 64–65
Binti Jua (gorilla), Brookfield Zoo, 68–69
blaming the victim, reducing, 135
Bloom, Paul, 1, 2, 4, 10, 11, 48, 153–54
Blue Eyes-Brown Eyes simulation, classroom, 197–99
Boehm, Christopher, 80
Borrowed Time (Monette), 161–62
Bowlby, John, 79
Bowles, Samuel, 125–26
brain regions
    associated with generalization of empathic concern, 87–88
    associated with parental care and empathic concern, 80–83
Bridgeman, Diane, 197
Briggs, Jared, 138–39, 163, 165
    experiment, 167–68
Bruneau, Emile, 175, 180–81, 182–86, 190–92
Bulletin Board broadcast, 14
Burnout, 146–47

Cameron, Daryl, 150
Campus Concerns broadcast, 14
Cardinal Rule of Policy, 150
caregiving behavioral system (Bowlby), 79
caring, valuing another's welfare, 71–72
child abuse and neglect, empathic concern as antidote, 128
chimpanzees
    de Waal on, 66
    Goodall on Gremlin, 67
Cialdini, Robert, 97–98
Cikara, Mina, 175, 177, 190–91
civil rights demonstrations, 208
Clark, Russell, 26, 50

close relationships, 128–31
    friendships, 130–31
    romantic relationships, 129–30
Color Purple, The (Walker), 161–62
Columbine High School, massacre in Littleton (CO), 197
compassion, 2–4, 12, 25
    feeling-with, 51
    Samaritan's, 9
compassion abuse, 157
compassion fatigue, 151
compassion meditation, 141–42
conflict out-groups, 180–82, 216
    direct test of empathy for members of, 182–86
    in-group bias toward, 185
    See also distant out-groups
conflict-resolution workshops, political conflicts, 200–1
conflict situations
    Buyer and Seller, 158–59
    dehumanization of out-group members, 191–92
    empathic concerns hurting chances in, 157–59
    in-group empathy in, 186–91
    Job Candidate and Recruiter, 157–58
    negotiations, 157–59
convergent validity, 13
convicted murders, empathic concern for, 137, 138
cooperative breeding, 84
cooperative learning, interpersonal and intergroup relations, 196–97
current need
    sympathy and, 93–94, 95
    See also need

Damasio, Antonio, 80–82
Damasio, Hanna, 80–81
Darwin, Charles, 77, 109
Davis, Mark, 54, 202
    Interpersonal Reactivity Index, 57, 188

Index • **257**

death camp survivors, Nazi Europe, 145

decentering, 53

Decety, Jean, 55

Dehumanization of conflict out-
groups, 191–92

depersonalization, strangers in
need, 148–49

derogation, reducing, 135

Des Pres, Terrence, 145

de Waal, Frans, 1, 46, 66, 67–68
The Age of Empathy, 1
chimpanzee, 66
Good Natured, 67
parental instinct, 79

Dickens, Charles, 206

Direct-Distress Index, 38–39

discrimination simulations, educational
settings, 197–99

dispositional empathy, 57, 213–14

distant out-groups, 180–82, 216
direct test of empathy for members
of, 182–86
if need clear, then no in-group
bias, 184
See also conflict out-groups

Dovidio, John, 26, 173, 176

Dufour, Nicholas, 180–81

educational settings, inducing
empathy in
cooperative learning, 196–97
discrimination simulations, 197–99
improving interpersonal and
intergroup relations in, 194–200
intergroup-dialogue classes, 199–200
Roots of Empathy program, 194–95

egoism, 110
altruism and, 110
threat to common good, 155–56

Einfuhlung (feeling into), 52

Eisenberg, Nancy, 22–23, 33, 109

Elephant Man, The (movie), 161–62

Elliott, Jane, 197–98

embarrassment, empathic, 101–4

emotion
anger, 82
appraisal theories of, 93, 105
beyond matching to catching, 50–51
catching another's, 50

emotional contagion, 48
empathic anger and, 98–99
empathic embarrassment and, 101–4

Emotional Response Questionnaire, 97,
100, 105

Emotional Response Scale, 18–20, 19*f,*
31–33, 32*f,* 35, 38

empathic accuracy, 44

empathic anger, 98–101, 105, 172–73

empathic attentional set, 53

empathic concern, 2–3
brain regions involved in
generalization of, 87–88
conditions for feeling, 61–72
current need, 93
defining, 11–12, 211
depersonalizing conditions that
inhibit, 149–50
developing a valid measure, 13–20
directions for future research,
214, 217–18
empathy-altruism hypothesis, 110
evidence of in-group bias, 175–80
evidence relating parental care
and, 80–84
examples of, 9–10
feeling-for not feeling as, 2–3
imagine-self perspective as source of,
56–57, 213
importance of, 215–17
inducing empathy with false
psychological feedback, 14–15
inducing empathy with perspective
instructions, 17–20
infant-like features increasing, 88–89
necessary conditions for feeling,
61, 62*f*

258 • Index

empathic concern (*cont.*)
  other proposed necessary conditions
    for feeling, 72–75
  oxytocin's role in, 86–87
  perceiving the other as in need (as
    necessary condition), 61–69, 62f
  personal distress versus, 25–28
  principal-component loadings of self-
    reported responses, 30t
  proposed necessary conditions
    (instead of valuing), 72–75
  schadenfreude versus, 11–12
  six-item index, 15–16
  sympathy and tenderness, 93–97
  valuing another's welfare and,
    62f, 69–72
  vulnerability, 93
  See also empathic concern and
    personal distress; empathy; feeling
    empathic concern
empathic concern and personal distress
  distinction as crucial, 27–28
  distinction as unimportant, 25–27
  evidence of distinctiveness, 28–29
  imagine-other and imagine-self
    perspective instructions, 37
  Katherine McDavis experiment, 33–34
  measuring emotional response to
    need, 38
  nature of reported distress, 38–40
  perspective taking and , 36–41
  self-report scale, 41
Empathic Concern Index, 15, 176–77
  adjectives for, 18–20, 19f, 30t, 31–
    33, 35
  evidence of induced-state validity of,
    15–17, 20
  gender and responses to, 20
  range of applicability of six-item
    index, 21–22
  sympathetic and tender, 96–97
  sympathy, 105

tenderness, 105
  using perspective instructions to
    induce, 20
Empathic Concern Scale (dispositional
  measure), 57, 202
empathic distress, 34–39, 97–98
Empathic-Distress Index, 38–39
empathic embarrassment, 101–4, 105
  probably not a form of empathic
    concern, 101–3
  support for doubt, 103–4
empathic joy, elation, 11
empathic-joy hypothesis, 112–13
empathic sadness, 97–98
empathy, 12
  avoiding terminological tangles, 3–4
  beyond matching to catching, 50–51
  bottom up or top down explanation of
    feelng-as, 48–49
  coming to feel as another person feels,
    48–51
  compassion as feeling-with, 51
  different meanings of, 2–3
  dispositional, 57, 213–14
  empathic concern and, 43
  feeling-as another as source of
    empathic concern, 51
  general disposition to feel for others, 57
  imagining how another is
    affected, 52–53
  imagining yourself in another's
    place, 53–57
  inducing with false physiological
    feedback, 14–15
  inducing with perspective
    instructions, 17–20
  intuiting or projecting oneself into
    another's situation, 52
  knowing another person's internal
    state, 44
  matching posture or expression of
    observed other, 45–47

Index · 259

mimicry and imitation, 45–46
neural matching, 46–47
psychological phenomena called,
  4, 57–58
similarity of feeling, 49–50
sources of sensitive response to
  suffering, 58–59
See also empathic concern
empathy-altruism hypothesis, 4,
  109, 111–21
  all-at-once combination, 119
  aversive-arousal reduction, egoistic
    alternative, 111, 116*t*
  avoiding empathy-specific
    punishment, egoistic alternative,
    111, 116*t*
  behavioral predictions from, 116*t*
  benefiting strangers in need, 131–35
  challenging doctrine of universal
    egoism, 109
  competing concerns, 123
  competing altruistic and egoistic
    predictions, 115–17
  current status of, 121
  egoism-altruism debate, 110
  empathic-joy hypothesis, egoistic
    alternative, 112–13, 116*t*
  empathy-induced altruistic
    motivation, 116*t*
  evidence supporting, 117–19
  gaining empathy-specific reward,
    egoistic alternative, 111–13, 116*t*
  implications for view of human
    nature, 123–26
  importance of ultimate goal, 113–14
  limits on the empathy-altruism
    relationship, 121–23
  logical structure of question about
    nature of motivation, 112*t*
  negative-state-relief hypothesis,
    egoistic alternatrive, 112
  new challenges, 119–21

other sources of altruistic
  motivation, 122
psychological escape, egoistic
  alternative, 119–20
scope of empathy, 121–23
self-other merging, egoistic
  alternative, 120–21
significance of, 109–10
testing against egoistic alternatives
  with experiments, 114–21
empathy and aggression
  Miller and Eisenberg's meta-
    analysis, 133–34
  recent research on relationship
    of, 134–35
Empathy and Moral Development
  (Hoffman), 9
empathy-attitude effect, extending range
  of, 165–66
empathy avoidance, 146–47
empathy bias, 216
empathy deficit, 1, 175
empathy gap, 175
empathy-induced altruism
  as fragile flower, 123
  in friendships, 130–31
  moral motivation and, 207–9
  paternalism, maternalism,
    and, 143–45
  planned orchestration, 209
  serious threat to common
    good, 155–56
  unplanned orchestration, 208
endogenous opioid peptides (EOPs), 86
extrinsic valuing, 71–72
Eyes on the Prize (documentary), 161–62

face validity, 13
factor analysis, 100
failure of empathy, 175
fairness, moral motivation, 207–8
Farmer, Paul, 144

260 • Index

favoritism, 155

feeling empathic concern
  adopting an imagine-other
    perspective, 73–75
  cognitive abilities for, 65–66
  evidence of link between valuing
    and, 70
  evidence perception of need
    required, 64–65
  innocence and, 63–64
  necessary conditions for, 62*f*, 75*f*
  perceived similarity and, 72–73
  perceiving the other as in need and,
    61–69, 75
  proposed necessary conditions instead
    of valuing, 72–75
  requires intrinsic not extrinsic
    valuing, 71–72
  role of imagine-other perspective, 75*f*
  species possessing abilities for, 66–69
  valuing the other's welfare and, 69–
    72, 76
  vulnerability as form of need, 64

Feldman, Ruth, 83–84

friendships, empathy-induced altruism
  in, 130–31

Fultz, Jim, 15, 29, 97–98

Galinsky, Adam, 157–58, 171–72

Galvanic Skin Response (GSR), 14, 28

Gandhi, Mahatma, 209

gender, responses to Empathic Concern
  Index by, 20

Gilbert, Daniel, 157

Golden Rule, 207

Goodall, Jane, 67

Good Natured (de Waal), 67

Gordon, Mary, 193
  Roots of Empathy program, 194–95

greedy, as epithet, 155

Halpern, Jodi, 144–45

Hardin, Garrett, 150

health, empathic concern can
  harm, 156–57

heart rate, respiratory sinus arrhythmia
  (RSA) and, 22–23

Hein, Grit, 176–77, 181

HIV-positive people, empathic concern
  for, 137–38

Hodges, Sara, 148–49

Hoess, Rudolf, Auschwitz, 147

Hoffman, Martin, 26, 33, 50
  empathic anger, 99
  Empathy and Moral Development, 9

Holmes, Sherlock, 121

homeless people, empathic concern for,
  137, 138

House Made of Dawn
  (Momaday), 161–62

human brain, triune (MacLean), 80–81

human parental care
  need and value-based, 82–83
  needs of infant and, 82

human parenting, attachment
  theories, 79–80

Hume, David, 48–49, 55, 59, 109, 175
  A Treatise of Human Nature, 48–49,
    55, 59, 109

Hygge, Staffan, 65, 148–49

imagine-other perspective, 52–53, 213
  as possible necessary condition for
    empathic concern, 73–75
  empathic attentional set, 53
  increasing empahy for stigmatized
    group, 137–39
  increasing situational attributions, 169
  reducing stereotyping of stigmatized
    group, 169–71

imagine-self perspective, 36–37, 54–
  55, 213
  changing places with another in
    fancy, 53–57

Index • 261

cognitive differences between
imagine-other and imagine-self
perspectives, 54–55
distinguishing imagine-self from
imagine-other perspective, 54–55
imagine-self perspective as source of
empathic concern, 56–57
neurophysiological correlates, 55
imitation, 45
infants, 45
mimicry and, 45–46
Implicit Association Test (IAT),
176, 181–82
induced-state validity, 13, 20
infants
catching another's emotion, 50
crying response, 50–51
imitation, 45
Insel, Thomas, 84
instrumental goal, stepping stone to
ultimate goal, 110
intergroup benefits, 215–16
acting to help a stigmatized
group, 168–72
empathic anger as response to out-
group suffering, 173–74
extending range of empathy-attitude
effect, 165–66
imagine-other perspective increases
situational attributions, 169, 174
imagine-self perspective can reduce
stereotyping, 169–71, 174
more positive attitudes and action
toward stigmatized groups, 161–68
perspective taking as means to induce
empathy, 168–71
questions about perceptual/cognitive
benefits, 172–73
three-step process for improving
attitudes toward stigmatized
group, 162–66
See also stigmatized groups

intergroup-dialogue classes
in educational setting, 199–200
intergroup liabilities, 215–16
dehumanization of conflict out-group
members, 191–92
direct test of empathy for members of
out-groups, 182–86
distant out-groups and limited in-
group bias, 184
evidence of in-group bias in empathic
concern, 175–80
evidence of in-group bias toward
conflict out-groups, 185
evidence not supporting in-group
bias, 177–79
evidence supporting in-group
bias, 176–77
in-group empathy can increase out-
group harm, 186–91
neuroimaging effects, 185
two forms of in-group bias, 180–82
two sorts of out-groups, 180–82
interpersonal and intergroup relations
empathy-induced altruism and moral
motivation, orchestrating, 207–9
in educational settings, 194–200
in political conflicts, 200–3
strategies using empathy to improve
relations, 193–94, 216–17
using media to induce empathy,
203–6
See also educational settings; media;
orchestration
interpersonal benefits, 215
decreased blaming of victims of
injustice, 135
feeling for members of stigmatized
groups, 135–40
for strangers in need, 131–35
in close relationships, 128–31
in friendships, 130–31
in romantic relationships, 129–30

262 · Index

interpersonal benefits (*cont.*)
  limit of benefit when interacting with
    stigmatized other, 139–40
  more sensitive parental care, 127–28
  reduced aggression toward target of
    empathy, 134–35, 147
  reduced derogation, 135
  See also stigmatized groups; strangers
    in need (benefits)
interpersonal liabilities, 215
  abstract needs, 150
  chronic needs, 150–51
  empathic concern causing unfair
    treatment, 151–54
  empathic concern can harm
    empathizer's health, 156–57
  empathic concern hurting
    empathizer's chances in conflict
    situations, 157–59
  empathic concern hurting common
    good, 154–56
  empathy avoidance, 146–47
  for close others, 143–45
  for strangers in need, 146–56
  in conflict situations, 157–59
  in everyday life, 153–54
  needs of non-personalized
    others, 147–50
  paternalism, maternalism and
    empathy-induced altruism, 143–45
  serious threat to common
    good, 155–56
  warm heart when needing a cool
    head, 145
  when assigning workers to
    tasks, 151–52
  when deciding who gets help, 152–53
  See also strangers in need (liabilities)
Interpersonal Reactivity Index, Davis,
    57, 188
intrinsic valuing of others' welfare, 71–
    72, 76

and parental instinct, 84–85
evolutionary basis of, 90–91
Isaacson, Walter, 153–54

Jigsaw Classroom (Aronson), 196–97
justice, moral motivation, 207, 208

Kahneman, Daniel, 124
Kelley, Harold, 129
Kelman, Herbert, 201
King, Martin Luther, Jr., 198, 209
Kozol, Jonathan, 209
Krebs, Dennis, 72

Lamm, Claus, 22, 87–88
La Rochefoucauld, Duke de, 109
Lerner, Melvin, 135
Lincoln, Abraham, 204
Lipps, Theodor, 52
Lishner, David, 89, 95, 103
Longtime Companion (movie), 161–62
loving, valuing another's welfare, 71–72
loving-kindness meditation, 22, 141

McAuliffe, William, 73–74
McClure, "Baby Jessica," rescue of, 10
McDavis, Katherine, 14, 21
  Campus Concerns appeal for
    volunteers, 70
  empathic concern and personal
    distress, 28, 33–34
  evidence of distinctiveness of
    empathic concern and personal
    distress, 28–34
  principal-component analysis of data
    from five additional studies, 29–
    33, 30t
McDougall, William, 16, 27–28, 77–80
  analysis of Samaritan parable, 27–28
  extending the parental instinct, 80
  human parental instinct, 78–80
  parental instinct, 77–78

Index · 263

sympathetic pain, 27
tender emotion, 27, 77–78
MacLean, Paul, 80–81, 145
mammalian neuroscience of parental
  care, 84
Manchild in the Promised Land
  (Brown), 161–62
Martin, Grace, 50
maternalism, empathy-induced altruism
  and, 143–45
Mead, George Herbert, 53
media
  addressing interpersonal/intergroup
    relations via, 203–6
  books, 161–62
  documentaries, 161–62
  inducing empathy via, 203–4
  movies, 161–62
  New Dawn (radio soap opera), 206
  Uncle Tom's Cabin (Stowe),
    204–6
meditation
  compassion, 141–42
  loving-kindness, 141
Miller, Rowland, empathic
  embarrassment, 101–3
mimicry, 45
  imitation and, 45–46
mirroring, neural, as evidence for
  perception-action model
  (PAM), 47
Mitchell, Harold, 138, 163, 165
Modern Racism Scale, 163
moral motivation, 207
  empathy-induced altruism and,
    207–9
Most Good You Can Do, The
  (Singer), 2
motivation, state versus trait, 110

Nazi Europe, empathy in death
  camps, 145

need
  ability of perceive another's need, 69–72
  current need, 64
  empathic concern requiring
    perception of, 64–65, 211
  forms of, 93
  species possessing ability to perceive
    need, 66–69
  vulnerability as form of, 64
  See also current need; vulnerability
needs of non-personalized
  others, 147–50
negative-state-relief hypothesis, 112
neural matching, 45, 46–47
neurochemistry
  of parental care and empathic
    concern, 83–84
  oxytocin, 83–84
neuroimaging responses to in-group and
  out-group members in need, 185
New Dawn (radio soap opera), 206
News from the Personal Side broadcast,
  17, 18, 35
nurturant care
  oxytocin and, 85–87
  tender feelings and, 84–90
Nussbaum, Martha, 52–53, 63

Obama, Barack, 1
Oliner, Samuel and Pearl, 208
Oliver Twist (Dickens), 206
Olson, Mancur, 124
One Flew Over the Cuckoo's Nest
  (Kesey), 161–62
Orange People-Green People
  discrimination simulation, 198–99
orchestration of altruistic and moral
  motivation, 207–9
out-groups
  distant and conflict, 180–82, 216
  See also conflict out-groups; distant
    out-groups

264 • Index

oxytocin (OT)
  as neurochemical basis for generalized empathy, 85–87
  evaluation of role in empathic concern, 87
  in other species, 84, 85–86
  in relations with strangers, 86–87
  in romantic relations, 85–86
  neurochemistry of parental care, 83–84

Paluck, Elizabeth, 206
parental and filial affections (Darwin), 77
parental care
  brain regions related to, 80–83
  empathic concern in, 127–28
  evidence relating empathic concern and, 80–84
  in other species, 78–79, 84
  neurochemistry of, 83–84
parental instinct
  character of, 77–78
  de Waal's grounding of, 79
  extending to nonkin, 80
  in humans, 77–80
  McDougall on, 77–80
  rat mothers, 84
  receipt of nurturance during childhood as necessary for, 85
  tender emotion as defining core, 94
parental nurturance, testing for extention, 89–90
parochial empathy, 175
Partners in Health, 144
paternalism
  dangers of, 144
  empathy-induced altruism and, 143–45
Payne, Keith, 150
peace workshop/camps
  Arab-Israeli, 201–2
  Sri Lanka, 201–2

Penner, Louis, 127
perception-action model (PAM), 46–47, 56
  neural mirroring as evidence, 47
  Russian-doll metaphor, 46
Pere Goriot (Balzac), 143
personal distress, 12
  eight-item index of, 29–33
  empathic concern versus, 25–28
  empathic distress versus, 34–39
  principal-component loadings of self-reported responses, 30t
  sympathetic pain, 94
  See also empathic concern and personal distress
Personal Distress Index, 31–33, 97–98
  adjectives for, 29, 30t, 31–33, 35
  eight items on Emotional Response Scale, 32f
personalizing contact with stigmatized group member, 136
perspective instructions
  inducing empathy with, 17–20
  limitation for inducing empathic concern, 20
perspective taking, 53
  empathic concern and personal distress, 36–41
  imagine-self and imagine-other, 54–55
  intergroup benefits of, 168–72, 174
Piliavin, Irvin, 26
Piliavin, Jane, 26, 33
pity, 2–3
political conflicts, 216–17
  conflict-resolution workshops, 200–1
  peace workshops and camps, 201–2
  storytelling, 202–3
Preston, Stephanie, 46, 78–79
principal-component analysis (PCA), 15
  assessing participants' empathic concern and personal distress, 29–33

Index • **265**

factor analysis, 100
self-reported emotional responses, 30t
Prinz, Jesse, 1, 4, 48
Prinz, Wolfgang, 46
Prisoner's Dilemma, 125–26, 154, 157
  outside the lab, 125–26
  test of value assumption of theory of
    rational choice, 125
Promises (documentary), 161–62
psychological empathy (Wispé), 52–53
psychological escape, 119–20

Quality Life Foundation, 152–53

Rain Man (movie), 161–62
Raisin in the Sun, A (movie), 161–62
rational choice theory, challenging value
  assumption of, 124–25
Regan, Dennis, 52–53
relationships, empathic concern in
  friendships, 130–31
  romantic relationships, 129–30
religion
  as source of concern and care, 140–42
  compassion meditation, 141–42
  loving-kindness meditation, 141
  Tibetan Buddhism, 141
  Western teachings, 140–41
respiratory sinus arrhythmia (RSA),
  22–23, 84
Rodin, Judith, 26
romantic relationships, empathic concern
  in, 129–30
Roots of Empathy program,
  Gordon, 194–95
rudimentary empathic distress reaction
  (in infants), 50–51
Russian doll metaphor, perception-action
  model (PAM), 46
Rwanda genocide
  New Dawn (radio soap opera), 206
  Tutsis and Hutus, 190, 206

Ryan, William, 135

Sadness Index, 97–98
Sagi, Abraham, 50
Samaritan
  compassion of, 9, 51
  McDougall's analysis of, 27–28
  parable of, 9
  sympathetic pain of priest and
    Levite, 27
Sandy Hook Elementary School
  mass shooting at, 2, 10
  parents of, 11, 63
Saxe, Rebecca, 180–81, 190–91
schadenfreude, 11–12
Schaller, Mark, 97–98
Schoenrade, Patricia, 15, 29
selfish, as epithet, 155
self-other merging, 120–21
sentient intentional agent
  (Tomasello), 65–66
shared physiology, 50
Shaver, Phil, 95
Shaw, Laura, 70, 146
Silk, Joan, 68
similarity, not necessary for
  empathy, 148–49
Singer, Peter, 2
Singer, Tania, 22, 87–88
Skutnik, Lenny, 156–57
Slovic, Paul, 149
Smith, Adam, 53, 59, 109, 148–49, 175
  The Theory of Moral
    Sentiments, 55, 56
social dilemmas, 154
  empathy as threat to common good
    in, 154–55
  Prisoner's Dilemma, 154
social perception
  mimicry and imitation, 45–46
  response matching, 45–46
Solomon, Robert, 208

266 • Index

Stevens, James, 138, 139, 163, 165
stigmatized groups
  adopting imagine-other perspective
    toward, 137–39
  improving attitudes and action
    toward, 161–68
  convicted murderers, 138
  drug dealers, 138–39
  feeling for members of, 135–40
  homeless people, 138
  limit of imagine-other perspective
    when interacting with, 139–40
  people with AIDS, 137–38
  personalizing contact with members
    of, 136
  sharing superordinate goal with, 136
  See also interpersonal benefits
stimulatory parenting, 83–84
Stocks, Eric, 103–4
storytelling, political conflicts, 202–3
Stotland, Ezra, 36–37, 52–53
Stowe, Harriet Beecher, 193, 204–6
strangers in need (benefits for)
  less aggression toward, 132–35
  more sensitive help for, 131–32
  reduced derogation and blaming of
    victim, 135
  See also interpersonal benefits
strangers in need (liabilities)
  abstract needs, 150
  chronic needs, 150–51
  empathy as threat to common
    good, 154–55
  empathy avoidance, 146–47
  empathy for one causing unfair
    treatment of others, 151–54
  needs of non-personalized
    others, 147–50
  when assigning workers to
    tasks, 151–52
  when deciding who gets help, 152–53
  See also interpersonal liabilities
Stroop, John, 115

Stürmer, Stefan, 177–79, 181
Summers, Sheri, 152–53
superordinate goals, 136
sympathetic distress (Hoffman), 12
sympathy, 3–4, 12, 25
sympathy and tenderness, 93–97
  as forms of empathic concern, 93
  empirical discrepancy regarding, 95
  testing proposed distinction, 95–97

Taylor, Shelley, 86
tender emotion (McDougall), 77–78,
    79–80
tender feelings, nurturant care
    and, 84–90
tending instinct, 86
tension-reduction analysis, arousal:
    cost-reward model, 26–27
theory of mind, research on, 44
Theory of Moral Sentiments, The
    (Smith), 55, 56
Tibetan Buddhism, 141
Titchener, Edward, 52
Tomasello, Michael, 65–66
Treatise of Human Nature, A
    (Hume), 48–49
triune, human brain (MacLean), 80–81
True Colors (documentary), 173
Tversky, Amos, 124

ultimate (versus instrumental) goal,
    110, 113–14
Ultimatum Game, 86–87
Uncle Tom's Cabin (Stowe), 161–62,
    193, 204–6
unfairness in everyday life caused by
    empathy, 153–54
unintended consequences, 110, 113

validity
  convergent, 13
  face, 13
  induced-state, 13

Index · 267

valuing
caring or loving, 71–72
evidence of link between empathic
concern and, 70
intrinsic, 76
intrinsic not extrinsic, 71–72
other's welfare, 62*f*, 69–72, 75*f*,
76, 90, 91
Vescio, Theresa, 169
Vitaglione, Guy, 99–100
Vollmer, Peter, 68

Vorauer, Jacquie, 139
vulnerability
as form of need, 64
tenderness and, 94, 95

Wispé, Lauren, 52–53
within-group variance, 21–22
workplace setting, treating others
unfairly in, 151–52

Zaki, Jamil, 2, 175, 202–3